MILLENNIUM

TRIBAL WISDOM AND THE MODERN WORLD

MILLENNIUM
TRIBAL WISDOM AND THE MODERN WORLD

DAVID MAYBURY-LEWIS

Design by **PAULA MUNCK**

VIKING

VIKING
Published by the Penguin Group
Viking Penguin, a division of Penguin Books USA Inc.,
375 Hudson Street, New York, New York 10014, U.S.A.
Penguin Books Ltd, 27 Wrights Lane, London W8 5TZ, England
Penguin Books Australia Ltd, Ringwood, Victoria, Australia
Penguin Books Canada Ltd, 10 Alcorn Avenue, Suite 300, Toronto, Ontario, Canada M4V 3B2
Penguin Books (N.Z.) Ltd, 182–190 Wairau Road, Auckland 10, New Zealand

Penguin Books Ltd, Registered Offices: Harmondsworth, Middlesex, England

First published in 1992 by Viking Penguin, a division of Penguin Books USA Inc.

1 3 5 7 9 10 8 6 4 2

"Cantares Mexicanos" from *Image of the New World* by Gordon Brotherston,
Thames and Hudson, London, 1979.

LIBRARY OF CONGRESS CATALOGING IN PUBLICATION DATA
Maybury-Lewis, David.
Millennium: tribal wisdom and the modern world / David Maybury-Lewis.
p.   cm.
Includes bibliographical references and index.
ISBN 0-670-82935-8
1. Indigenous peoples.   2. Human ecology—Philosophy.   3. Wisdom.
4. Social perception.   I. Title.
GN380.M39   1992
306'.08—dc20   91–40489

Printed in the United States of America
Designed by Paula Munck

This book is dedicated to the memory of my father

Sydney Allan Maybury-Lewis

THE MILLENNIUM TEAM GRATEFULLY ACKNOWLEDGES

THE ONGOING COLLABORATION OF

CULTURAL SURVIVAL

IN PROMOTING GREATER UNDERSTANDING

OF INDIGENOUS PEOPLES

FOR FURTHER INFORMATION ON THE CULTURES DISCUSSED
IN THIS BOOK OR ON THE PRESENT SITUATION
OF INDIGENOUS PEOPLES AROUND THE WORLD, READERS MAY CONTACT:

CULTURAL SURVIVAL
53A CHURCH STREET
CAMBRIDGE, MA 02138
TEL: (617) 495-2562

CULTURAL SURVIVAL, U.K.
4 ALBION PLACE
GALENA ROAD
LONDON, W6 OLT
TEL: (081) 741-8090

CONTENTS

PREFACE

How could I refuse an offer to make a television series about tribal peoples? I have, after all, studied them all my life and come to respect their different ways of viewing the world. The "Millennium" series and its accompanying book give me an opportunity to tell a wide audience that tribal peoples have not tried (and failed) to be like us, but have actually chosen to live differently. By examining the roads they took that we did not, we can get a better insight into the choices we ourselves make, the price we pay for them, and the possibility of modifying them.

Anthropologists originally went to study tribal peoples because they were seeking the most exotic societies they could reach to try to understand alien worlds where everything was different except for the basic humanity of their hosts. They went in search of answers to big questions. What makes us human? Why are other societies so different from ours? What kind of sense lies behind their customs and what does this tell us about our own, and about human nature in general? Moreover, a hundred years ago tribal peoples were considered "primitive," so it was felt that a study of their societies would also tell us something about the history of humankind. Anthropological research led to different conclusions, however, for it established that, although tribal people did not possess the technology of the industrial world, they were no less intelligent or rational than citizens of supposedly more advanced nations. It established, in fact, that there are no reasonable grounds for considering tribal ways of life "primitive" in comparison with those of other societies. The word *primitive* has therefore all but dropped out of anthropological use.

Nowadays the majority of anthropologists do not study tribal peoples but pursue their inquiries into the nature of human nature by carrying out research in all kinds of societies, including our own. In fact, there is considerable debate among scholars about how to define a tribe and whether it is useful to speak of "tribal peoples" at all. There is no need to go into that argument here. I simply want to make it clear that when I write in this book about tribal peoples, I am using the phrase as a kind of shorthand to refer to small-scale, preindustrial societies that live in comparative isolation and manage their affairs without any centralized authority such as the state. I am one of those anthropologists who went on a romantic impulse to study such peoples. I was intrigued by them precisely because they lived at and beyond the fringes of the modern world, and I have been fascinated ever since by tribal ways of doing things.

Of course there is no single "tribal" way of life, any more than there is a single way of doing things that is common to all "modern" societies. Yet the societies that I am here calling "tribal" do share certain characteristics, as do modern industrial ones. It is to these generalities that I refer when I write broadly in this book of the contrast between "tribal" and "modern" societies. These words are used to refer to what Max Weber called "ideal types," which help us to understand processes and institutions without pretending to describe them. So this book looks at the consequences of industrialization and modernization by contrasting societies that have undergone this process with others that have not.

Such broad characterizations are necessary in order to make my arguments clear. Inevitably, however, they do not deal with exceptions and variations. These could be discussed, and would be if I were writing a scholarly treatise, but are out of place in a book intended for the general reader. There is one possible misunderstanding, however, that I want to dispel from the outset. The title of our series and of this book refers to "tribal wisdom." This should not be taken to imply that tribal societies are the repositories of all wisdom and that modernization has been a great mistake. I am not holding up an idealized "tribal way of life" as some sort of Eden from which we moderns have strayed. On the contrary I, like most anthropologists who have lived with tribal peoples, do not wish to exchange my way of life for theirs. It is, however, equally true that most tribal individuals, though they may envy us our creature comforts, would not wish to exchange their way of life for ours either. The point, then, of writing about tribal wisdom is to correct a long-standing misperception. We in the modern world have tended to assume that *our* societies have a monopoly on wisdom and that the study of tribal and even "traditional" peoples was a kind of excavation of human backwardness. The purpose of this book is to show that we have much to learn from them, just as they do from us; it is to encourage a mutuality of thinking that seems to me to be essential if we are all to flourish in the next millennium.

To this end, the makers of the series and I have tried to give the points of view of people living in tribal societies so that the viewer and the reader can get a sense of them as human beings, grappling as we all do with the existential problems of living. We have taken care to ask them for the stories and incidents that they think are significant and to elicit their commentaries on them, and it is on these that our tribal vignettes are based.

I need also to clarify two other usages that give rise to endless confusion. One has been perpetuated in the major languages of the world by Christopher Columbus, who thought he had landed in Asia when he arrived in the Americas.

He therefore referred to the natives of the Americas as "Indians," and the designation has been applied to them ever since. The indigenous inhabitants of Canada and the United States understandably resent the term "Indian" and prefer to be referred to as "Native Canadians" or "Native Americans." It would, however, be absurd to refer, for example, to colonial laws about Native American slavery, or to the Native American policies of countries that have specifically designated Indian statutes. I therefore use the term "Indian" where it is historically appropriate and use alternative designations such as "indigenous peoples" or "Native Americans" when writing in the modern context.

Even the term "Native American" has its problems, for Latin Americans also resent the way in which the citizens of the United States so often use "America" and "American" to refer exclusively to themselves, as if Mexicans, Peruvians, Brazilians, and so on were not Americans, too. Here again it is not always possible to avoid the unfortunate usage, since I know of no other adjective to refer to United States-ers. But readers from the United States should be aware that I sometimes use American in its technically correct sense to refer to peoples and things of the Americas.

I had all the usual misgivings when I was invited to collaborate in the making of this series. It would turn my life upside down. I would have to put my other work on hold. My friends regaled me with horror stories of megalomaniac film directors and insensitive cameramen. I decided to take these risks, however, because of the confidence I felt in the Canadian producers who were in charge of the series. The idea for it came from Richard Meech, whom I have known since his days at Harvard, where he says he first began to think about making a series of this kind while studying history and anthropology. He teamed up with Michael Grant in order to do it, and I have watched their collaboration with admiration. It was my respect for their judgment and good taste that persuaded me to join them and I have not been disappointed. They have been the kind of colleagues one hopes to have when one has to work under pressure, and I am immensely grateful to them both.

They in turn had the good sense to take the project to one of the most experienced executive producers of epic series, Adrian Malone, who, I am delighted to say was captivated by the idea and agreed to join the "Millennium" team.

It was my particular good fortune that Laurie Hart decided not to take up her academic position at Haverford until the fall of 1991 and was therefore able to work with me on the book. Without the benefit of constant dialogue with her and of her efficient and imaginative work on the text, this book could never have been completed in time, nor would I have survived the writing of it. I also relied heavily on Victor Barac in Toronto, who put his own anthropological writing aside and provided me with notes and texts on such a wide range of topics that I only hope they will enrich his own lectures for years to come. Mark Johnston and Stephen

Milton also gave me invaluable help in developing ideas and checking facts. Meanwhile, Michael Grant took immense pains with the layout of the book and Richard Meech managed to help me edit and rewrite – all at a time when they were both working day and night on the series itself.

I want also to thank the specialists on the various peoples depicted in the series and discussed in this book, who were generous with their advice and even with their unpublished writings. Kaj Århem advised me the Makuna, Carol Beckwith on the Wodaabe, Aneesa Kassam on the Gabra, Joel Kuipers on the Weyewa, Juan Negrin on the Huichol, and Walter van Beek on the Dogon. I hope they will feel we have done justice to the peoples they helped us to present.

I am also grateful to the anthropologists who gathered at Harvard years ago to help us plan the series: Jason Clay, Vincent Crapanzano, Michael Fischer, Mary Hebert, Catherine Lutz, Peter Metcalfe, Renato Rosaldo, and Aram Yengoyan. They will see that our original ideas have been much modified, but I hope that they will recognize in the final product the freshness and originality with which they helped us launch the whole enterprise. So many other anthropologists have helped us over the years that it is impossible to thank them all personally. I do wish, however, to acknowledge the help of Ted Macdonald and Mac Chapin, colleagues whose recent assistance has proved invaluable.

I want also to thank Jenny Rathaus and Gail Fielding, who were in charge of the daunting logistics of putting this book together, and Mariana Chilton for her research assistance in the final stages. Furthermore, I was exceedingly fortunate to have Dawn Drzal assigned to edit this book by Viking Penguin. I am grateful for her suggestions, her calm, and above all her sense of humor, which kept us all going through the intense pressures of the past few months.

Finally, my thanks are due to my wife Pia, who has had to live with a zombie during the writing of this book but managed not to let this dampen her enthusiasm for the project and even to remind me from time to time of the excitement that drew me to it in the first place.

Cambridge, Massachusetts 21 July 1991

THE SHOCK OF THE OTHER

I met my first aliens in early childhood, and they fascinated me. I was a small boy, traveling with my family in what was then British India and is now Pakistan. My father was a British engineer who built and inspected canals in a constant struggle to make the desert bloom. I loved the months when we went on tour. Every few days the contents of our entire household, from carpets to crockery, would be packed into huge chests and loaded onto the backs of twenty-seven protesting, government-supplied camels. The camels would go off in the evening and walk through the Sind Desert to the next government bungalow listed on my father's inspection schedule. We followed next morning, transported over the rutted tracks in an Armstrong Siddeley, a car with fenders so high off the ground that I had to be lifted into it.

But even the marvels of the car could not distract me from the camelmen. They were my first experience of "the other." They were local men who spoke only Sindhi and could not even talk to our house servants, sophisticates who spoke Urdu, the national language. The house servants looked down on them anyway, referring to them disdainfully as *jungli* (people of the jungle). The camelmen certainly looked wild to me: tall men, their long hair only partly restrained by untidy turbans, wearing loose shirts over their baggy trousers. I was discouraged from spending too much time with them, so they were irresistibly fascinating. I loved hanging around their camp. They tolerated me and played with me when they had time. They taught me how to wrestle and I remember happy bouts in which I always ended up sitting on the chest of my well-muscled opponent, who professed that he was pinned and quite unable to get up.

Then came the day of departure. The whole household was packed up and handed over to my camelmen friends. I can still smell the smoke of the fires as evening came on and the reek of the animals, and hear the bubbly, grumbly noises that camels make. At last, they were ready to leave. The long camel train would go slowly into the darkness as my friends sang to ward off the evil spirits. They left our compound with a surging chorus that died away plaintively into the night, and I would suddenly miss them, though I knew I would see them again

David Maybury-Lewis spent his childhood in British India (now Pakistan). For a few months every year his family went on tour in the Province of Sind, where his father helped build and maintain the canal system.

Every few days, the family packed its entire household onto camels managed by Sindhi-speaking camelmen, who were considered wild men (*jungli*) by speakers of Urdu, the national language.

the next day. I was seven years old when I was sent from India to go to school in England. After that there were no more camels and I forgot the camelmen, or thought I did.

Perhaps that vague hankering for exotic peoples that impelled me later on to take up anthropology actually came from my early affection for my alien friends. But by the time I was graduating from college my imagination no longer lured me toward the east. It was the Indians of the Americas whom I wanted to study. At a conference, held providentially in Cambridge, England, where I was an undergraduate, I met a German professor who had settled in Brazil and who invited me to come and work in the Amazon. Herbert Baldus spoke in glowing terms of all the work that remained to be done in the Amazon regions, but warned me of the bureaucratic delays and difficulties I would face if and when I went to Brazil to try to do it. He ended up suggesting that, since I was English and the international frontiers in the Amazon were at that time unmarked and unguarded, I simply go to British Guiana, walk across the frontier, and do my research on the Brazilian side. To this day I do not know if he was serious, but his suggestion fired my imagination. I had no training in anthropology yet. I spoke Spanish but no Portuguese. I was not sure which Indians I would meet or where or why, but the idea of walking across an unmarked frontier into an unknown jungle to work among unstudied tribes fascinated me.

The author is on the far left.

I had to go about it in a rather more prosaic way. I got a job teaching English in São Paulo, Brazil's largest city, and about a year after my conversation with Professor Baldus I presented myself to him in his office. If he was surprised, he did not show it. Instead he welcomed me and my wife with open arms and started to teach us anthropology. He urged us to follow up the work of an explorer-anthropologist, also of German origin, who studied the tribes of central Brazil. The name of my predecessor had been Kurt Unckel, but he had adopted an Indian name and was known to anthropologists therefore as Curt Nimuendaju.

Nimuendaju loved the Indians among whom he worked and eventually felt more at ease in their company than he did when he returned to what he considered the decadent world of urban Brazil. He was particularly fascinated by the Indians of central Brazil. These peoples have lived as hunters and gatherers at the edges of the jungles on the high plateau of central Brazil since time immemorial. Seventeenth-century chroniclers were referring to them when they reported tribes of huge Indians in the interior of the continent, men who could run for days across the savanna without tiring and who carried tree trunks on their shoulders for sport. Eighteenth-century writers reported that these Indians fiercely resisted the gold miners and the colonists who invaded their territory. Even in the twentieth century they were remote enough and tough enough to have kept their lands and their lives intact. But the frontier was catching up with them. Nimuendaju lamented that he felt their days were numbered. Above all, their intricate social systems, which had served them so well for so long, were breaking down, he said, under the pressures of modern life.

Those Indians were reported to organize themselves in an interesting way.

T H E M O N S T R O U S R A C E S

Before the age of exploration and expansion, European ideas of people in distant lands were informed more by fancy than by fact. The wellspring of these imaginings was the ancient Greeks, the first of the Western peoples to write about their exploits in foreign lands. Although many of their accounts were fictitious, written as exercises in training for the art of rhetoric, they nonetheless served as the basis for the earliest compilations of accounts of exotic peoples. By far the most influential of these, the one that introduced the subject to a European readership and was to remain the main source of such ideas for over fifteen centuries, was Pliny the Elder's *Natural History.* This thirty-seven-volume compendium, completed in A.D. 77, included the most complete catalog of what he termed the "monstrous races." "Monstrous" peoples were distinguished by their peculiar appearance and by their unusual behavior. The *Blemmyae,* for instance, were men with faces on their chests who lived in Libya. The *Amyctyrae* were "unsociable" people who lived on raw meat and had large, protruding lower lips that could be used as umbrellas for protection against the sun. The *Sciopods,* or "shadow-foot," were one-legged people from India who used their single large foot for the same purpose. *Troglodytes* were Ethiopian desert cave dwellers who lacked speech but were extremely swift and could outrun game. Another popular race was the *Cynocephali,* also cave dwellers, who lived in India, had dogs' heads, communicated by barking, dressed in animal skins, and hunted with bows, javelins, and swords. In some accounts, they had big teeth and breathed flames.

During the Greek and Roman eras the "monstrous races" were more objects of curiosity than of serious contemplation or study. However, the spread of Christianity in Europe and increasing missionary zeal produced mounting pressure to place these exotic peoples in a properly Christian framework of understanding. Who were they anyway? Were they rational? Did they have souls? Were they descendants of Noah, or were they antediluvian? Were they perhaps descendants of the cursed Cain? Could they be converted? Could they be saved? Could they even be considered human? All these questions presented themselves to devout Christians intent on spreading the gospel. When Columbus returned from his first voyage to the Americas it was believed that he had discovered the western passage to India. Soon afterward there appeared the first graphic depictions of native Americans, which, not surprisingly, resembled medieval European pictures of the "monstrous races" of India. The earliest voyagers to America clearly carried with them preconceptions about what the "Indians" must look like. Unfortunately, they also brought predispositions that were to prove catastrophic for the indigenous peoples of the New World.

CAPVT. VI.

Von den Wunderbaren Leuten/so in Guiana zu finden.

VOn der Provintz Juvaipanoma,im König-reich Guiana, zwischen dem See Cassipa, vnnd dem grossen See Parime gelegen / bezeuget Herr Ralegh in den hievorn gemelten Büchlein (wie Jodocus Hondius,in seiner offtgedachten Land-Tafel / mit fleiß anzeiget) daß es allda eine art von Menschen oder Leut habe / so ohne Hälß vnd Köpff seyn / darinn ihre Augen vnd ander theil deß Ange-sichts / auff ihrer Brust stehen / seyn sonsten starcke / wüste/Barbarische Leut.

Indians of Guyana

illustrated in

Nuremberg edition of

The Discoverie of

***Guiana* by**

Sir Walter Raleigh

(1599).

Title page of an

edition of

Travels of Sir John

Mandeville,

circa 16th century.

Their societies were divided into halves or "moieties," such that everybody in them had to belong to one moiety or the other. Social life for them was therefore an elaborate set of exchanges between the two halves of their society. Actually it was not quite so simple. They liked to set up various systems of moieties. So for one activity an individual would be in moiety A as opposed to B, but for another he would be in C as opposed to D (where C/D crosscut the membership of A/B), and so on, through any number of different moieties for different purposes. Similar kinds of social systems are found in many other parts of the world, so I was interested in discovering whether there is some kind of human tendency to set up such systems and if so, under what circumstances and what this tells us about human beings.

In order to do this I had first to study such a system in operation, but this proved to be harder than I had at first thought. I wanted to study a central Brazilian tribe that had a dual organization that was *not* breaking down. The only sure way to do that was to study one that had very little contact with the outside world. But such a people might not welcome outsiders and they probably would speak only their own language, so it was not clear how one could talk to them. I thought I could solve these problems by studying the Xavante. They had moved away from the settlers in the nineteenth century by burying themselves in the heart of Brazil and were in the process of being recontacted. They were also thought to have been one people together with the Xerente, who had stayed behind when the Xavante disappeared into central Brazil. The Xerente had therefore had long contact with Brazilians and some of them were sure to speak Portuguese. My wife and I planned to work among the Xerente, speak to them in Portuguese, and learn their language. Then we would go off to work among the Xavante and hope that they could understand us when we spoke to them in Xerente.

All of this took a while. By the time we had studied anthropology, lived with the Xerente, learned their language, and received some funds to go and work among the Xavante, we already had a baby son. We decided to take him with us into central Brazil, but with some misgivings. After all, the Xavante had a fierce reputation and many of their communities had not yet made peace with the Brazilians. We were not sure what sort of a welcome we would get when we sought them out. I had nightmares in which I was surrounded by strange Indians to whom I could not talk. And the Xavante were not just any Indians. They had acquired a reputation in Brazil for being especially ferocious. Settlers avoided their territory. The Brazilian Indian service had sent an expedition to make peaceful contact with them, but the Xavante had killed the expeditionaries. Only their Xerente interpreters escaped to bring back the news. The Indian service had persisted and eventually established posts in Xavante country. We hoped that the Brazilian air force would fly us to one of these. After that, it would be up to us.

My mentor, Herbert Baldus, defended the Xavante. He wrote a controversial article in a major São Paulo newspaper entitled "Are the Xavante Bellicose?," arguing that they were not particularly fierce. All they were doing was defending themselves, and they had good reason to fear the arrival of outsiders. We agreed with him, but it was one thing to agree and quite another to test our opinions by dropping in on the Xavante to see whether they could easily distinguish between friendly outsiders and unfriendly ones. Besides, the Xavante were shrouded in myth. Everybody was agreed that they were tall and tireless. Some said they slept like bats in the trees as they wandered over their lands. Others insisted that their feet were fixed backward onto their legs, which is why people had such difficulty following their trail.

We tried to keep our perspective. Bound by the romantic tradition of the West, we could not just *visit* the Xavante. We had to organize an "expedition" to them. The Brazilian authorities insisted that we should constitute ourselves an expedition, which could be duly authorized to proceed by the National Council for the Fiscalization of Artistic and Scientific Expeditions into the Interior. We felt a little incongruous – graduate students with minimal funds, no equipment to speak of, and a small son now approaching his first birthday – to be offering ourselves as an Expedition to be Fiscalized, but that was the only way it could be done. Our one special item of equipment was an army surplus radio transmitter and receiver, which we hoped to use to call for someone to come and get us out if our son got sick. It was impounded by the Brazilian customs and delayed us for months while we tried to get it out. We finally liberated it a day or two before we were to leave for the interior. It never worked properly in the field.

It was in 1958 that we found ourselves, at long last, in a Brazilian air force Beechcraft, flying to the airstrip that supplied the Indian post named Pimentel Barbosa, on the Rio das Mortes. The names were not auspicious: the post was named after the leader of the expedition whose members had been killed by the Xavante, and it was located on the River of Deaths. We were appropriately apprehensive, but our nervousness gave way to excitement as the plane flew over the great horseshoe village and we saw our first Xavante come running out of their beehive-shaped huts. We landed at the airstrip and the crew flung our baggage, rather hurriedly we thought, out onto the rank grass. They took off hastily as the Xavante came loping toward us.

It was the young men who arrived first, running easily like athletes, with their long hair streaming behind them. They were well built and stark naked, except for small white cylinders that they wore in their earlobes and tiny palm-leaf sheaths that they wore on their penises. We waited for them, feeling an immense loneliness. Our gear, which now lay in a litter around our ankles, looked pathetically inadequate to sustain us for a year in the wilderness. Even our two tin cabin trunks, containing presents for the Xavante, gathered with care and (what was for us) great expense, now seemed puny and insufficient. The Xavante gathered around us, eyeing our belongings with interest and pointing out the Xerente sling, woven from palm fiber, in which my wife was carrying our son. Hesitantly, I spoke to them in Xerente.

"Let's go," I said. "Let's pick this stuff up and take it to your village."

To my relief and amazement they burst out laughing. They had never expected anyone who literally dropped in on them from the sky to speak to them in an intelligible language. My Xerente was understandable, but it sounded so funny to their ears that they doubled up with laughter every time I opened my mouth. This was disconcerting but, I thought, it was better to be welcomed as a figure of fun than not to be welcomed at all.

We were among the Xavante at last. After all those years of anxious preparation, we had reached the edge of our world. We were finally living among the "other."

Anthropology has always claimed that we learn a great deal about ourselves from studying the "other." But, in order to differentiate between self and other, there has to be some common background against which difference is conceived. For anthropologists, this common background is the notion of humanity itself. In learning about the other, about many "others," our conception of humanity is enlarged and enriched. We gain insight into the plasticity of human culture. We begin to see that our way of life is determined not so much by nature but by culture and history. Only then can we see that our way of life is just one of many possible ones. Only then can we pass informed judgment on our own way of doing things. In studying the other, we begin to learn how to separate fact from fantasy, not only about ourselves and others but also about humanity itself.

Europe has a long tradition of speculation about other peoples that goes back to the writings of the Greek geographers, writings and ideas passed down through Rome and the heirs of Rome to Christian Europe. These ideas are not uniquely Western: we find similar fantasies and reactions among the Chinese or the Arabs, who, when confronted by the Europeans, found them every bit as peculiar and uncivilized as did the Europeans the Indians of the New World.

The ancient Greeks, from whom we inherited the word *barbarian*, applied this term to all peoples who did not speak Greek and had therefore not reached the pinnacle of Hellenic civilization. But some Greeks were sufficiently open-minded to realize that the superiority of their own culture was a matter of point of view. The geographer Herodotus, who wrote in the fifth century B.C., observed that even the Persians, whom the Greeks detested, considered themselves in every way superior to everyone else in the world. Herodotus considered each society to have its advantages and disadvantages, and he made no categorical distinction between "great civilizations" and smaller groups or tribes. It is part of his message that we cannot tell who will become "great" or what the contribution of the presently peripheral peoples will be. He was so reluctant to impose Greek standards on his neighbors that Plutarch accused him of "sympathizing with barbarians."

Still, like later observers of exotic peoples, Herodotus is inclined to look for poetic extremes. The Ethiopians, according to him, are the "tallest and best looking" people in the world; the Androphagi the "most savage." He wants to provide the reader with mirror-images of his own society, especially concerning sex roles and sexual practices. If Greek women stay at home, Sauromatae women, descended from Scythian fathers and Amazon mothers, campaign on horseback like men; Egyptian women go to market and trade, while Egyptian men weave. The extremes are used to show us the variability of the human condition and the importance of culture. He rarely condemns alien practice, reserving his disapproval for what we might call abuses of human rights: extreme maltreatment of women, indifference toward the sick or old, abuses of power.

The writers of early medieval Europe were familiar with fragments of the works of Herodotus and other ancient authors, but they did not read them as testimony to the wide range of cultural practice. Their interest lay in the fabulous and bizarre, which they took as evidence of the monstrous character of everything foreign. An enormous anxiety about foreign peoples had developed in Europe as a result of confrontations pitting Christians against non-Christian Europeans, against Islamic Arabs, and against the invading Mongols. The old dichotomy between the civilized and the barbarian was recast in a Christian mold. The old tolerance for other religions common in the Greco-Roman world was gone. The monotheistic religions of Europe and the Near East divided the world between the faithful and the heathen, and the former dealt severely with the latter. As for the European explorers, who set out in their new, fast sailing ships to discover the limits of our world, they were not at all sure what these distant and fallen peoples would look like. They expected the monsters of their medieval imaginings – people with dogs' heads, or headless people with eyes in their torsos, or people with a single eye and a single foot, the latter broad enough when raised to shade them from the sun. They even claimed to find them. People with heads like dogs were reported from India, as were people so dainty that they ate no meat at all but survived on the smell of apples. Others claimed to have seen people with eyes in the middle of their shoulders and mouths in the middle of their breasts. The explorers were especially fascinated by cannibals and Amazons and reported meeting them all over the world.

The Christian view of other peoples was derived from the story of the fall from paradise, according to which humanity, originally innocent and perfect, has fallen into decline. All people (and peoples) were, in medieval Christian theory, descended from one point of origin, but some, it could be said, had sunk relatively further into decline than others. This was the scholastic solution to the problem of human difference. In the biblical story, there are two separate peoplings of the earth – one by Adam and Eve after their expulsion from paradise, and another by Noah after the flood. So the various peoples on this earth

FOURTEENTH-CENTURY MAP OF THE WORLD AND SIXTEENTH-CENTURY ATLAS

A MAP OF THE WORLD USED BY THE ARAB HISTORIAN IBN KHALDŪN IN HIS *MUQADDIMAH*, OR "INTRODUCTION TO HISTORY," 1375–79. FROM OUR CONTEMPORARY PERSPECTIVE, THE MAP IS UPSIDE DOWN: EUROPE AND THE MEDITERRANEAN ARE IN THE LOWER RIGHTHAND QUARTER; CHINA IS IN THE LOWER LEFT QUARTER; THE LARGE AREA IN THE UPPER HALF IS DESCRIBED IN ARABIC WRITING AS "EMPTY BECAUSE OF THE HEAT"; THE CENTER OF THE MAP LIES SOMEWHERE IN THE ARABIAN PENINSULA, PROBABLY WHERE MECCA WAS THOUGHT TO BE LOCATED.

Indispensable instruments of expansion, accurate maps showing cities, ports, and marine and overland trade routes were a product of Renaissance craft and science. This map of Atlantic Europe and North Africa is from an early sixteenth-century Catalan atlas commissioned by Charles V, last of the Holy Roman Emperors.

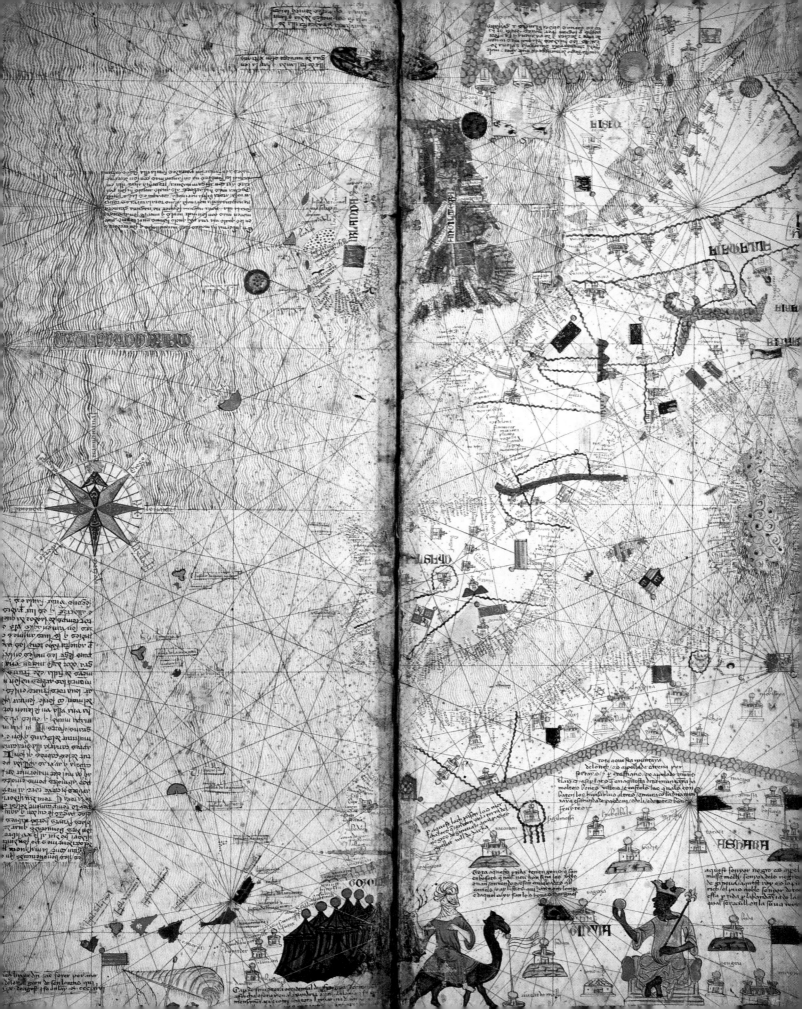

On Friday, October 12, 1492, Columbus and his crew met the Arawak people. Neither group could effectively communicate with the other; Columbus's translator could speak the languages they thought he would use in China. The Uruguayan novelist Eduardo Galeano, in the first part of his *Memory of Fire* trilogy (1985), dramatizes the event:

He falls on his knees, weeps, kisses the earth. He steps forward, staggering because for more than a month he has hardly slept....

■

Then he raises the flag. On one knee, eyes lifted to heaven, he pronounces three times the names of Isabella and Ferdinand.... the scribe Rodrigo de Escobedo, a man slow of pen, draws up the document.

■

From today, everything belongs to those remote monarchs: the coral sea, the beaches, the rocks all green with moss, the woods, the parrots, and these laurel-skinned people who don't yet know about clothes, sin, or money and gaze dazedly at the scene.

■

Luis de Torres translates Christopher Columbus's questions into Hebrew: "Do you know the kingdom of the Great Khan? Where does the gold you have in your noses and ears come from?"

■

The naked men stare at him with open mouths, and the interpreter tries out his small stock of Chaldean: "Gold? Temples? Palaces? King of kings? Gold?"

■

...he tries his Arabic, the little he knows of it: "Japan? China? Gold?"

■

The interpreter apologizes to Columbus in the language of Castile.

■

Columbus curses in Genovese and throws to the ground his credentials, written in Latin and addressed to the Great Khan. The naked men watch the anger of the intruder with red hair and coarse skin, who wears a velvet cape and very shiny clothes.

■

Soon the word will run through the islands: "Come and see the men who arrived from the sky! Bring them food and drink!"

must be descended from the various sons of Noah. Unless, of course, they are antediluvian remnants.

The most extraordinary meeting of all took place in 1492, when Christopher Columbus and his men set foot in the Americas. At that moment they reunited without knowing it two portions of humanity that had been separated for about forty thousand years, ever since the American Indians had lost touch with their Asiatic forebears. But Columbus met no monsters. To the contrary, he was favorably impressed by the first Americans he met, the gentle Arawaks. He admired their appearance and their modesty (though they all went naked), their friendliness, and their generosity. More ominously, he added that they were likely to make good and skilled servants, for they were quick to repeat whatever was said to them in languages they did not understand. From the very first moment, Indian servitude was in the minds of the European invaders.

The Indians soon learned that the invaders wanted gold, land, and slaves. They were amazed by the newcomers' lust for the precious metal. One Aztec chronicler wrote that the Spaniards grabbed for the gold as if they were monkeys. He added that "they thirsted mightily for gold; they stuffed themselves with it; they starved for it; they lusted for it like pigs." But the Spaniards brought worse than gold fever with them. They brought pestilence and oppression. The Indians sickened and died from alien diseases before being subjugated by alien power.

The Aztecs, who ruled despotically over a mighty empire in what is now Mexico, were devastated by the arrival of the Spaniards. These strange beings were preceded by fearful omens. A comet, a great fire, portentous lightning, the sudden boiling up of the lake on which their city stood, strange voices, men with two heads, dust storms, a rain of stones. Their emperor Montezuma was terrified. He feared not just the end of his reign but the end of the world. Perhaps the strange beings from the east were gods? They were certainly fantastic enough: clothed in metal, led by huge dogs, perhaps physically connected to their horses. But gods would not throw down the oracles or mistreat the deities of the Indians. Gods would not lust after gold the way the Spaniards did. No, they were not gods. They were more alarming still, for gods have some interest in humans and can be placated by them. These beings were aliens, ruthless and possessing strange powers.

Those Indians who received the Spaniards courteously discovered their mistake too late. So did those who allied with the Spaniards to throw off the yoke of the Aztecs. They now had to live through the nightmare of being conquered by fantastical creatures who considered their subjects scarcely human. Indian chroniclers describe the experience. Before, as they wrote, "the Indians had no sickness; they had no aching bones; they had no burning chest; they had no abdominal pain; they had no consumption; they had no headache. At that time the course of humanity was orderly. The foreigners made it otherwise when they arrived here." The Indians saw their world destroyed. As the same chronicler wrote in despair, "Let us therefore die! Let us therefore perish! For our gods are already dead."

Many of them did die. It is impossible to say how many in the absence of reliable censuses, but it is certain that the invasion of the Americas produced the greatest demographic disaster that the world has ever known. By the end of the sixteenth century, the Indian population of the Americas had been reduced by half. Those who survived faced a future of slavery, serfdom, or forced labor unless they were sufficiently remote to defend themselves at the margins of European settlement.

The Spaniards were only the first of the European invaders to set about enslaving the Indians, but this was not done without some misgivings. Bartolomé de Las Casas, the bishop of the Indies, was appalled by the cruelties of the conquerors and by the decimation of the Indian populations that they came to rule. He urged the Spanish court to protect its Indian subjects, insisting that they were rational beings who should not be mistreated or casually enslaved. In response to his urging, Charles V of Spain summoned a council of fourteen leading theologians to

INDIGENOUS POPULATION   PAST

Area or People Affected	European Contact Population BEFORE	Population AFTER
North and South America	60 – 70 million	5 million by 1900
Area that is now United States	5 million	250,000 by 1900
Australian Aborigines	300,000 in 18th century	60,000 by 1900
Hawaiians	300,000 in 18th century	70,000 by 1900
Andaman Islanders	2,000 in 1900	269 today
Congo	8 – 12 million killed between 1900 and 1921	
Yanomami (Brazil-Venezuela)	12,000 in 1987	0 by year 2,000
Tehuelche (Patagonia)	—	0 today
Tasmanians	—	0 today

INDIGENOUS POPULATION   PRESENT

Number of indigenous people (worldwide)	200 million
Percentage of world population that is indigenous	4 percent

Distribution of Indigenous People

North America	2.5 million
Central and South America	25 – 30 million
Scandinavia	60,000
New Zealand	240,000
Australia	250,000
Philippines	6.5 million
Burma	11 million
Thailand	500,000
India	51 million
China	67 million

THEIR REASON FOR KILLING AND DESTROYING SUCH AN INFINITE NUMBER OF SOULS IS THAT THE CHRISTIANS HAVE AN ULTIMATE AIM, WHICH IS TO ACQUIRE GOLD, AND TO SWELL THEMSELVES WITH RICHES IN A VERY BRIEF TIME AND THUS RISE TO A HIGH ESTATE DISPROPORTIONATE TO THEIR MERITS. IT SHOULD BE KEPT IN MIND THAT THEIR INSATIABLE GREED AND AMBITION, THE GREATEST EVER SEEN IN THE WORLD, IS THE CAUSE OF THEIR VILLAINIES. AND ALSO, THOSE LANDS ARE SO RICH AND FELICITOUS, THE NATIVE PEOPLES SO MEEK AND PATIENT, SO EASY TO SUBJECT, AND THAT OUR SPANIARDS HAVE NO MORE CONSIDERATION FOR THEM THAN BEASTS. AND I SAY THIS FROM MY OWN KNOWLEDGE OF THE ACTS I WITNESSED. BUT I SHOULD NOT SAY "THAN BEASTS" FOR, THANKS BE TO GOD, THEY HAVE TREATED BEASTS WITH SOME RESPECT; I SHOULD SAY INSTEAD LIKE EXCREMENT ON THE PUBLIC SQUARES.

From Bartolomé de Las Casas's
Brief Account of the Devastation of the Indies (1542).

D. FR. BARTHOLOME DE LAS CASAS
*Del Orden de Predicadores, Obispo de Chiapa,
Varon apostolico, y el mas zeloso de la felicidad
de los Indios.
Nació en Sevilla el año de 1474, y murio en Madrid
el de 1566.*

Valladolid where, in 1550, they listened to a learned debate concerning the justifications for the Spanish treatment of the Indians.

The debate dragged on through 1550 and 1551, exhausting the judges and the contestants alike. The debaters were Las Casas himself and Juan Ginés de Sepúlveda, his opponent. Sepúlveda invoked Aristotle's doctrine of natural slavery to justify the conquistadors' treatment of the Indians. According to Aristotle some people are naturally inferior and can therefore properly be enslaved by others. War is justified against people who are naturally inferior but refuse to submit. They may be conquered and enslaved by their betters. Sepúlveda therefore went to some lengths to show why the Indians were inferior and could legitimately be enslaved. He took it for granted that the king of Spain had a right and duty to take the Catholic faith to the heathen Indians and was bound to wage war on them if they refused to accept that faith. To support his case, he insisted that the Indians committed sins, such as idolatry and cannibalism, that showed the rudeness of their nature and justified enslaving them in order to bring them to Christianity and civilization.

Las Casas replied with a massive rebuttal of Aristotle's view that there were degrees of humanity, with lesser breeds condemned to serve their superiors. He also showed that Aristotle's ideas about natural slavery (ideas that were still being used to justify the enslavement of Africans as late as the nineteenth century) did not apply to the American Indians. He pointed to their remarkable achievements, their rationality, and their aptitude for the Christian faith. It was after all only thirty years earlier that Cortés and his men had entered Mexico City in wonderment. The Aztec emperor might have been terrified of the aliens from the east, but they, for their part, were astounded by the Aztec capital. It was a city much larger, more spacious, and more impressive than anything in contemporary Spain, then the most powerful nation of sixteenth-century Europe. Its inhabitants were obviously skilled architects, craftsmen, and gold- and silversmiths. They were also citizens of an empire with a hierarchy of authority, an effective system of administration, and an elaborate economy. It was difficult to find grounds for classifying them as naturally inferior or even as barbarians, unless one focused on particular customs that put them beyond the pale.

The Aztec practice of human sacrifice was such a custom. That the ancient Greeks, from whom we derive so many of our ideas about civilization, also practiced it was a fact ignored by most of the European theorists who insisted on the barbarism of other peoples. Cannibalism was another custom that was regularly and obsessively imputed to American Indians, few of whom actually ate their fellow humans. In fact, the colonists manipulated this accusation quite cynically and regularly sent back reports of cannibalism among Indians who did not practice it in order to make "just" war on them and enslave them.

Las Casas insisted that Spanish condemnation of Indian customs was ill-

LINNAEUS'S CLASSIFICATION OF THE GENUS *HOMO*

The eighteenth-century Swedish botanist Carolus Linnaeus is credited with devising the first scientific system of biological classification and nomenclature. His book *Systema Naturae,* published in 1735, was the first attempt to establish a standardized system by which all known life forms could be named and classified according to their similarities and differences. Linnaeus's classification distinguished two species of humans, "sapiens" and "monstrous," and regarded "racial" divisions as equivalent to subspecies. His system conflated cultural and biological characteristics and assumed a congruence between the anatomical, physiological, natural, moral, civil, and social aspects of humanity that is regarded as quite untenable today.

informed and, as we would now say, ethnocentric. That is, the Spanish used their own standards to judge Indian practices that they did not understand and that had usually been misrepresented. This insistence on the need to understand other people's customs before passing judgment on them is an essential aspect of modern anthropology, but it was an unusual position to promote in the second half of the sixteenth century.

This enlightened attitude, while rare, was not confined to Spain. Jean de Léry, a French Calvinist pastor, wrote a sympathetic account of the Tupinamba Indians in his *History of a Voyage to the Land of Brazil,* published in 1578. The tolerance he displayed in his book was even more remarkable because the Tupinamba did practice ritual cannibalism. They kept captured warriors for years at a time. Such men came and went at will, even married and had children with the women of their captors and thought it beneath them to try to escape the heroic death that awaited them. On an appointed day they would be killed in simulated combat and their hosts would then eat them to partak of their heroic essence. Europeans, who routinely practiced judicial torture and unspeakable cruelties on each other at the time (and had been known to kill and eat each other in the religious wars then raging), were horrified by this Tupinamba custom. It therefore took considerable independence of mind for Jean de Léry to write of it so dispassionately and to conclude that the Tupinamba, in what he took to be their observance of the laws of nature, produced conditions of life for the average person infinitely better than those of contemporary France. The conclusion was especially daring since it was assumed that life in sixteenth-century France was governed by the laws of God and King. De Léry's conclusion was taken up by his contemporary, the great French essayist Montaigne, who wrote an essay on cannibalism in which he stated: "We may call them barbarous, in respect of reason's rules, but not in respect of us that exceed them in all kinds of barbarism."

One solution, then, to the problems posed by the Americas was a kind of reasoned tolerance of other people's ways of life and a willingness to question the absolute rightness and superiority of one's own. Learned men, in the spirit of the Enlightenment, were willing to rethink their ideas about the world and about mankind. Some argued, like Herodotus, that each society inevitably holds its own way of life to be normal and natural and that there are no reasonable grounds on which to decide whether one society is better than another. This idea did not, however, appeal very much to a Christian Europe whose faith was already troubled by the new outlook of the Renaissance. Nor did it match the mood of those who were in the forefront of science in the eighteenth and nineteenth centuries.

Scientific and technological advances ushered in the Industrial Age, accompanied by a new faith in the possibility of a comfortable life on this earth. People came to believe that history was not a decline or regression from a previous state of perfection. It was instead a matter of progress, at least in the modernizing West. The theory of evolution provided a framework in which the march of history could be understood. It revolutionized the modern view of the human place in the scheme of things. More than that, it offered the exciting prospect of a grand theory of human history derived from scientific principles. As the European powers established their empires over most of the globe, reports came pouring in to them about the peoples in their colonies. So Western scholars felt that at last they had both the data and the theory they needed to make sense of human history. Darwin's *Origin of Species* was followed by a spate of books on the origins of civilization and the history of humankind. These evolutionary theorists invariably placed tribal societies at the bottom of the ladder of development. Other exotic societies were placed on various rungs and the writer's own society was always at the top. The theories, then, came to be considered as the "scientific" justification for imperialism. Europeans and North Americans had tended anyway to think it was the natural order of things that stronger and more "advanced" peoples conquered weaker and more "backward" ones in order to bring civilization to them. Here, then, was the scientific evidence, a classification which demonstrated that tribal peoples existed in a state of "savagery." Evolutionary theory made the world into a living museum in which theorists claimed to see the human past as they examined other societies that were still mired in the stages

that preceded "civilization." The reasoned tolerance that characterized the thinking of earlier scholars as they tried to understand ways of life quite different from their own gave way in the nineteenth century to evolutionary disdain.

The "scientific" evidence for these social evolutionary schemes turned out to be highly suspect. The criteria for ranking societies boiled down to one, namely technology, and in productive and military technology the West had no competitors. But there was simply no evidence for a universal progression in social life: no necessary march from polygamy to monogamy, from pantheism to monotheism, from tribe to state. In fact, there was so little accurate information on the history and workings of tribal societies that the whole evolutionary scheme was at bottom simply biased speculation.

Modern social and cultural anthropology was pioneered by scholars who, fascinated by societies unlike their own, were aware of these problems and were determined to try to understand these societies without prejudgment. But how was this to be done?

Franz Boas decided to find the answer. Born and educated in Germany, he studied geography and anthropology and became interested in how human perceptions are formed. How are people in other societies conditioned literally to "see" things differently from ourselves? What, in essence, are the processes that shape a people's way of life (what anthropologists, beginning with Boas, came to call "their culture")? To investigate these questions he went to some of the remotest people he could think of, the Eskimo of Baffin Land in the far northeast of Canada. He lived with them alone for a year, struggling to learn their language

MANU NATIONAL PARK AND ITS INDIAN RESIDENTS

AT THE HEIGHT OF THE RUBBER BOOM AT THE TURN OF THIS CENTURY AN ECCENTRIC IRISH-PERUVIAN, CARLOS FITZCARRALD, OBTAINED A CONCESSION TO GATHER RUBBER FROM THE INACCESSIBLE UPPER URUMBAMBA-UCAYALI RIVER DRAINAGE. THE MASHCO INDIANS IN THE AREA COULD NOT EASILY BE SUBJUGATED OR CONVERTED TO RUBBER GATHERERS, SO MANY OF THEM WERE SIMPLY KILLED, AND THE REST FLED DEEPER INTO THE JUNGLE. WHEN THE RUBBER BOOM COLLAPSED, MOST NON-INDIANS ABANDONED THE AREA, SO TODAY THERE IS ONLY A SMALL CATHOLIC MISSION SETTLEMENT ON THE ISTHMUS OF FITZCARRALDO. MOST OF THE MANU WATERSHED REMAINS ISOLATED AND SPARSELY POPULATED BY THE SEVERAL HUNDRED REMAINING INDIGENOUS RESIDENTS.

IN 1977 UNESCO ACCEPTED THE PERUVIAN GOVERNMENT'S REQUEST TO ESTABLISH 1.9 MILLION HECTARES AS A BIOSPHERE RESERVE. UNESCO SUBSEQUENTLY DECLARED MANU A WORLD HERITAGE SITE FOR "THE PRESERVATION OF REGIONAL BIOLOGICAL AND CULTURAL INTEGRITY."

MANU'S INDIGENOUS POPULATION CAN BE DIVIDED INTO TWO GENERAL

CATEGORIES. MOST OF THE MACHI-
GUENGA, PIRO, AND AMARAKAIRE
INDIANS LIVE IN AND AROUND THE
PARK AND ARE IN REGULAR CONTACT
WITH NONINDIGENOUS AGENCIES,
INSTITUTIONS, AND INDIVIDUALS.
OTHERS LIKE THE PREVIOUSLY ISO-
LATED YAMINAHUA ESTABLISHED
REGULAR CONTACT IN THE EARLY
1980S; SINCE THEN THEIR POPULA-
TION HAS BEEN REDUCED BY ABOUT
50 PERCENT DUE TO EPIDEMIC DIS-
EASE. THERE ARE INDICATIONS THAT
THE ELUSIVE MASHCO-PIRO WILL
SOON ESTABLISH REGULAR CONTACT,
AND NUMEROUS AGENCIES ARE
MAKING EFFORTS, AMOUNTING TO A
VIRTUAL COMPETITION, TO BE THE
FIRST TO CONTACT THEM.

THREE MASHCO-PIRO WOMEN HAVE
IN FACT SOUGHT CONTACT WITH THE
OUTSIDE WORLD. THEY EMERGED ON
THE BANK OF THE MANU RIVER AT
A PLACE CALLED PAKITSA, RIGHT
OPPOSITE THE STATION MANNED BY
OFFICIALS OF MANU NATIONAL PARK.
WHY DO THESE THREE WANDER ON
THEIR OWN? ARE THEY OUTCASTS? AN
ADVANCE GUARD? IF SO, WILL OTHERS
FOLLOW, AND HOW MANY YEARS WILL
IT TAKE THEM TO MAKE UP THEIR
MINDS?

THE NOBLE SAVAGE

European accounts of other peoples tended to extremes: either the "aliens" were monsters or they were idealized into "noble savages." Although the theme of the "noble savage" was fully developed in the literature of eighteenth- and nineteenth-century Europe, the concept is rooted in ancient sources. Greek writers such as Homer idealized the Arcadians. The idealization of "primitive" people was one way of pointing out that "civilized" life had departed from the innate goodness of primitive life. Because the ancient Greeks were idealized by later Europeans, eighteenth- and nineteenth-century artists often depicted contemporary "savages" as ancient Greeks.

and to learn how to see things through their eyes. Later he came back to study the Indians on the other side of Canada, in British Columbia. In 1889, when he was 31, he received a teaching appointment in the United States and soon moved to Columbia University, where he became the founder and leader of American cultural anthropology.

Boas set high standards for this new kind of anthropology. Field workers, he insisted, should live with the people they study, learn their language, and communicate with them through it. Anthropologists should take the other seriously enough to be able to put themselves mentally in the place of someone from that culture. Only then would they be ready to write a scientific account of the culture of the other, to show how all its aspects, its art, religion, technology, and social organization relate to one another. Only then would anthropologists be able to claim (and communicate) a genuine "understanding" of the people studied, of their psychology and their qualities of mind. Boas's insistence on sensitive, rigorous, and comprehensive fieldwork has become the hallmark of modern cultural and social anthropology. As he and his students pursued their investigations, they became more and more convinced that the grand generalizations of the social evolutionists should be scrapped. Cultural anthropology would provide a new foundation for understanding the "other" that was both sensitive and scientific.

The new findings indicated that there were no scientific grounds for believing that tribal peoples had mental capacities inferior to our own. So, around the turn of the century, Boas took up the battle against racism; it was not a very propitious moment to do so. At that time, most people in Europe and the United States found social evolutionary theories quite congenial and were content to relegate other peoples, especially tribal peoples, to the level of savagery. Furthermore, racism was on the rise everywhere in the world that considered itself civilized. Serious people in the United States worried about the future of the republic if its racial stock were debased by the arrival of immigrants from "inferior" races. Physical anthropologists provided the "proofs" of inferiority. Psychologists claimed to develop tests that measured the mental capacity of peoples of various racial stocks and cultural backgrounds. Nordics and Anglo-Saxons always scored gratifyingly well on their tests. Other cultures and races did not. Congress passed immigration laws, based on the tests, to limit the numbers of "inferior" peoples who could enter the country. In Europe, the matter-of-course racism of the imperialists was soon to be joined by the more virulent strains of racist thought and action that found expression in fascism and nazism.

The battle against racism occupied Boas throughout his life. He felt that cultural anthropology was a science that only made sense if it was practiced in the service of a higher tolerance, not that he saw much evidence of that tolerance during his own lifetime. He died in 1943, during the great war against the worst racists of them all – entrenched, to Boas's great sadness, in the country of his birth. He collapsed at a dinner being given in his honor in New York and in his last moments urged the dismayed friends who gathered round him to keep up the fight against racism and intolerance. Boas's concerns were far from my mind when I went to Brazil in search of the Xavante. In my youthful innocence I believed the battle against evolutionary disdain for tribal peoples had been fought and won. Besides, my wife and I were caught up in the drama of mounting an expedition into the unknown in order to make friends with Indians who were reputed to be hostile and likely to be unpredictable.

When we got there, our whole view of being and working with the Xavante began to change. They accepted my wife Pia quite easily. She went about with the

The "other" on display. The Kwakiutl family at the 1893 World's Columbian Exposition in Chicago.

Kwakiutl men at the Exposition.

women on endless journeys to gather the wild fruits and roots that are the basis of their diet. They watched our son Biorn learn how to walk and saw him absorbed into the eddies of children that flow around Xavante villages. As for me, I made them laugh because I was so incompetent in the ordinary skills of the backwoods. I never knew where I was in their terrain. I was an indifferent hunter and a hopeless tracker. This meant that when I traveled with Xavante men, as I did often since they were nomads who kept on the move for large parts of the year, I had to stay close to them for fear of getting lost. Ordinary Xavante never bother to stay in sight of their hunting or traveling companions. They just keep an eye on their trail and carry on at their own pace. So they were amused by my childish dependence on them, by my naive questions, phrased in my rudimentary Xavante, in short, by just about everything I did or did not do. Eventually some of them became quite protective of me, and I found myself seeking their company as I would that of my own friends back home. With them I felt secure.

This was particularly true of the chief's sons, my "brothers," and of his son-in-law, my "brother-in-law." A Xavante man goes to live in his wife's house. That is why, if he has more than one wife, as often happens, he prefers to marry women who are sisters. So it was Apewen's son-in-law who was living in the old man's house, and it was he who often looked out for me, especially when we were out on a trek, traveling slowly through the wilds as Xavante have done ever since they can remember. But it was the old man's sons who were my real Xavante family. The older ones, Waarodi and Pahiriwa, intimidated and patronized me. The youngest, Surupredu, took me out hunting and nearly killed me with exhaustion. It was the middle one, Sibupa, whom I considered my special friend.

Sibupa was less flamboyant than his older brothers. Less self-important, I thought. He was tough enough, but more reflective than the others. When he spoke in the men's council, his speeches were more than impressive oratorical performances – which are expected among Xavante leaders. They touched on the

THEATRE

DATE   ABSOLUTELY UNIQUE!
PRIMITIVE PAGEANTRY!
NEVER BEFORE FILMED!

Presenting The WEST COAST PREMIERE of

'Latuko'

WE SAW PRIMITIVE MAN

ON-THE-SPOT NATIVE SOUND!

Print by Technicolor

SEE Present day primitive man. A fully authentic...completely different picture!

SEE Savage pageantry...ceremonial sacrifice..entirely unstaged and unrehearsed!

SEE Stark realism...native hunters track down vicious African game in wildest terrain!

Presented by The
AMERICAN MUSEUM OF
NATURAL HISTORY

The Edgar M. Queeny Expedition
Photographed by Mr. Queeny
and Fort B. Guerin Jr.
Script, Charles L. Tedford
Sound, Jack Clink
Film Editing, William K. Chulack
Narration, Paul E. Prentiss

YOU MUST BELIEVE YOUR EYES...INCREDIBLE AS IT MAY SEEM!

Advertisement for the 1950 film *Latuko*, a documentary about the "Lotuko" people of Sudan, shown by the American Museum of Natural History. Their 1987 catalog commented that: "This film was censored by censorship boards across the country when it was released; male nudity and secondarily, cruelty to animals were cited as the reasons. However, the only indecent aspect of the film is the ethnocentric narration that accompanies it."

essence of what it means to be Xavante in a time when that was becoming increasingly difficult. I liked him and thought him something of a philosopher. We were delighted when the Xavante decided that his name ought to be continued in our son, to be known thereafter as Sibupa.

I was given the chief's name, Apewen, meaning "beautiful return," and Pia received the tongue-twisting name of his wife Arenwainon. Neither of us could pronounce it correctly in the Xavante fashion, but it did not matter much since women's names are never used among them anyway. As we began to feel accepted by the Xavante and to see the world through their eyes, we also began to understand that their world was in imminent peril.

Nowadays, when we go back to the Xavante, the elders point us out to the young people and say "these two lived and traveled with us here in the days when there were no Brazilians in these parts." Indeed we did, but the settlers were not long in coming. We soon realized that the real drama of central Brazil lay not in the discovery and "pacification" (as the Indian service called it) of "savage tribes" but in

The author with his Xavante brother, Sipuba, 1990.

the life-and-death struggle of the Indians to survive the savagery of the invaders who were flocking to their territory.

The Xavante had known this for a long time. Their ancestors fought the gold miners in the eighteenth century and, more recently, led their people westward into the heart of Brazil, away from the frontiersmen and the settlers, seeking a land where they could live and let live. Yet even as Pia and I went up beyond the frontier to visit them for the first time, ominous developments were taking place that would soon change the Xavante world forever.

Brazil was building a new capital in the interior. When it was inaugurated in 1960, the new city of Brasilia was linked by an all-weather road to the old city of Belem at the mouth of the Amazon. When the armed forces seized power in 1964 they set about realizing the age-old Brazilian dream of developing the interior of the country. They built the transamazon highway and started work on feeder roads into the wilderness. Central Brazil was becoming accessible. Not easily, and certainly not comfortably, but accessible nonetheless. It was no longer stray back-woodsmen the Xavante had to deal with, but cattle ranchers, mining companies, and land speculators who came in private airplanes and were backed up by their private armies of hired gunmen.

Brazil's surviving Indians, who had been protected by their remoteness, began all of a sudden to feel the pressures of the outside world. They were harried, killed, or driven off their lands. Brazil suddenly found itself accused of genocide in the world's press. Its government replied that these allegations were untrue. It had no intention of killing or annihilating the Indians. What had happened were merely regrettable incidents at a frontier that was impossible to police or control. The Indians were just victims of progress.

But what kind of progress is it that rolls over people and crushes their way of life? Why are tribal peoples constantly victims of a progress that is defined and imposed on them by outsiders? Is it not possible to imagine a kind of progress that would include our fellow human beings, even those whose ways of life seem strange to us, and let them join us in it? It was to address these questions that Pia and I founded Cultural Survival in 1972. It started as a small organization that bore witness to the horrors of the frontier in order to make the world aware of them and, we hoped, to put an end to them. Cultural Survival has grown over the years, denouncing abuses and seeking alternatives. Colleagues have joined us in the organization and worked in different parts of the world trying to mitigate the ferocious onslaught of our "progress" and help the peoples at the frontier to sur-vive it with their lives and their dignity intact.

And so it was that I found myself back in South America nearly twenty years later, this time in Peru. One of our colleagues in Cultural Survival, Ted Macdonald, had been working for some time with indigenous organizations in that country. It was through him that we learned about the tragic fate of the Yaminawa Indians. The Yaminawa too had fought to defend themselves and their dwindling territory in the remote jungles of southeastern Peru. They killed oil-men, woodcutters, and their neighbors the Machiguenga, but in 1984 they were finally forced out of their refuge. Pneumonia and respiratory diseases caught from outsiders killed off half the tribe. Others drifted downriver, dead or dying in their canoes until they were found by Peruvian officials of the Manu National Park. The park officials and leaders of Peru's Indian organizations were deeply concerned and committed to preventing such a disaster from happening again. Yet what could be done to avert it? We went to the Manu Park to try to help solve the problem.

The problem was compounded by a mystery. There are other peoples in the jungles where the Yaminawa used to live. Among them are the Mashco-Piro, an extremely elusive tribe with whom few Indians in the park can communicate. The

"These nymphs, I want to perpetuate them, with their golden skins, their searching animal odor, their tropical savors." So wrote Paul Gauguin as he sought the "noble savage" in French Polynesia. In 1897, he painted this masterpiece. A few months later he attempted suicide. Was he disillusioned with the disease and drunkenness his civilization had brought to Polynesia, or did he despair of a world not ready for his questions — *Where do we come from? What are we? Where are we going?* — the title of this painting.

Machiguenga catch sight of them now and again and sometimes leave small gifts for them, which the Mashco-Piro take, leaving bananas in return. They say that the Mashco-Piro paint themselves black from head to foot, and that they are neither fierce nor aggressive, preferring to flee from contact whenever possible.

Their shyness is understandable given that all the Indians of this part of Peru had horrifying experiences with the outside world at the time of the rubber boom in the early years of this century. It was common practice for the rubber bosses to take Indian families hostage and torture a man's relatives if he brought in less rubber than he was ordered to. Eventually they tortured at will, for fun perhaps, or in a gruesome spiral of terror that represented the final reductio ad absurdum of the conquest, when neither profit nor progress is served and power and cruelty obey their own logic.

Yet the mystery of the Mashco-Piro remains. Other tribes have emerged from the jungles and discovered that the rubber bosses and the system they imposed is long gone. The Mashco-Piro still hesitate. That is, most of them do. Three Mashco-Piro women have in fact sought contact with the outside world. They emerged on the bank of the Manu River at a place called Pakitsa, right opposite the station manned by the officials of the vast Manu National Park. They have been there (or wandering in that vicinity) for years now, yet nobody knows who they are or why they are there. They seem to be women of three different generations. A grandmother, her daughter, and her granddaughter? But then where are the rest of the family? Why do these three wander on their own? Are they outcasts? An advance guard? If so, will others follow, and how many years will it take them to make up their minds?

One day the others, the shy Mashco-Piro still hiding in the jungle, will come out for a meeting with our civilization, from which there will be no turning back. It was this thought that brought us into the park – the representatives of the national and local Indian organizations, Ted, and me. Could we help the Mashco-Piro avoid the fate of the Yaminawa? Could Cultural Survival do anything? We could certainly try. Meanwhile we promised our Indian friends that we would make no contact with the Mashco-Piro on this trip if we could avoid it. Our mission was to help prepare for the time when they emerged from the jungle, not to encourage (or entice) them to come out, and certainly not to infect them with whatever microbes we might be bringing with us from the outside world.

Day after day we went deeper into the jungle. There was no one to be seen now, for we were in the Manu Park, which is closed to outsiders and whose Indian inhabitants keep well out of sight. What were we doing here? The thought oppressed me. Our intentions were certainly honorable enough, but could we help? Might we actually do harm? I found myself thinking of the French painter Gauguin, who lived in Peru until he was seven. Was it these silent forests and this brilliant light that he could never forget, that drew him as a painter back to the tropics in later life? Was it the vanishing Indians, glimpsed in early childhood, that gave him such intense sympathy for the disappearing culture of the Polynesians? Gauguin translated his deep appreciation of Polynesian life into a new aesthetic understanding, with the result that his art, at once emotional and philosophical, was not easily appreciated by his European contemporaries. They were disturbed and frightened by the flood of sunshine in Gauguin's paintings, by the apparently innocent and yet deeply troubled world they depicted.

All this was summed up in a great painting Gauguin completed in 1897. He had been ill. His daughter had died. He returned from a brief stay in Paris to Tahiti and found the island changed. French influence and administration were fast destroying native Tahitian life and culture. Gauguin was no longer the naive romantic who had come to Polynesia in search of the primitive. He was a close observer of the realities of the Polynesians and a despairing sympathizer with their way of life. In this mood he painted the picture he entitled *Where do we come from? What are we? Where are we going?* It is a painting influenced by both Tahitian and Christian cosmologies that tries to express Gauguin's sense of the beauty and the futility of life. He intended to commit suicide when it was done. In fact he tried and failed to do so. Instead he lived on, continuing to paint, continuing to act as an advocate for the Polynesians and their art until he died in poverty in the Marquesas.

Chugging up that remote river in Peru where the Mashco-Piro had appeared, I felt I understood Gauguin. I, too, had set out for the tropics on a romantic quest. I, too, had ended up seeing my civilization through the eyes of others – and had been horrified. But surely some things had improved since Gauguin's day. The sadistic rubber bosses were gone. Instead we were traveling with leaders of Peruvian Indian organizations, looking for ways to ensure that the tragedies of the past were not repeated in the future; looking, above all, for ways to protect the dignity of the others whom we had not yet seen, to give some mutuality to our relationships with them.

Then I heard a shout. Chachon, our pilot, standing in the bow of the boat, called out "Mashco-Piro-oooo..." and pointed. I looked and could see nothing but the Peruvian jungle on the far bank. Then I saw a woman. Then two more. They had strong faces and sturdy bodies, not naked and painted black but clothed in shapeless garments encrusted with jungle dirt. They stared at us. We stopped the boat on the other side of the river and stared back. We were face-to-face with the Mashco-Piro – people, yes, but so different from ourselves that it was hard to know how to reach out to them. A sense of intrusion weighed on me. No matter that I knew we were not the first and that we came with better intentions than most. We were still interlopers. After us would come others. The animals in the forest would die out. The Indians might be killed off. We came like the plague.

But was this not why I took up anthropology? To meet people at the edge of our world, to try to understand them? Well, this time there would be no meeting. I could not do what I most wanted to – establish some friendly contact, try to bridge the gulf between us. We had promised not to contact them, and we kept to our promise and to our side of the river. But it made our meeting, if it was a meeting, almost unbearable for me. We were forced to be voyeurs, to stare at them without communicating with them, the way we do with animals in the zoo. How different this was from my meetings with the Xavante after so many years of mutual recognition. I wondered what they were thinking. How could they be sure that we were different from the rubber gatherers, the miners, or any of the other outsiders who force themselves on the tribes of the jungle? One of them gestured to us to come over. Another one put her hand to her mouth and called – but to whom? Finally they lost patience and went shouting back into the jungle.

I was sad to see them go, for I longed to meet them all, men, women, and children, to get a sense of what kind of people they were. But perhaps, after all, it is better for them to stay where they are, to keep on fleeing from us just a little longer. How much time do they have?

AN ECOLOGY OF MIND

"I am become death, the destroyer of worlds," thought Robert Oppenheimer, remembering the lines from the *Bhagavad Gita* as he stood near Alamogordo, New Mexico, and witnessed the unearthly power of the first atomic explosion on July 16, 1945. Oppenheimer was director of the atomic-energy project at Los Alamos from 1942–45, when the Western allies were racing to build a bomb since they feared that Hitler's scientists might build one first. After the use of the bomb against Japan, Oppenheimer became such an outspoken opponent of the use of atomic energy for military purposes that he was considered a security risk and removed from his position. Oppenheimer had realized all too quickly that our cosmology changed forever when that first bomb went off. The extended vistas of time that had been opened up for us by nineteenth-century science – the millions of years of human existence behind us, the prospect of millions yet to come – looked as if they might at any moment end with a bang. Humankind was capable, still is capable, of putting an end to itself.

Since then we have all lived with that awful knowledge. It has even become commonplace. We discuss the prospect of mutual assured destruction in seminars, hoping that its very finality will render it impossible. Atomic warfare could make our planet uninhabitable very quickly. But we are increasingly aware of another danger, just as apocalyptic but more insidious. We may be making the planet uninhabitable gradually, without even being quite sure that we are doing so. The signs are all around us but we are not sure how to read them. Our experts, like Montezuma's priests trying to interpret the portents as the Spaniards were advancing on them, quarrel over their precise significance. Meanwhile, ordinary people sense that enormous changes are taking place. The globe is warming up and is increasingly polluted. We cannot take fresh air or clean water for granted anymore. Even our vast oceans are starting to choke on human garbage. The rainforests are burning. The ozone layer is being depleted at rates that constantly exceed our estimates. Are we making our own earth uninhabitable, not in one grand moment of atomic destruction as we have feared, but simply by being bad stewards of it, by foolishly destroying the very environment that nurtures us? This is the new specter that is coming to haunt us.

How have we come to this? A hundred years ago science seemed to hold such promising possibilities. The confidence in reason that spread through Western Europe in the eighteenth century was bolstered by the scientific advances of the nineteenth century. People believed that humankind was about to be released from its bondage. Human beings would master nature and make it produce more easily and plentifully for them. They would live better and think better – more scientifically that is. Eventually, when rationality and progress had conquered the globe, war would become a thing of the past, since it was so clearly irrational. This in its turn would ensure a better future for us all.

The nineteenth-century optimists who thought this way may have been naive about human beings, but they were quite reasonable about science, which has provided us with material benefits that would have seemed truly fantastic to our ancestors. Why then has our science, which has been so dramatically successful in so many fields, proved less successful in dealing with the environment?

The answer lies in the belief that human beings are the masters of this world. This idea was central to medieval Christianity, which took seriously the words of the Bible in which God's creation of humankind is described:

> In the image of God He created him; male and female He created them.
>
> Then God blessed them, and God said to them, "Be fruitful and multiply; fill the earth and subdue it; have dominion over the fish of the sea, over the birds of the air, and over every living thing that moves on the earth."
>
> And God said, "See, I have given you every herb that yields seed which is on the face of all the earth, and every tree whose fruit yields seed; to you it shall be for food."

In this way the Bible assured human beings that, although they might be sinners, they were nevertheless created in God's image to have dominion over this earth. Scholars in the Middle Ages took up this theme. There was a pattern to nature, they argued, giving it a design of harmony and balance stemming from God. Out of love for his creation, God made the various species permanent and abundant and thus not capable of change or susceptible to extinction. The apparent disorder and flux of the natural world (the killing of prey by predators, the superfluous production of offspring by fish or insects) were explained as being maintained by an underlying harmony that corresponded to God's design. This design included what was known as the Great Chain of Being, according to which all living forms were part of a series that ranged from the simplest organisms to the most complex and most perfect, which was man. Humankind was therefore central to God's plan for this world, just as this world was considered to be the center of the universe. Ironically, though, it was the new and irreverent sciences emerging in the eighteenth and nineteenth centuries that gave humankind, for the first time, the means to exercise that dominion over the earth that the Bible had promised but which had until then been conceptual rather than actual. Whether man's dominion was guaranteed by the Bible or by science, the result was the same – the natural world was his to exploit.

Armed with the new science and confident of biblical authority, Western Europeans set out on a grand mission to subdue nature and press it into the service of humankind. The initial phase of European expansion, and its subjugation of foreign peoples, was driven by the search for gold, silver, spices, and other precious commodities. But the economic and demographic explosions that accompanied the birth of industrial capitalism soon led to the rapid depletion of Europe's own resources, triggering a new phase of imperialism to seek minerals and fossil fuels to meet the growing demands of European industries. Furthermore, industrial Europe came increasingly to rely on the foods that were grown overseas. So to maximize both efficiency and profit, capitalist methods of production were transplanted to the colonies. This meant that the indigenous inhabitants of those colonies had to be converted from their traditional modes of life to others more suited to industry and the global market.

Such a grandiose undertaking had to be directed by people who were convinced of the rightness of what they were doing. The Europeans saw themselves as the bearers of progress. They considered therefore that it was a moral imperative, virtually an act of generosity, to force native peoples to live according to European dictates. Similar attitudes persist to the present day, only now they are no longer justified in terms of Christianity or civilization, but rather in terms of development. Assaults on tribal ways of life are invariably justified in the name of "development." Societies that have for centuries been oriented toward self-sufficiency and long-term management of their resources are considered backward. Worse, they are stigmatized as being "obstacles to development." Accordingly, official state policies toward tribal peoples all over the world stress that they need to be "brought into the twentieth century," – their lands and presumably their attitudes need to be "developed." At the very least they must not be allowed to "stand in the way of development."

The irony is that many of the environmental disasters in the world are brought about in the name of "development." Meanwhile tribal peoples come under increasing pressure to abandon practices that have served them well since time immemorial and to adopt those which are contributing to the crisis. The few remaining nomadic peoples left on this earth are a case in point.

The prejudice against nomads is very old. It is true that sedentary peoples have often envied nomads their freedom and their political independence and even

THE GREAT CHAIN OF BEING

THE MEDIEVAL CONCEPTION OF NATURE RESTED UPON THE IDEA OF THE GREAT CHAIN OF BEING, ACCORDING TO WHICH ALL EXISTING THINGS WERE HIERARCHICALLY ARRANGED IN A SERIES OF LEVELS THAT EXTENDED FROM THE LOWLIEST EARTHLY FORMS RIGHT UP TO GOD. IN BETWEEN WERE THE ELEMENTS, THE PLANETS, THE STARS, AND THE VARIOUS ORDERS OF ANGELS. AFTER NEWTON, HOWEVER, WESTERN SCIENCE GRADUALLY SEVERED THE CONNECTION BETWEEN MATTER AND SPIRIT THAT HAD BEEN THE BASIS OF WESTERN COSMOLOGY SINCE ANCIENT TIMES.

YET, DISSATISFIED WITH ORTHODOX SCIENTIFIC "REDUCTIONISM" – THE IDEA THAT HIGHER LEVELS OF REALITY ARE TO BE EXPLAINED BY LOWER LEVELS – MODERN SCIENTISTS SUCH AS STEPHEN J. GOULD AND HIS COLLEAGUES PROPOSE A NEW HIERARCHICAL MODEL OF NATURE. ACCORDING TO THIS MODEL, THE WORLD IS CONSTRUCTED, AS GOULD SAYS, "NOT AS A SMOOTH AND SEAMLESS CONTINUUM, PERMITTING SIMPLE EXTRAPOLATION FROM THE LOWEST LEVEL TO THE HIGHEST, BUT AS A SERIES OF ASCENDING LEVELS, EACH BOUND TO THE ONE BELOW IT IN SOME WAYS AND INDEPENDENT IN OTHERS."

MEDIEVAL THOUGHT, TRIBAL THOUGHT, AND MODERN SCIENCE COME TOGETHER IN VIEWING THE NATURAL WORLD AS A VAST AND COMPLEX SYSTEM OF LINKAGES WHERE, IN CHIEF SEATTLE'S FAMOUS WORDS, "EVERYTHING IS CONNECTED."

Medieval European conceptions of nature such as the Great Chain of Being included both "natural" and "super-natural" entities. In this alchemical engraving from Robert Fludd's *Utriusque cosmi* (1617), the universe is depicted as a complex series of levels linking terrestrial and celestial domains with humanity (the ape), wisdom (the female figure), and spiritual being (the cloud with Hebrew letters and protruding arm). The Latin headline at the top reads: "Mirror of virginal nature and the image of the art."

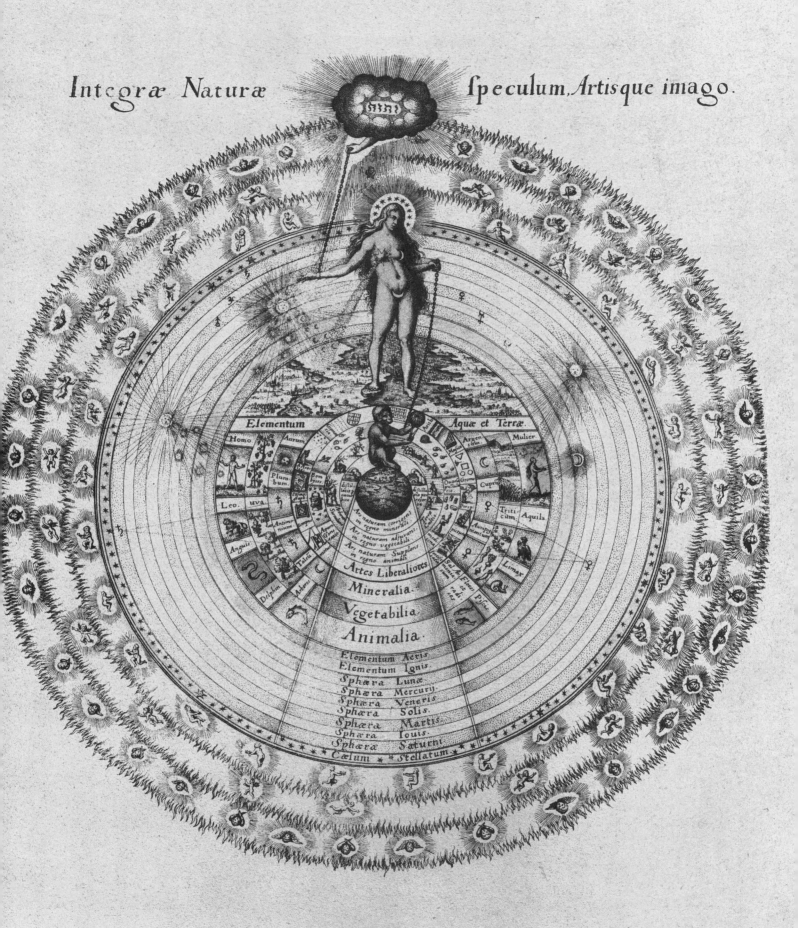

idealized their simplicity or their poverty; but more often the nomads have been hated and feared. Nomads could use their mobility as a strategic resource, enabling them to prey on their settled neighbors. The Mongols did this so effectively in the thirteenth and fourteenth centuries that they conquered China, the Near East, and eastern Europe before their empire broke up. Even smaller and less-organized groups of nomads could control the resources of important trade routes, such as salt in Africa or silk in Asia.

The days of nomad power are long gone, but the prejudice against them persists. Their way of life, their diffuseness, their mobility seem strange and awkward to us. They are also inconvenient to nation-states: as groups, they straddle national boundaries and disrupt the imaginary map of homogeneous national identities. They live in unpleasant places, where it is very cold, or barren, or too hot, or too "far" from the centers of our cosmopolitan world.

Nomad societies lack the capacity for unlimited expansion that agricultural societies possess. Nomad populations tend to remain constant over long periods of time; agricultural populations, in favorable conditions, explode. There are clear reasons for this. The balance between people and animals, and between animals and the resources that feed (and water) them, is precarious among mobile populations, who must constantly strive to maintain this balance. As a Somali saying runs, "Abundance and scarcity are never far apart; the rich and the poor frequent the same house."

Nomads have been forced by circumstance to stay in tune with their environment. Their very survival depends on it. It is therefore especially ironic that modern environmental disasters are routinely blamed on them. Drought and famine on an unprecedented scale have recently decimated nomad populations and the herds on which they depend, especially in Africa. Yet nomadic pastoralists of both East and West Africa are accused by their governments and by earnest development agencies of degrading the soil and helping the deserts to encroach upon the farmlands at their edges. They are said to do this by overgrazing. Nomads normally hold common rights in pasture land; it is therefore supposed by outsiders that, since this land is a resource available to all, it is the responsibility of no one in particular. The theory goes that nomads refuse to limit the size of their herds or to accept any limitations on their movements, with the result that they destroy their own environment and enlarge the desert. A publication of the Food and Agriculture Organization of the United Nations was fierce in its criticism of West African nomads at a time when a terrible drought was ravaging the region. They were said to be a social, economic, and political burden on their respective countries – people who take care of nothing, shun all manual work, refuse to pay their taxes, are reluctant to sell their animals, and fail to make the economic contribution to countries that their governments have a right to expect.

In fact the nomads take elaborate care of their grazing lands. If they are reluctant to sell their animals, this is not, as the bureaucrats think, because they are irrational, but rather because they understand the necessities of pastoralism better than city dwellers do. They know how many animals they need as a safeguard against emergencies, and they keep them, in spite of the calculations of outside experts. They keep steers, too, that city folk think should be slaughtered for meat since they can no longer be used for breeding; but this too makes sense because herding is labor intensive and steers help keep the herd together.

One of the few remaining nomadic peoples of Eastern Africa are the Gabra, who live in northern Kenya. A space traveler who touched down in Gabra country might wonder if she had landed on the wrong planet, for the limitless red expanses of the Chalbi Desert seem more like Mars than our own green earth. But the Gabra consider this wilderness their land, and they see it as a place of freedom and fertility. There is water for those who know where to look, good grasses and bad grasses, and protective trees standing like shrines under the sheltering sky. Above all, it is a good land for camels, and it is their camels that define the Gabra.

Gabra keep cattle and goats, but they may be tended by herders as far away as two hundred miles from the community. The camp travels with the camels as the animals meander through and around the Chalbi Desert, constantly moving on in search of forage or to get away from their own dung. Their aversion to dung is not just a whim on the part of these notoriously whimsical beasts, for ticks collect in the dung and make the camels' lives miserable. They may even do worse than that, for the ticks sometimes carry a disease that can be fatal to camels. So the camels must move and the people with them.

If possible, the Gabra pick a new site that can be reached in a day, so as to avoid spending a night in the open with their huts and all their possessions loaded on their camels. They are not averse, however, to moving fifty miles or more when necessary. Every eight years or so they make pilgrimages over long distances to their sacred sites in southern Ethiopia, where Gabra men go through the ceremonies that enable them to graduate from one age-set to the next. On such journeys the community must camp out, building thorn fences for their smaller animals, while the camels, the cattle, and the Gabra themselves sleep out under the enveloping skies.

But there is drama even in routine migrations. People become restless once the decision to move has been made, and women often get up in the middle of the night to begin dismantling their households. If there is no moon, they have to do this by touch in the darkness, which is possible because everything in the household has its place and is packed and loaded in a certain order. The men tie upright poles onto the camels and the women then roll up everything in the household, even the outer skins of the huts themselves, and pack them between the poles. The poles are then bound together and lashed tight by ropes on the

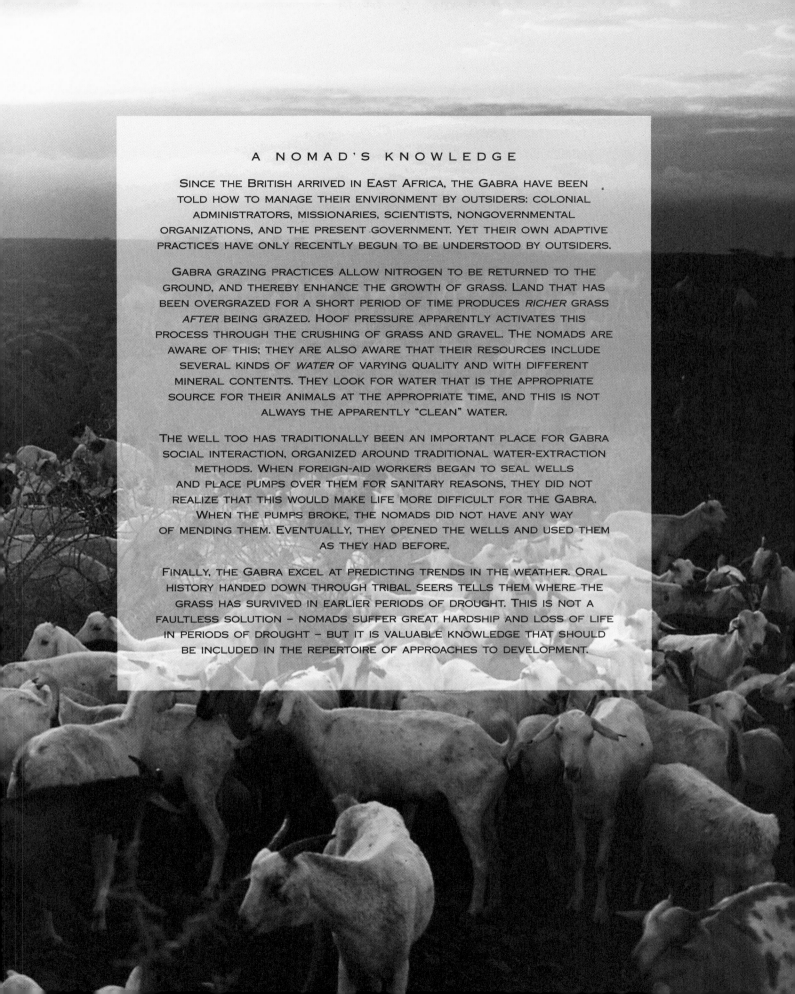

A NOMAD'S KNOWLEDGE

Since the British arrived in East Africa, the Gabra have been told how to manage their environment by outsiders: colonial administrators, missionaries, scientists, nongovernmental organizations, and the present government. Yet their own adaptive practices have only recently begun to be understood by outsiders.

Gabra grazing practices allow nitrogen to be returned to the ground, and thereby enhance the growth of grass. Land that has been overgrazed for a short period of time produces *richer* grass *after* being grazed. Hoof pressure apparently activates this process through the crushing of grass and gravel. The nomads are aware of this; they are also aware that their resources include several kinds of *water* of varying quality and with different mineral contents. They look for water that is the appropriate source for their animals at the appropriate time, and this is not always the apparently "clean" water.

The well too has traditionally been an important place for Gabra social interaction, organized around traditional water-extraction methods. When foreign-aid workers began to seal wells and place pumps over them for sanitary reasons, they did not realize that this would make life more difficult for the Gabra. When the pumps broke, the nomads did not have any way of mending them. Eventually, they opened the wells and used them as they had before.

Finally, the Gabra excel at predicting trends in the weather. Oral history handed down through tribal seers tells them where the grass has survived in earlier periods of drought. This is not a faultless solution – nomads suffer great hardship and loss of life in periods of drought – but it is valuable knowledge that should be included in the repertoire of approaches to development.

camel. All of the packing and loading is done entirely by women. Men take no part in it other than to restrain the camels if they become unruly or to help lift some item that is too heavy for the women.

Gabra live their entire lives in these unending cycles of migration. The movement is necessary in order to live off their land, but the Gabra love their desert and see it as a supportive environment where people like themselves can live with dignity. They know how to use their land and to conserve its resources. They move even before they are forced to in order to ensure that the land is replenished for the future. So when the rains come they leave their dry-season pastures and move to the highlands. They could stay where they are, but then the area would be overgrazed when the dry season came round again.

They manage their pastures by setting controlled fires to drive back the bush. Because their herds soon denude an area of edible grasses, leaving only unpalatable ones, Gabra burn off the bad grasses to allow the good ones to flourish in the ash. They are also careful of trees. Full-grown acacia trees are protected, for example, and called "bulls," for they regenerate the landscape just as bulls regenerate the herd; another tree whose supple branches make it particularly useful for hut construction is also protected against overexploitation; trees whose spreading roots stabilize underground water sources are considered sacred and treated as shrines.

This sense of the sacred permeates the Gabra landscape and protects it. Aneesa Kassam, who studies the Gabra, writes that their philosophy of life can be summed up in their idea of *finn*, meaning fertility and plenty. The sky god sends rain to bless the earth, make the grass grow, and ensure that animals and humans have enough to eat and can grow fat. *Finn* is the earth and the cycle of life that takes place upon it. Human beings contribute to *finn* as they care for the earth and for their animals, as they exchange livestock, nourish friendships, exchange ideas, tell tales, or sing songs. They and their wanderings are part of a constant cycle of creation and replenishing.

Not too long ago, the Gabra were briefly the victims of well-intentioned experts. While Kenya was still a British colony, the authorities decided to prohibit the Gabra from firing their grasslands in the old-fashioned way. The result was a buildup of deadwood that caused a huge fire that raged out of control and destroyed a large part of the forest on Marsabit Mountain. Since then, the Gabra's own small controlled fires have been looked upon as a useful and intelligent practice. Nowadays Kenyan ranches are using the Gabra combination of camel browsing and range firing to keep the grasslands under control.

In part because of vindications like this one, the Kenyan government has begun to realize that taking the nomads off the land is not necessarily a wise thing to do and may, in fact, even begin a process of ecological degradation. It has become clear that, if the deserts of Africa are spreading, it is not because of the nomads and their way of life – for their survival has always depended on cultivating a harmonious relationship with their environment. The fault is more likely to lie in efforts to squeeze the "economic contributions that their governments have a right to expect" out of regions that have traditionally been used by nomadic herders. Such is the legacy of Western-style development thinking. It is often disastrous for indigenous peoples because planners neglect or scorn their knowledge and so belittle one of humankind's greatest attributes – adaptability. Humans can live almost anywhere, given ecological knowledge and the appropriate social relations. The best development planning takes account of both the interests and the expertise of those in the areas to be "developed." Where this is done, indigenous peoples do not suffer needlessly from a "development" in which they have had no say. The Kuna Indians of Panama are such a people. They live packed closely together on coral islands off the Panamanian coast, but they draw their livelihood from the jungles of the mainland as well as from the sea. They are blessed by geographical accident since the isthmus of Panama was literally the center of the Spanish empire in the New World. To the north lay the riches of Mexico, to the south Peru and the silver mines of the Andes. In colonial times all communication between Spain and its South American possessions involved a transatlantic voyage to Panama, an overland journey to cross the isthmus, and then another voyage down the west coast of Peru. Yet the Kuna lay off this well-beaten track, sheltered behind a mountain range cloaked in dense jungle. They were never conquered and to this day they live in their own territory, accessible only by plane or launch or (increasingly) by cruise ship. But the tourists who arrive are strictly controlled by the Kuna. They are encouraged to come to the picturesque islands and to buy Kuna handicrafts, especially the beautiful reverse-appliqué *mola* blouses that Kuna women make, but they may not stay for long. If they stay overnight at all, it must be in hotels owned and managed by the Kuna.

It is, however, the land that defines them. In the words of one of the present Kuna chiefs: "The land is our culture. If we were to lose this land, there would be no culture, no soul." The Kuna not only conserve the land but they also respect and protect it. So the idea of a road linking them with Panama City was seen as a mixed blessing: it would certainly make it easier for the Kuna to go to town, and more important, to take their wares to town, but it would also open the way to invasion of Kuna territory by land-hungry peasants. The Kuna decided to bar the way by establishing a biosphere reserve at Udirbi, just where the road enters the Kuna domain. Young Kuna professionals garnered support from an impressive array of national and international institutions to set up the park, which represents an extraordinary coming together of Kuna culture and Western science. The Kuna have always maintained reserves within their forests, which they see as sanctuaries for malevolent spirits who would harm the Kuna if they were disturbed but also serve as areas where healers and shamans go to gather plants and herbs and as regenerators of fertility in the Kuna's own clearings. Meanwhile, Western scientists are delighted to work in and help protect a tract of virgin forest that is incredibly rich in plant and bird species. In fact, the Kuna encourage scientific tourism in the Udirbi park, in the hope that this, together with the influence of the scientists working there and the international agencies that support them, will serve to protect their land and their way of life.

Yet Western science, for all its pride in its own achievements, is only now beginning to understand that peoples who had no "science" of their own could nevertheless have developed a profound knowledge of their corner of the natural world. This is nowhere more true than in the rainforests, yet it is in the rainforests that the clash between Western arrogance and traditional wisdom is most violent. The rainforests of the Americas are literally going up in smoke, being destroyed to make room for cattle ranchers who provide fast food for the fast-growing cities of the affluent world. The rainforests of Asia are being destroyed to provide wood and paper and chopsticks. They are being destroyed because we fail to see them as storehouses of knowledge, as a sacred trust, the way we think of our great libraries. Shamans, of course, see them that way and are now being joined by ethnobotanists, scientists who specialize in studying the botanical knowledge of other peoples. That this knowledge is truly remarkable is no accident. We do not know exactly how the Amazonian Indians learned of the chemical properties of the various drugs they use, but it derives from a genuinely speculative interest in their environment coupled with elaborate classification of its properties. It is this genius for classification that led Claude Lévi-Strauss to argue, in his famous book *The Savage Mind*, that the thinking of such peoples is not so "savage" after all. Yet Western scientists ignored it until recently, supposing that tribal peoples simply chanced upon their discoveries.

Charles Lamb, an English writer of the early nineteenth century, parodied this kind of reasoning in a famous satirical essay on roast pork. This delectable dish originated, he suggested, in ancient China. People had never known the delights of roast pork until the day when a peasant's hut burned down, killing the pigs inside it. His son tried to rescue one of the pigs by pulling it out of the fire. Alas, the pig was already well roasted and much too hot to touch. The slow-witted son burned his hand, let out a cry and sucked his fingers to soothe the burn. What a delicious flavor! From then on people in that part of China built huts, filled them with pigs, and burned them down in order to feast on this new delicacy.

This story is hardly more farfetched than believing that Indians of the Americas learned to process bitter manioc by a kind of lucky fluke. Manioc (also known as cassava) is a tuber that was domesticated by the Indians in Brazil and spread all over the world after the conquest of the Americas. Bitter manioc, the most common and most important variety, is deadly poisonous for it has a high content of prussic acid. The Indians of the Brazilian rainforests nevertheless cultivated it in their gardens after they discovered how to prepare it for eating. The process involves peeling the flesh of the manioc and squeezing the poisonous juice out of it. The Indians invented a press for doing this which consists of a long hollow tube, almost the size of a man, made out of flexible matting woven from the leaves of forest palms. The manioc pulp is packed into the tube, which is then hung from a post outside the house. The bottom of the tube ends in a loop into which a stick is inserted and twisted. Twisting the loop works as a tourniquet, tightening the tube and squeezing the juice out of the manioc through the matting. The poisonous juice is carefully collected in a container and put where it is inaccessible to children or pets. After some hours an edible sediment collects on the bottom of the container, and the sediment – which is tapioca flour – is kept. Meanwhile the manioc pulp left in the tube is now also edible. It was the Indians who thought of toasting it on a flat container until it acquired the consistency of toasted bread crumbs and could easily be carried as a staple snack by travelers.

It is hard to imagine the kinds of accident that would have led to the invention of a process like this one. Indians biting into manioc tubers and falling down dead? Others stamping on the offending tubers in a rage? Biting them for revenge? Discovering that without their juices they were harmless? Hardly. The secrets of manioc were obviously discovered in the course of a patient exploration and systematic experimentation with the environment that has been going on for hundreds of years among the inhabitants of the rainforest.

Indigenous chemists discovered innumerable varieties of poisons derived from toxic plants that are unlikely even to have been sampled as food. Curare is the best known of these. It is prepared from the bark, stems, and roots of plants that must be singled out in the tangled jungle. Each people that uses it has its own way of preparing it, but the poison is generally smeared onto the tips of darts that can then be fired through a blowgun at birds or animals that are being hunted. It is especially useful in dense jungle because it acts so quickly: animals on the ground cannot run far when they are mortally wounded and so elude the hunters. Monkeys in the jungle canopy do not die and stay up there, clinging to the branches, because curare is a lethal relaxant. The monkey loses its hold and comes crashing down.

The principle active ingredient of curare is tubocurarine, which is currently much used as a muscle relaxant during surgery. This is not the only discovery that has found its way from the folk remedies of tribal peoples into the pharmacopoeia of modern medicine. Many of our antibiotics, tranquilizers, sedatives, anesthetics, pain relievers, and laxatives have come to us from the same source. So have digitoxin and digoxin (used to combat heart failure), ergotamine (against migraine), salicin (for pain and inflammation), morphine (for pain), and a host of others.

Tribal Pharmacology and the Burning of the Tropical Rainforest

The tropical
rainforest is home to
approximately
70 percent of the
million or so species
of higher plants that
are believed to
inhabit the earth.
Scientists have
named only about
250,000 of these
species, which are
becoming extinct at
a rate faster than
we can name them.
Of those plants that
have been named,
only a tiny fraction
have been scientifi-
cally studied. Among
these are many of
our most important
drugs. Tribal
peoples, on the
other hand, use
thousands of species
of higher plants in
their medical prac-
tices. Many of these
have not yet been
botanically named,

let alone studied by scientists. We are just beginning to appreciate how much more tribal peoples know about plants and their properties than we do.

The conflagration of the tropical rainforest threatens not only countless species of plants but also the cultures and individuals who know their properties and use them in their daily lives. What we are witnessing makes the burning of the library of ancient Alexandria look insignificant by comparison. It is as if the greatest medical library in the world is burning faster than we can read its contents, which we have just begun to catalog.

A Sampling Of Plant Medicines

Plant Sources	Use In Traditional Cultures	Use In Medical Sciences
Horse chestnut	Inflammations	Antiinflammatory
Indian snakeroot	Tranquilizer	Circulatory stimulant
Belladona	Dilate pupil of eye	Anticholinergic
Papaya	Digestant	Proteolytic; mucolytic
Autumn crocus	Gout	Antitumor agent; antigout
Lily of the valley	Cardiotonic	Cardiotonic
Tumeric	Choleretic	Choleretic
Common foxglove	Cardiotonic	Cardiotonic
May apple	Cancer	Antitumor agent
Paradise tree	Amebicide	Amebicide
Cotton	Male contraceptive	Male contraceptive
Goldenseal	Astringent	Hemostatic; astringent
Henbane	Sedative	Anticholinergic
Toothpick plant	Asthma	Bronchodilator
Indian tobacco	Expectorant	Respiratory stimulant
Rattlebox	Skin cancer	Antitumor agent
Opium poppy	Analgesic; sedative	Analgesic
False hellebore	Hypertension	Antihypertensive
Quinine	Malaria	Antimalarial; antipyretic
Yellow azalea	Antihypertensive	Antihypertensive; tranquilizer
Nasturtium	Chronic bronchitis	Antitussive
Chinese stephania	Sedative	Analgesic; sedative
Levant wormseed	Anthelmintic	Ascaricide
Squill	Cardiotonic	Cardiotonic
Holy thistle	Liver disorders	Antihepatotoxic
Nux vomica	Toxic stimulant	Central nervous system stimulant
Cocoa, cacao	Diuretic	Diuretic; vasodilator
Kuntze (Tea)	Diuretic; stimulant	Diuretic: bronchodilator
Common periwinkle	Cardiovascular disorders	Cerebral stimulant
Pierre ex Beille	Aphrodisiac	Adrenergic blocker; aphrodisiac

The drugs that interest the indigenous peoples most of all, it seems, are the psychotropic ones. They have developed scores of different mind-altering substances. These are invariably compounds – and not simple ones either. They are mixtures of substances drawn from plants and creepers, blended through proper processes and in the proper proportions to give the desired effect. Nor are the effects particularly enjoyable, in the usual sense of the word. One of the most common hallucinogens used in the Amazonian regions causes those who drink it to vomit at once. The physical effect may ultimately feel cleansing, but it is initially wrenching, as are the mental consequences. People hallucinate and are often terrified of what they see and feel. They do not, then, take these drugs casually or for momentary pleasure but in order to know what is unknowable in their ordinary state, to see with the inner eye that understands the connectedness of things.

It is this connectedness that tribal peoples seek. Practical knowledge of the environment, of crops and medicines, of hunting and fishing, is a byproduct of it. For us it tends to be the other way around. We have prospered both intellectually and materially by separating ourselves from our environment and by seeking to dominate it. This sense of mastery is usually associated with the scientific and industrial revolutions of the nineteenth century and also, ironically, with the theories of evolution that were formulated at that time and have provided many of our current ideas about the interconnectedness of living forms.

It was Charles Darwin and Alfred Russel Wallace who, in the 1850s, developed a theory of natural selection and brought a concern with evolutionary process into the mainstream of scientific thinking. In broad outline, their theory proposed that species had to adapt to the constraints of the environment or face extinction. According to this evolutionary perspective, living forms are constantly subject to a process whereby nature "selects" the most "fit" varieties, while the unfit eventually die out.

This theory, which came to be known as "the survival of the fittest," was often taken to imply that man owed his place at the top of the evolutionary ladder to the peculiar fitness that human beings had demonstrated. And if European man stood astride the globe in the nineteenth century, then this too was taken by social Darwinists as evidence that he – and it was *he* – was especially fit to dominate other races.

But evolutionary theory can be read quite differently. Both Darwin and Wallace focused in their theories on the place of human beings within nature. Wallace especially was trying to develop a systematic way of thinking about the natural world that would include human beings as a part of it. The story of Darwin and Wallace is the stuff of scientific high drama. They developed their evolutionary theories independently, but somehow Darwin contrived to get the credit and the limelight, overshadowing Wallace in life as well as for posterity. Yet

In the Brazilian rainforest, a Kayapo woman prepares for the maize festival by painting her face with a pigment containing crushed ants. Encoded in this ritual is part of the Kayapo canon of ecological wisdom: out in the woman's jungle garden, foraging ants protect her plantings of manioc and maize; attracted by manioc nectar, ants cut down the wild vines that choke the crop. Thus, they not only weed the garden, they fertilize it, for the rotting vines enrich the soil.

it is quite possible that if the scientific world had taken its cue from Wallace rather than Darwin then the whole interest in cybernetics (the theory of feedback systems) might have developed a hundred years earlier. Wallace, after all, compared the process of natural selection to the workings of a steam engine with a governor. Just as the governor checks and corrects irregularities in the engine before they become evident, so no imbalance in the animal kingdom can ever become too great, because it would make itself felt early on by rendering existence difficult and extinction sure to follow. Natural selection therefore operated, for Wallace, with built-in principles for self-correction that he was interested in investigating. But he was concerned that the unique development of the human brain, which for the first time in history allowed a species some partial escape from the laws of natural selection, might be a mixed blessing. Our complex forms of cooperation and communication allow us a guiding hand in how we are to evolve, but also give us unusual powers of destruction and self-destruction.

The implications of these ideas were not taken up in Wallace's time, but they are becoming increasingly influential in our own. One of the first to be strongly influenced by them was a British anthropologist by the name of Gregory Bateson, who did fieldwork in the Pacific in the 1930s. After the Second World War, Bateson met Norbert Weiner, the inventor of cybernetics, and himself became interested in the idea of feedback. So he began to look not only at social processes but also at psychological, biological, and ecological ones as feedback systems.

This led him to studies of communication among human beings, to investigations of schizophrenia and to theories concerning family psychotherapy. It also led him to study communication among dolphins and to try to unravel the puzzles of interspecies communication as well. Bateson refused to be restrained by the boundaries of conventional academic investigation. He was convinced that all things are connected and so he spent his life trying to develop a scientific understanding of those connections.

Such theories are the basis for our latest ecological thinking. But the idea of the interconnectedness of things has been central to the tribal way of looking at the world since time immemorial. For example, human beings have, for the greater part of the history of our species on this earth, lived by hunting and gathering. They have thus been predators in a much more immediate sense even than we are today, when those of us who eat meat rarely go near a slaughterhouse. Yet peoples who lived by hunting and gathering did not – and do not to this day – consider themselves the lords of creation. On the contrary, they are more likely to believe in (and work hard to maintain) a kind of reciprocity between human beings and the species they are obliged to hunt for food.

The Xerente Indians, whom I have been visiting for years, love to hunt peccary, the wild pig of central Brazil. They think of peccary as being very like human beings. They are sociable, always travel in flocks, and are dangerous when confronted. They live like humans, but in the underworld, and the Xerente tell many stories of people who visited the peccary world and of some who never came back. One tale that was very popular with Xerente audiences was that of the man who was an unlucky hunter. One day he wounded a peccary and, to his surprise, the peccary begged for his life, asking the hunter to let him go back to his family in

If you put God outside and set him vis-a-vis his creation and if you have the idea that you are created in his image, you will logically and naturally see yourself as outside and against the things around you. And as you arrogate all mind to yourself, you will see the world around you as mindless and therefore not entitled to moral or ethical consideration. The environment will seem to be yours to exploit. Your survival unit will be you and your folks or conspecifics against the environment of other social units, other races and the brutes and vegetables.

If this is your estimate of your relation to nature *and you have an advanced technology,* your likelihood of survival will be that of a snowball in hell. You will die either of the toxic by-products of your own hate, or, simply, of over-population and overgrazing. The raw materials of the world are finite.

From Gregory Bateson, *Steps to an Ecology of Mind* (New York: Ballantine, 1972).

STEPS TO AN ECOLOGY OF MIND

the underworld. The hunter agreed, and the grateful peccary promised to reward him. Henceforward, he said, he would see to it that the hunter always found peccary when he and his fellows went out hunting. The hunter's friends could kill them but the hunter himself must refrain, for he had a pact with the peccary.

So the young Xerente became famous as a man who could always find peccary when he went out. The hunting parties he led would come back loaded down with wild pig, but he himself would never bring any. Predictably, his wife started to complain. How was it that he was so good at finding peccary and so bad at hunting them? It was humiliating for her to have to accept handouts from everybody else's game and never be able to give any in return. At this point in the telling the men, who always gathered to listen when it was being told, regularly broke out into exasperated comments. "Just like a woman! They never understand!" they would say. I thought the young wife was being quite reasonable, especially since her husband never tried to explain his problem to her, but I kept my thoughts to myself. Anyway, she kept up her nagging until one day her husband could stand it no longer. He drew his bow and mortally wounded a peccary. The wounded animal turned on him and upbraided him for breaking his compact with the pigs. Then he took the hunter down with him into the peccary world, from which he never returned.

This Xerente story is what our theologians would call a "hard" parable. It tells of a difficult choice between two obligations. The hunter's wife is humiliated because she cannot reciprocate when other women give her peccary meat – a delicacy among the Xerente. She does not understand that her husband has, in a sense, already provided the meat she receives from the others and he, Xerente-like, does not bother to enlighten her. Nor does he bother to tell her of his pact with the peccary, which puts him under a competing obligation. The moral of the story is, however, crystal clear. The human covenant with the animal world is fundamental and takes precedence over human social relations.

The reciprocity between hunter and hunted is even more elaborately expressed in the ideas of the Makuna Indians of southeastern Colombia. They are one of several Tukanoan-speaking groups living along the Negro and Vaupes rivers contacted by Wallace and the naturalist Henry Bates during their famous expedition to the Amazon and its tributaries in the 1850s.

Wallace was impressed with the Tukanoan Indians – especially with their physical beauty, their care for one another, their self-sufficiency, and their independence from the artifices of civilization. Wallace saw them as living as closely as possible to a "true state of nature." Had he been able to spend more time with them, he would have discovered that their "state of nature" involved a sophisticated view of the interconnectedness of everything in the natural world (including human beings) that paralleled his own ideas.

The Makuna believe that human beings, animals, and all of nature are parts of the same One. Their ancestors were fish people who emerged in the form of anacondas from the Water Doorway at the east of their world. They swam upriver until they entered the Pira-Parana and the Apaporis rivers. The ancestors came ashore along these rivers and turned into people in the birth houses of the clans that make up Makuna society. Out of their bodies or by their actions these ancestors created everything in the world, the hills and forests, the animals and the people. They carved out river valleys by pushing their sacred musical instruments in front of them.

People, animals, fish all share the same spiritual essence and so, Makuna say, animals and fish live in their own communities, which are just like human communities. They have their chiefs, their shamans, their dance houses, birth houses, and "waking up houses" (places where they originally came into being as species). They have their songs and dances and their material possessions. Above all, animals and fish are just like men because they wear ritual ornaments, consume spirit foods – coca, snuff, and the hallucinogenic brew called *yage* – and use the sacred *yurupari* instruments in their ceremonies. When shamans blow over coca, snuff, and other spirit foods during human ceremonies, they are offering them to the animal people. When human beings dance in this world, the shaman invites the animal people to dance in theirs. If humans do not dance and shamans do not offer spirit food to the animal people, the animals will die out and there will be no more game left in this world.

Fish people, like animal people and human beings, have their own communities inhabiting their own territories. The owners of their houses are anacondas and water monsters, known as the fathers of the fishes. When humans think the fish are spawning, they are actually dancing in their birth houses. That is why it is particularly dangerous to eat fish that have been caught at the spawning places, for then one eats a person who is ceremonially painted and in full dance regalia. If a human being does this or enters a fish house by mistake, he will sicken and die, for his soul will be carried away to the houses of the fish people, like the Xerente who was borne away by the peccary.

The Swedish anthropologist Kaj Århem, who is a modern authority on the Makuna, describes their ecological practices and cosmological speculations as an "ecosophy," where the radical disjunction – so characteristic of Western thought – between nature and culture, men and animals, dissolves.

It is clear that Makuna beliefs have specific ecological consequences. The sacredness of saltlicks and fish-spawning places, the careful reciprocity between humans and their fellow animals and fish, all mediated by respected shamans, guarantee that the Makuna manage their environment and do not plunder it. Århem suggests that the Makuna offer a lesson to the industrialized world. We need an ecosophy of our own, imbued with moral commitment and emotional power, if we are to protect the resource base on which we depend and ensure not

V E N A N C I O

The Makuna Indians live in the Vaupés region of eastern Colombia, where dense rain-forests crowd the headwaters of the Amazon. Venancio spent thirteen of his formative years at a Catholic mission school far away from his village of Santa Isabel. His father, Ignacio, is a revered shaman of the area. It was his decision to alternately send a son out to school and keep a son in the village to learn Makuna ways.

"I always knew I would come back," says Venancio, now thirty-two years old. "It was when I had children that I asked myself the question, Will they be Colombians or Makuna? Then I realized I would have to come back and learn from my father."

What Venancio is learning from Ignacio is the history and mythology of his people and a different way of seeing the world. As Ignacio says, "The whites only see with their eyes and hear through their ears. We Indians can see and hear with our minds."

The guns of professional hide hunters and those of railroad passengers killed more than a million buffalo a year in the 1870s. By the mid-1880s the buffalo had vanished from the Great Plains, and with them the hunting cultures of the Sioux, Comanches, Arapahos, Cheyennes, and others.

only our own survival but that of our fellow creatures on this earth.

We, unlike the Makuna, tend to forget our environment except when we want to extract wealth from it or use it as the backdrop for a scenic expedition. Then we take what we want. There is no compact, none of the reciprocity so characteristic of tribal societies. For the most part we mine the earth and leave it, for we do not feel we belong to it. It belongs to us. This rootlessness and the waste that goes with it are particularly shocking to traditional societies.

The Indians of the western United States were outraged by the way in which the invaders of their territories squandered the resources that they themselves used so sparingly. The Indians on the plains lived off the buffalo, killing only as many as they needed and using every bit of the dead animals. They ate the meat, made tents and clothes from the hides, and used the bones to make arrow-straighteners, bows, mallets, even splints for setting fractures. They made butter from the marrow fat and cords from the sinews. When the white buffalo hunters came, it was more than an invasion. It was a sacrilege. These men slaughtered the herds with their powerful rifles, often taking only the tongue to eat and leaving the rest of the animal to rot.

The deep sadness of the Indians over this slaughter was expressed in a speech, delivered in 1854 to an assembly of tribes preparing to sign away their lands under duress to the white man. The speaker was Chief Seattle, after whom the city of Seattle is named. The moving words of this statesman-poet speak as much to us about our own predicament as they did to his fellow chiefs about their defeated civilization. "What is man without the beasts?" he asked. "If all the beasts were gone, man would die from a great loneliness of spirit. For whatever happens to the beasts, soon happens to man. All things are connected."

Chief Seattle understood only too well the vast differences between the ways in which the white man dealt with the world and the Indian lived in it. He feared the consequences of the white man's victory:

> We know that the white man does not understand our ways. One portion of the land is the same to him as the next, for he is a stranger who comes in the night and takes from the land whatever he needs. The earth is not his brother, but his enemy, and when he has conquered it, he moves on. He leaves his fathers' graves behind, and he does not care. He kidnaps the earth from his children. He does not care. His fathers' graves and his children's birthright are forgotten. He treats his mother, the earth, and his brother, the sky, as things to be bought, plundered, sold like sheep or bright beads. His appetite will devour the earth and leave behind only a desert.

It is above all a vastly different attitude toward the land that separates our industrial civilization from that of tribal peoples. Among tribal peoples, land may be used but it cannot be bought or sold. As Chief Seattle said: "The idea is strange to us. If we do not own the freshness of the air, and the sparkle of the water, how can you buy them?" It is different among "civilized" folk, where land is a commodity and most of it is owned by a few people, whose interests do not necessarily lie either in the community or the land itself, but simply in turning a profit.

The earth is not yet a desert, but a dispassionate observer might well wonder if the modern world is not deranged in its restless quest for unlimited growth and its assumption that we may use this earth as if we were not part of it. We have become accustomed to the idea that growth is the measure of success: Darwin took high rates of reproduction as the criterion of a successful species, but even Darwin's theories have now been revised. We now know that disastrous consequences threaten those species that cannot regulate their rate of reproduction and that overexploit the resources of their environment.

We are protected from this knowledge by cities. We take shelter in this man-made environment and act as if it were independent of the natural world. It is small wonder then that our cities are coming to resemble cancers, growing uncontrollably, invading the land and threatening to destroy it. On a sunlit morning the cities on the dark side of our planet are visible from space by the light

Chief Seattle (1788-1866)

they produce but the cities on the light side cannot be seen. They are shrouded from view in a pall of their own pollution.

Yet cities are the symbols of modern civilization. Until recently the largest cities in the world were also the richest. They were the showplaces of the twentieth century, the engines of our progress, the focus of our thoughts and the bearers of our dreams. Not everybody lives in them, of course, though in poorer countries it increasingly seems as if everybody is trying to. Today it is in Third World countries that huge cities are to be found, their populations swollen by the poor and the desperate, their resources overtaxed, their water and air threatened. It is as if cities are becoming modern Frankenstein monsters that we built to serve us and over which we are losing control.

WILLIAM IRWIN THOMPSON ON NATURE

In a recent interview on *Ideas,* a national radio show of the Canadian Broadcasting Corporation, the cultural historian William Irwin Thompson spoke about the idea of "nature":*

When we say "nature," we're really influenced by the Sierra Club calendars, the Elliot Porter photographs, Ansel Adams, which are influenced by Constable and by Gainsborough....a kind of 18th-century gentlemanly vision of the great estate and the park...[but] that's a cultural idea. It has nothing to do with nature. In the 19th century, nature was objective and the observer was subjective and had no value. All value therefore came by decreasing subjective contamination to achieve a reading of nature which was pure and true, and the most pure was where human was least present. ...We now have the same thing, only we call it deep ecology, that nature is at its purest when it's not contaminated by trailer parks...by weekend hikers...by selling pharmaceuticals from the Amazon rainforest.... But there is no such thing as that nature, that's a fiction. Nature is the horizon of culture. Every time you change cultures, you change the horizon....if one really wants to understand what's going on in the shifting horizons of our culture, one has to understand nature as going in two directions simultaneously. One is the return to nature, with the Greens, and the other is the destruction of nature in the cyberpunk landscape of things like *Blade Runner* or *Neuromancer.* And unless you look at both of those edges of our culture and ask yourself what is nature, I don't think you'll really come up with the transformation that's going on right under our nose.

*Taken from transcripts of the *Ideas* program "The Age of Ecology." Part II, 10–11. Copyright © 1990 The Canadian Broadcasting Corporation.

It is true that poets and reformers have always hated cities, hated them for their arrogance and impersonality, for their slums and tenements. The great Spanish poet Federico García Lorca reacted with horror when he visited New York in the 1930s. He wrote:

> The New York dawn has
> four columns of mud
> and a hurricane of black doves
> that paddle in putrescent waters.
> . . . .
> The light is buried under chains and noises
> in impudent challenge of rootless science.

Chief Seattle would have agreed with him. He said: "There is no quiet place in the white man's cities. No place to hear the unfurling of the leaves in spring or the rustle of insect wings." Yet the clatter and clang that so distressed Lorca and grieved Chief Seattle is to others the sound of progress, the guarantee of civilization or, at the very least, of an escape from rural squalor.

The problem, as Lorca perceived at once, is not science but a "rootless science" that gives us a false sense of mastery over an earth to which we feel we do not belong. We do not treat the cities as our tribal lands, and we have no shamans to tell us how to ensure that our relationship to them and to their surroundings is harmonious. We do have scientists who warn us about our abuse of the earth, but we ignore what they say, especially if the solutions they suggest cost us in money or convenience. Our science could be our salvation, but it cannot save us unless we are deeply convinced of Chief Seattle's words: "Whatever befalls the earth befalls the sons of the earth. Man did not weave the web of life, he is merely a strand in it. Whatever he does to the web, he does to himself."

A POOR MAN SHAMES US ALL

A flotilla of canoes cuts through the green waters of the western Pacific. A fresh breeze fills their sails so that they race along, lifting their outrigger floats clear of the water. Their crews sing with the exhilaration of it all and little boys lean out and play with the water, excited by the bounce and buoyancy of their speeding craft. But the *toliwaga*, the master of each canoe, does not join in the singing. He is more than the captain of the ship. He is also its master of ceremonies. It is up to him to perform the continuous rituals on which the success of the expedition depends, and it is he who must be strictest in respecting the taboos that surround the expedition.

The fleet presents an impressive sight as it makes for a big, sheltered bay on the eastern tip of New Guinea. A village is coming up over the horizon, its beautifully carved and painted houses standing amid the palms, surrounded by mango and breadfruit trees. There are nets drying on the glistening white sands of the beach, but they are obscured now by the throngs of people running down to the shore to watch the arrival of the visitors.

Sixty canoes in full sail come sweeping into the bay. There are five hundred people in them, all male, for they come from the western part of the Trobriand Islands where it is not customary for women to accompany such expeditions. They have come to trade, but this is no ordinary trading fleet. The precious items they bring are arm bracelets and necklaces made from beautifully polished shells. But their hosts have similar bracelets and necklaces themselves, all carefully worked and ceremonially handled. The canoes wait in the bay while the master of the fleet mounts a platform and makes an impassioned speech to the crowd on the beach. He urges them to be generous, to give more valuables to their visitors than ever before. As he finishes his speech a conch-shell horn is blown from the shore, sounded by his trading partner, who then wades into the water and offers the first necklace to the visiting dignitary. Soon horns are being blown up and down the beach, as men detach themselves from the throng and wade out to their partners with welcoming gifts. It is only when all these gifts have been given that the visitors can come ashore.

The visitors from the islands now anoint themselves with coconut oil and put on their finest ornaments. They make themselves as seductive as they can, performing their personal ceremonies and casting their private spells to ensure a successful outcome in the transactions they are about to undertake. Then they seek out their partners among their hosts and give them arm bracelets in exchange for the necklaces. They also seek out other partners from whom they expect arm bracelets and give them necklaces. The exchanges go on for days, until the fleet puts out to sea again to sail hundreds of miles back to their home villages in the Trobriands. Eventually their hosts will mount a similar expedition of their own and sail through the archipelago at the eastern tip of New Guinea until they arrive at the Trobriand Islands themselves to reciprocate the trade.

The whole system of visits and exchanges is called the *kula*. It was first described in detail by Bronislaw Malinowski, a Pole who grew up in Kraków, moved to England, and became one of the leaders of British anthropology in the

One of the large canoes the Trobriand Islanders use on their long-distance voyages.

1920s and 1930s. His marvelously vivid accounts of the way of life of the Trobriand Islanders have become classics in anthropology, none more so than his book *Argonauts of the Western Pacific* (1922). In it he describes the kula and the elaborate arrangements it entailed. It takes months to prepare a major kula expedition. The participants, often from villages separated by days of voyaging, have to decide who is going and when and where to. The canoes have to be built and launched and the departure feasts organized. Then the fleet puts out to sea, leaving behind the shallow lagoon of the Trobriands and sailing over waters that are now a dark and ominous green. The voyages are dangerous. Canoes can be blown off course and, if they are unlucky, out into the open ocean never to be seen again. They can smash up and sink in storms or heavy seas. They can be seized by giant octopuses or chased and destroyed by the live stones that lie in wait for sailing canoes. They have to run the gauntlet of witches who like to eat shipwrecked sailors, and they must at all costs avoid the islands where the women are so beautiful, big, and strong that no man can survive the violence of their passion. No wonder the whole enterprise of the kula is punctuated by rituals and surrounded by taboos. No wonder the individuals who venture out on these hazardous voyages take special precautions and use their own spells as well as the communal rituals to bring them safely through and to ensure a successful outcome.

But what is a successful outcome, when the intrepid traders come bearing valuables their hosts already possess, and for which they will receive similar items in return? In fact, what is the point of the kula? It is clearly not trade in the ordinary sense of the word. Nor can it be dismissed as a confused kind of trading practiced by people not modern enough to know how to trade properly, for the people in this part of the world are famous for being astute in ordinary commercial transactions. The Trobrianders know all about trading, which they call *gimwali* and which they consider to be sharply distinct from kula. It is in their eyes a severe censure of a man to say that he behaves in the kula as if he were engaged in gimwali.

Men do not take part in the kula to make a profit in the ordinary financial sense. They do it for social gain, since the kula system gives its participants far-flung networks of partners and partners' partners along the paths that will be traveled by the bracelets and the necklaces. These networks link individuals from different tribes, speaking different languages, over a wide area of the western Pacific. The more successful an individual is in these exchanges, the more kula paths he can become part of and the more extensive will be his networks. Wherever he is likely to go, he will find a kula partner. If he becomes famous within the kula system, his name will be known by people beyond the horizon whom he has never met, but who have received valuables that have passed through his hands.

The valuables themselves vary in quality. Both the necklaces and the arm bracelets are ranked in terms of the size, color, polish, and smoothness of the shells. A man acquires prestige by passing on especially beautiful ornaments. He must be a skillful negotiator to get others to pass on such high-ranking valuables to him. That is why men make themselves irresistibly beautiful and persuasive, in order to "seduce" their kula partners into parting with the most beautiful ornaments they have. A man who is good at the kula will multiply his networks and make himself "strong" within the system, eventually obliging others to wait on his timing and on his decisions about which valuables to pass on, when, and to whom. A strong man no longer acquires renown by receiving and passing on a famous ornament. Now it is the ornament whose fame is enhanced by passing through the hands of a man of renown.

Annette Weiner, a modern authority on the kula system, tells us that Trobrianders still engage in it. Young men holding positions in business and government in Port Moresby, the capital of Papua New Guinea, enter the kula in order to spread their fame, and candidates may run for office in the legislature on the basis of their renown in the kula. The Trobrianders say, moreover, that kula for them is like a bank. What does this system have in common with banks as we know them? It not only depends on credit and confidence in order to function at all, but it also enables a skillful investor to build up his capital. All the same, the kula is in a fundamental way quite the opposite of a modern bank. Banks are part of an economic system that depends on the ownership and accumulation of money, which can be exchanged for goods and services. Kula is central to a system where ownership is of minor importance, and where wealth and prestige accrue to men who give well and in that way succeed in mobilizing networks of people who are obligated to them.

The crucial importance of giving in human affairs was brilliantly analyzed by the French anthropologist Marcel Mauss in his *Essay on the Gift*, published in 1925. Mauss was gathering data for his essay when he read Malinowski's work on the kula, which he promptly included, for it provided an independent confirmation of his conclusions. Mauss pointed out that, since earliest times, the exchange of gifts has been the central mechanism through which human beings relate to one another. The reason is that the essence of a gift is obligation. A person who gives a gift compels the recipient either to make a return gift or to reciprocate in some other way. Obligation affects the giver as well. It is not entirely up to him whether or when he will bestow a gift. Even in the modern world, which prides itself on its pragmatism, people are expected to give gifts on certain occasions, at weddings, at childbirth, at Christmas, and so on. People are expected to invite others to receive food and drink in their houses and those so invited are expected to return the favor.

Mauss argued that the life of traditional societies revolves around such expectations. People are enmeshed throughout their lives in systems of gift exchange and it is through these exchanges that they fulfill their social obligations. In fact, the English language and others closely related to it show that in northern Europe not so very long ago people did not draw hard and fast distinctions between obligations which we would consider "debts" and others which we would not, or even between obligations which make us feel guilt if we do not discharge them and others which are formal debts that need to be repaid. So the German word *schuld* today means both "debt" and "guilt." The German word *gelt* means "money" today, but it is related to the English word *guilt*. The Danish word *gaeld* means "debt," and it is related both to German *gelt*, "money," and English "guilt." Debt and guilt were thus closely related ideas among the peoples of northern Europe,

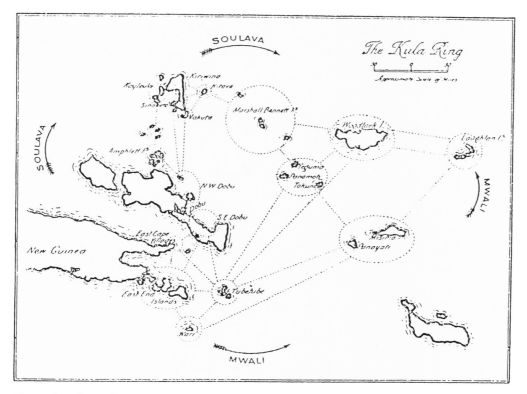

The "Kula Ring" of the Trobriand Islanders. The *soulava* (necklaces) are traded in a clockwise direction, while the *mwali* (armbands) are traded in a counter-clockwise direction. By having the necklaces go one way and the armbands the other through the islands, the kula system keeps the greatest number of people active in maintaining trade connections.

ideas that later became entangled with notions of money as a means of paying debts and assuaging guilt.

Mauss pointed out that traditional societies depended on these feelings of obligation, these debts that were constantly being repaid and creating new debts in their turn. Gifts were the means used to create these obligations. It was gifts that bound people to one another and made society work. It follows that in such societies a rich person is not somebody who accumulates wealth in money and goods but rather somebody who has a large network of people beholden to him. Such networks are the instrument through which prominent people can demonstrate their prestige. They are also the safety net that sees an individual through the crises of life.

In modern societies these networks have shrunk, just as the family continues to shrink. There are fewer and fewer people to whom we feel obligated and, more ominously, fewer and fewer who feel obligated to us. When we think of a safety net, when our politicians speak of it, we refer to arrangements made by abstract entities – the state, the corporation, the insurance company, the pension fund – entities we would not dream of giving presents to; entities we hope will provide for us (and fear they will not). The immediate reciprocities of Trobriand interaction have given way in our larger and more impersonal societies to "mechanisms of redistribution." We know they do not function very well. What does function well in our society is the market.

Even occasions like Christmas, the time of gift-giving par excellence, where sentiment is supposed to reign supreme, become moments of marketing frenzy. Most of us do not need the gifts we get at Christmas in a material sense. What we do need is to keep alive the feeling that there are people who care about us enough to give us presents or send us cards. But we do not create widening networks of people indebted to one another out of our personal need for such exchanges; we simply go on a buying spree. We do not of course go shopping to prevent the stores from going bankrupt, but that seems to be the major effect of our festival of sentiment. In traditional societies people have to care about others, even about people they may not like or do not know, because the system depends on it. Modern societies do not.

Yet modern societies produce more goods, make their members more comfortable physically, and give them choices and possibilities in their lives that far exceed the capacities of traditional ones. So what is the problem? Surely the commercialization of Christmas is a small price to pay for all the goodies that appear under the tree. The problem is that people seem to be diminished in the modern way of living. We can produce an extraordinary range of goods, but we do not have a distribution system, or a belief in one, that is able to counteract the poverty within our affluence. Our economics does not operate as if people mattered. The notion of wealth that comes from giving things away is strange to us. No matter whether we think such behavior is saintly or silly, most of us agree that it is unworldly.

This attitude is not shared by the Weyewa people on the island of Sumba in eastern Indonesia. Joel Kuipers, an anthropologist who is currently working among them, tells us that their society is organized around the fundamental principal of exchange, whether in personal, social, or cosmic relationships. Like all Sumbanese, the Weyewa say that everything has its pair, its opposite, and life is lived in the dynamic tension between the pull of one side and the push of the other. The Weyewa divide their social world into people who give wives to us and people who take wives from us. This distinction between wife-givers and wife-takers is for them a cosmic principle, part of the permanent structure of life, not a momentary contrast that is important only at the time of a marriage. Marriages do not create the categories of wife-givers and wife-takers but rather continue them and rearrange them. Weyewa find Western-style romance literally inhuman. They feel that selecting and marrying a spouse without the elaborate exchanges between givers and takers that are necessary on Sumba is like animals coupling. It is something done outside of society, something that has no social consequences and no moral sanction.

On Sumba, marriage produces the largest and most elaborate exchanges in a system that is built on exchange. Female goods are offered by the wife-givers to the husband's clan; cloth and pigs accompany the bride to her husband's residence. Male goods are given in return by the husband's people to the wife's clan: cattle and gold to compensate her family for the reproductive powers they are losing. The necessary exchanges are so complex and costly that a young man

In this painting by an unidentified crew member of Captain Cook's *Endeavour*, a Maori tribesman exchanges a crayfish for a handkerchief. Although the painting depicts a simple exchange of gifts, it also indicates a merging of tribal and market economies. The crayfish was locally caught, the handkerchief was most likely manufactured in a British textile mill.

looking for a wife must have the support of his kinsmen if he hopes to accumulate the required outlay. He and his father then hold what is essentially a fundraising party. The kinsmen who come to the feast are, by participating, promising to contribute to his bridewealth. So many animals and so much treasure are exchanged at marriage, so many social ties cemented, that divorce is understandably rare. The business of trying to undo it all is too complicated.

Less common but even more spectacular exchanges occur during Weyewan stone-dragging ceremonies. It is customary in Sumba for distinguished men to organize a reburial of the remains of one of their ancestors. This involves a massive mobilization of people to drag a twenty-five-ton rock from the quarry where it has been cut to the site where it will mark the new tomb. Stone-dragging is a true test of wealth, of how many people – exchange partners, people who "owe him one" – a man can call on for the biggest exchange of all, the one between the living and the dead. A great stone-dragging involves such a wide range of personal relations and social obligations that it is called "a cloth of extraordinary weave," and the Sumbanese are master weavers.

Why is any man willing to do this? The debts he will incur are enormous, debts that he himself will never be able to repay in his lifetime, debts that will flow through to his children and his children's children. Does he hate his children or is he simply indifferent to them? Is he mortgaging their future to enhance his own prestige? The truth is quite the opposite. He is doing all he can to widen the exchange networks for future generations to ensure their wealth and prosperity.

THE STONE-DRAG

Lende Mbatu, powerful patriarch of the Weyewa people of Sumba, Indonesia, has made a promise to the spirit of his dead father to drag a twenty-five-ton rock in order to construct a new tomb in his honor. Over four hundred men are needed to drag this "burden of dreams" from the quarry to its final resting spot more than one mile away.

The economic and social obligations Lende must bear are considerable. It is not a question of having enough money to finance the event since the Weyewa do not have a cash-based economy. Weyewa society is organized around the principle of exchange, where wealth is measured in terms of the number of people with whom you have exchange relations. Lende is about to find out just how wealthy he is: Does he have enough exchange partners who feel obligated to help him? The stone-drag will be a public test of his wealth and status.

Lende's exchange partners arrive in great numbers. The stone is successfully dragged to its new location. Animals are slaughtered and a great feast is prepared. Lende is delighted. He has fulfilled his promise to his father, and he has increased his stature and wealth within the community. Lende looks around at the hundreds of laborers and guests and says to himself, "My corrals are all empty but my wealth is all around me."

At the same time he is raising or confirming his own status in the eyes of all the participants. The more "others" with whom he exchanges favors, knowledge, and cooperation the "wealthier" he is. As one senior Weyewan put it: "I'm not a rich man according to most human reckonings but I am rich in ability and I am rich in knowledge, I'm rich in favors and I'm rich in cooperation with others."

Such a man is rich by Sumbanese standards and therefore has standing in the community. When he goes to the homes of his "kinsmen" to request their help in pulling the stone, he is bringing them something already – his stature. These kinsmen may have only a very distant blood-tie to his clan but they are considered kinsmen because they are exchange partners. He may find them involved in a lesser ceremony of their own. If so he will chant in ritual language, exhorting them to maintain their unity (and also their unity with him). He knows that his presence heightens the occasion, but he speaks humbly when asking for their support and their labor. The kinsmen know that by helping him they will in fact increase his stature, but they will also increase their own because he will now owe them.

A Weyewan elder explained the nature of Sumbanese exchange economics in terms that would have gladdened the heart of Marcel Mauss. "It's the custom of life everywhere on this earth [i.e., in his society] that we exchange our belongings and we don't hang on to what we have. It's our custom to exchange. We exchange favors and we exchange meat and we exchange labor – how else could it be?... You offer me one hundred people or I offer you two hundred people in support – in this way we exchange labor, and this after all is the only way we can reach our goals.... If it wasn't like this what else could we do?" It is important to note that the exchanges are never quite equivalent. One guest might bring a huge tusked pig to the feast and receive a Sumbanese cloth in return. Another might bring a water buffalo and receive a small pig in return. Yet everyone is happy. A guest would be mortified if he received an equivalent countergift for it would mean that his exchange relationship was over, that the accounts were now balanced. The idea is to maintain an ongoing debt-credit relationship where sometimes you will owe and at other times you will be owed. Extend that to a few hundred people and you will begin to see what wealth is on Sumba – the more people you have such relationships with the larger your human resource base is. One of the mysteries of such a system is how people remember all the complicated debits and credits extended to so many people and across so many generations. One of the marvels of the system is that they do.

But Weyewans are not ignorant of the encroaching modern world and its radically different style of economic practice. The Dutch controlled Sumba from the middle of the nineteenth century. After independence in the 1960s the Indonesians took over what the Dutch began. The official view of the Indonesian government is that stone-dragging and feasting are wasteful, backward, and, furthermore, dangerous. People can be killed or maimed by a runaway stone. The government says that the Sumbanese should save their animals instead of killing them for meat exchanges and sell them in the marketplace to raise money. With the money they could send their children to school, pay taxes for government services, and generally improve their lives.

The Weyewans know this argument well – they know that "the moon rises differently and the sun sets differently now," that times are changing, and that the modern world is pressing them to do things differently. They also know, however, that the path of their ancestors is the one they must follow. So they save up their animals, but not to sell. They save them for the celebrations that accompany the fulfillment of promises made to their ancestors; then they give them away to exchange partners or slaughter them to feed the people who rallied round and dragged the stone. The animal blood darkens the earth as proof to the ancestors that they too are being repaid for the lives of the living. The animals create solidarity both among the living and with the dead. To treat them as commodities to be bought or sold at market would not merely threaten the moral economy of exchange, it would destroy it. Kinsmen would compete with each other in the marketplace, each trying to outsell the other. The endless cycle of reciprocity, of mutuality, would be broken forever.

People everywhere have had to rely on one another. It has been like this since the beginning of time. Sometimes this dependency was forced through systems of slavery or serfdom. Sometimes it was maintained by subtler pressures – obligations, gifts, guilt, social indebtedness. But in the modern world we shroud our interdependency in an ideology of independence. We focus on individuals, going it alone in the economic sphere, rather than persons, interconnected in the social sphere. As Marcel Mauss put it, "It is our western societies that have recently turned man into an economic animal." What happened?

A truly revolutionary change swept Western Europe during the Renaissance and eventually came to dominate and define the modern world. It was a social revolution centering on the rights of the individual. It may seem paradoxical to speak of a *social* movement that glorifies the individual, but it is not really. All societies recognize the fact that humanity is made up of people who possess distinct personalities. All societies likewise have their individualists, men and women with powerful personalities who influence others and are willing and able to flout convention. But traditional societies denounced individualism as antisocial. In Western Europe, by contrast, a belief in the rights and dignity of the individual slowly came to be regarded as the most important aspect of society itself. Individualism was no longer considered antisocial. It was instead regarded as the engine that drove modern society and transformed stagnant feudalism into dynamic capitalism.

The change did not come quickly and there was plenty of opposition to it.

Medieval Europeans had an organic view of society as a hierarchical arrangement of persons, ordained by God and watched over by his church. People were supposed to know their place and do their duty on this earth and to seek personal salvation in the afterlife. The dignity of the individual lay in his or her relationship with God. It was a worldview that elevated faith over reasoning and acquiescence over inquiry, and it could not survive the emergence of the scientific spirit.

By the sixteenth century Europeans were beginning to question the authority both of the church and of the ancients. Leonardo da Vinci summed up this mood when he wrote, "Whoever appeals to authority applies not his intellect but his memory." Europeans increasingly applied their intellects in their efforts to understand the world around them. The spirit of scientific inquiry eroded the old certainties and led people to challenge those who tried to maintain those certainties by force. Protestants broke away from the Catholic church. It is true that they often established intolerant orthodoxies of their own, but the very existence of rival claimants to truth called the old dogmas into question. The Protestants, moreover, insisted that people did not need the church to mediate between them and God. Each person could do this for himself, provided that he studied and properly understood the holy scripture. Such ideas undermined the hierarchy of the church and exalted the role of the individual.

Meanwhile, the organic unity of medieval society was being weakened by economic forces, among which the rise of a "money" economy was paramount. What resulted was a thoroughgoing reorganization of the medieval system of duties and rewards. The whole feudal system of occupations had been seen as part of an unchanging divine order in which work was performed for the nobility by peasant farmers and artisans in exchange for protection and sustenance. With the breakup of the feudal system and the rise of towns, occupational specialists were freed to sell their services on the open market, for money. They no longer considered themselves locked into a fixed and divinely ordained occupational role for life. Henceforth, work came to be seen as a means for obtaining money. The vast and sweeping process in which money came to be the universal means of exchange, for land as well as labor, was called "rationalization" by Max Weber and "commodification" by Karl Marx. It was intensified by the European expansion, which created a global economy on the basis of plantation labor in the colonies. Ever-increasing pools of labor were now producing goods for people in far-off lands in an increasingly abstract world market. Thus the religious individualism of the Protestants came at a time when the spoils of empire and of worldwide trade were bringing new wealth to the towns of Western Europe and to the traders and manufacturers who lived in them.

These tendencies were nowhere more evident than in the Netherlands, so it is not surprising that Amsterdam became the principal center of emergent capital-

This painting of the Tulipmania of 1636–37 satirizes the folly of a society that chases wealth through speculation. Here the frenzied buyers of tulip futures are caricatured as monkeys.

ism in the sixteenth century. The Netherlands had broken with the feudal past by wresting its independence from Spain, the dominant Catholic, conservative power in Europe. The country became a haven for religious dissenters, where a certain tolerance encouraged the pursuit of free inquiry and where, above all, the handsome profits made by Dutch traders led to the development of those institutions required by a capitalist economy.

The most important of these was the bank. There had been banks elsewhere, of course – especially in Italy, which had been controlling the trade of the Mediterranean ever since anybody could remember – but their activities were hampered by the strictures of the Catholic Church against charging interest, which was considered usury and therefore sinful. Banks started as places where people could change money. Their very name comes from the word for bench or table, the one at which the money changers sat to ply their trade. Early banks contrived to receive interest on loans by pretending it was the fee charged for changing money. Later they arranged for people to deposit money with them and to transfer funds to other people by arrangement – quite a convenience, for it meant that businessmen did not have to carry around large quantities of cash, which in those days was usually in coin. But these transfers were still highly personal matters. Both parties had to go down to the bank and meet face-to-face like kula partners. There they would complete their transaction in the presence of a notary and it would be duly noted by an employee of the bank.

The Wisselbank (Exchange Bank), founded in Amsterdam in 1609, changed these procedures. It allowed merchants, for example, to settle their bills without having to follow a tangled trail of IOUs. Previously, when a merchant tried to collect cash from a debtor, he was often told that the debt had been passed on to someone else. It was up to the creditor to pursue the chain of indebtedness and

Hans Holbein's *The Ambassadors*

What distinguishes oil painting from any other form of painting is its special ability to render the tangibility, the texture, the lustre, the solidity of what it depicts. It defines the real as that which you can put your hands on. Although its painted images are two-dimensional, its potential of illusionism is far greater than that of sculpture, for it can suggest objects possessing colour, texture and temperature, filling a space and, by implication, filling the entire world.

Holbein's painting of *The Ambassadors* (1533) stands at the beginning of the tradition and, as often happens with a work at the opening of a new period, its character is undisguised....

It is painted with great skill to create the illusion in the spectator that he is looking at real objects and materials.... The two men have a certain presence and there are many objects which symbolize ideas, but it is the materials, the stuff, by which the men are surrounded and clothed which dominate the painting.

Except for the faces and hands, there is not a surface in this picture which does not make one aware of how it has been elaborately worked over – by weavers, embroiderers, carpet-makers, goldsmiths, leather workers, mosaic-makers, furriers, tailors, jewellers – and of how this working over and the resulting richness of each surface has been finally worked over and reproduced by Holbein the painter....

Works of art in earlier traditions celebrated wealth. But wealth was then a symbol of a fixed social or divine order. Oil painting celebrated a new kind of wealth – which was dynamic and which found its only sanction in the supreme buying power of money. Thus painting itself had to be able to demonstrate the desirability of what money could buy. And the visual desirability of what can be bought lies in its tangibility, in how it will reward the touch, the hand, of the owner.... The gaze of the ambassadors is both aloof and weary. They expect no reciprocity.

From John Berger, *Ways of Seeing* (Harmondsworth: Penguin, 1972).

try to collect from the person at the end of it. The Wisselbank did away with all that. People could now do business, indeed were very soon obliged to do business, through the bank. The transactions, however, were simplified because the bank did not require that business be done in person.

In Naples, Genoa, and Venice earlier banks had offered transfer services, but it was in Amsterdam that a full-blown system of writing checks on the Wisselbank was developed. The bank was the centerpiece of Amsterdam's money markets, which, in the seventeenth century, were the hub of the capitalist world. It protected the currency of the Dutch republic and gave it a stable exchange rate that proved immensely valuable in international trade. Bank money guaranteed in Amsterdam came to be used all over the world without hesitation. It not only set the exchange rate for other currencies, but it actually had to be used for certain transactions in other countries. In Russia, for example, all customs dues had to be paid in Dutch bank money. And it was not only Dutch money that was accepted everywhere; so were checks written on accounts in the Wisselbank. Coins no longer changed hands. Money had become abstract.

So abstract, in fact, that the Dutch nearly bankrupted themselves in the early seventeenth century through a frenzy of trading intended not to acquire commodities but quite simply to produce wealth. At that time tulips, now grown by the thousands in the Netherlands, were rare and exotic flowers. Owning a tulip was considered the height of fashion throughout Europe. By 1634, Dutch nurseries were producing enough tulips to bring the price of the flowers down to the levels where ordinary people could afford them. Suddenly, people with modest incomes could buy flowers that had previously been seen only in the houses of the incredibly rich. But the interesting thing about tulips is that if you let a tulip bulb grow longer than usual it often produces extra bulbs. You might buy one and get four or five extra, but you would not know for sure until the end of the season. So people started buying tulips furiously. Soon, most of the buyers had no wish to own any flowers at all. They were just trying to make a profit by buying one bulb and hoping to sell a whole slew of them. Since no one knew what the value of a bulb and its offshoots would be at the end of the season, sales were based on guesses as to its future worth. This is the "futures trading" that is a common practice in stock exchanges nowadays.

In the Netherlands it led to a huge rise in tulip prices. One farmer paid for a single viceroy tulip with two measures of wheat, four of rye, four fat oxen, eight pigs, a dozen sheep, two oxheads of wine, four tons of butter, a thousand pounds of cheese, a bed, some clothing, and a silver beaker. Competition was fierce, too. One group of florists went from Haarlem to The Hague to buy a black tulip. They persuaded the owner to sell it to them for fifteen hundred florins. As soon as the deal was made, however, the men from Haarlem trampled their purchase under their feet, for they already owned a black tulip and had come solely to wipe out

The European conquest of the "New World" had far-reaching consequences for the world economy. Worldwide trade replaced traditional subsistence and redistributive economies. In this picture, armed overseers watch over African slaves as they "wash for diamonds" for their Brazilian owners.

the competition. The original owner was so shocked that he took to his bed and died soon afterward.

Tulip prices kept rising, but one day in 1637 they peaked. The market crashed. Many Dutchmen lost the savings they had invested in tulip speculation, and the crisis brought the country to the edge of bankruptcy. If the market had become abstract, it had also become impersonal. A Dutch merchant writing as late as 1699 remarked that there was a kind of reality in transactions where gold, silver, piasters, ducats, and the like changed hands. He contrasted this tangible worth with the illusory quality of a transaction through which all of these precious metals were taken to the bank in exchange for a line of writing in a book. The illusions, however, were only beginning. Soon the banks were not just facilitating transactions between people who knew each other, they were taking money that was deposited with them and lending it to third parties who had no connection at all with the original depositors. The modern system of strangers financing strangers with profit as the primary motive had begun.

These banking and trading activities incurred the censure of both the Catholic Church and the Calvinists. Traditional Catholicism held that interest payments were sinful; that money should only represent value and not become a source of profit in itself; and that speculation in money was especially wicked. Interestingly enough, the Calvinist ministers who succeeded the Catholics in Amsterdam also thought that their parishioners were steeped in sin. The ministers felt that the burghers prospered by ignoring traditional Christian values that, among other things, emphasized fair dealing with the members of one's own community. They denounced the most prosperous capitalists from their pulpits on Sundays and even on occasion expelled them from their congregations. In fact, from 1581 until 1658 bankers were officially prohibited from taking communion, together with other shady figures such as pawnbrokers, actors, acrobats, and brothel keepers. A banker's wife could take communion, but only if she declared her repugnance for her husband's profession.

Did this induce some kind of schizophrenia in the Dutch? I think probably not. I suspect that their wealthy capitalists went to church on Sunday, heard their methods and their morals roundly condemned, felt better for it, and went back to making money on Monday, much as the rest of us do nearly four hundred years later (that is, if we bother to go to church at all). After all, the Dutch were becoming enormously prosperous, and they were not about to abandon the habits and institutions that brought them their riches. The ministers told them it was their Christian duty to live for one another, but their financial transactions had brought them a long way from the love-thy-neighbor world conjured up in the Sunday sermons.

Individualism, while not yet quite respectable, was increasingly tolerated because it was central to a new way of looking at the world – a way that, among other things, seemed to bring considerable material reward. The separateness of the individual began to be recognized in small and subtle ways. Separate chairs replaced benches in people's homes. People wanted better mirrors to have a firmer sense of what they looked like. In art, the self-portrait became more common. This recognition of the needs and rights of the individual went hand in hand with a weakening of the ties that bound people together in families, in guilds, in communities. The new individualism came into conflict with the ideals of Christian charity, which preached that the needy should be helped by the more affluent.

There are still societies in the world that operate on this principle. They too have their banks, as we saw with the modern kula participants, but these function quite differently from ours. They are people banks more than money banks; or, in the case of the Gabra, whom we met in the last chapter, they are camel banks (since people depend on camels in order to survive in the Chalbi Desert). The government of Kenya tried to set up a conventional bank in the Gabra country, hoping the Gabra would use it to build up savings that would tide them through lean years and perhaps even decide to abandon their "backward," nomadic lives, but the Gabra made little use of it. They said they had their own bank – a camel bank.

The Gabra constantly lend camels among their own people. They will also lend them to outsiders in time of dire need. During the last, particularly vicious drought they lent many camels to the neighboring Boran. In fact, many Boran came to live with the Gabra during those difficult times. Whether the lending is between Gabra and Boran, or among the Gabra themselves, the ties created along the lending paths endure for generations, and a herder must therefore know the genealogy of his animals so as to know to whom he is indebted. Camel-lending is the most precious form of credit extended in these parts, a way of cementing the relations between families and clans or of establishing relations with strangers.

Selling camels or camel products is thus as abhorrent to the Gabra as usury was to medieval preachers, and for the same reason. It undermines the morality that holds society together and therefore threatens to destroy society itself. Lending camels, on the other hand, enables more than thirty thousand people – most of them strangers – to help one another to survive, even to thrive according to their own lights, in one of the harsher environments of the world. In fact, since the system is extended outward to the Boran and others, it embraces many more than this number, which is the core population of Gabra.

A cynic might say that the Gabra have little alternative. After all, they live in an environment that looks like the surface of Mars. It is tempting, and much too easy, for us to sit back in relative comfort and think of the Gabra system as an "ecological adaptation." It certainly is that, but consider the pain of lending when one's own survival and that of one's family is so precarious. Consider, too, the anguish of parting with animals one has raised and called by name. Would not there be a temptation *not* to lend, but to hoard and turn a deaf ear to the

BORU AND THE STRANGER

"CRY FOR THE EYE THAT HAS CRIED FOR YOU
AND FEEL MERCIFUL FOR
THE HEART THAT HAS FELT FOR YOU."

IT IS ONE OF MANY PROVERBS OF THE GABRA
PEOPLE, PASTORAL NOMADS WHO INHABIT A VAST
AREA NEAR THE CHALBI DESERT IN NORTHERN
KENYA. THEY MOVE ACROSS AN ARID, BOULDER-
STREWN LANDSCAPE IN SEARCH OF WATER
AND GRASSES FOR THEIR SHEEP, GOATS, CATTLE,
AND CAMELS. THEIR ANIMALS ARE THEIR CURRENCY.
OTHER GABRA ARE THEIR SECURITY.

BORU WAS THIRTEEN WHEN A STRANGER SHOWED
UP IN HIS *OLLA*, OR VILLAGE, WITH A PRESENT
OF TOBACCO, COFFEE, AND CLOTH FOR HIS FATHER.
"IT IS THE APPROPRIATE GIFT WHEN ASKING
FOR A CAMEL," BORU'S FATHER EXPLAINED TO HIM.

THE STRANGER'S FAMILY HAD FALLEN ON HARD
TIMES. THE DRY SEASON HAD BEEN VERY LONG, THE
RAINY SEASON PAINFULLY SHORT, AND MANY OF
THEIR ANIMALS HAD DIED. "OUR ANIMALS ARE FEW,
FOR WE, TOO, HAVE SUFFERED FROM THE DROUGHT,"
BORU HEARD HIS FATHER TELL THE STRANGER,
"BUT WE WILL GIVE YOU A CAMEL."

THE GABRA KNOW THEIR ANIMALS INTIMATELY. THEY
KNOW HOW EACH WAS ORIGINALLY GIVEN,
LOANED, OR OBTAINED — AND THEY KNOW THEIR
ANIMALS' OFFSPRING. OBLIGATIONS ARE CARRIED
FROM GENERATION TO GENERATION, BUT EVEN
IF THERE HAS NEVER BEEN EXCHANGE BETWEEN
FAMILIES, NEW RELATIONSHIPS MUST BE
FORMED, FOR A GABRA IS BOUND TO GIVE TO
ANOTHER GABRA IN NEED.
AS THEY SAY, "A POOR MAN SHAMES US ALL."

SOME GABRA WAYS OF GIVING

DABARE
AN OUTRIGHT GIFT OF
FEMALE STOCK (CAMELS OR
CATTLE) THAT HAVE NOT
GIVEN BIRTH. IT CAN CROSS
MANY GENERATIONS AND
MAY NOT OCCUR WITHIN
ONE'S FAMILY.

GATTI
AN ANIMAL LOANED, USU-
ALLY IN TIMES OF CALAMITY.
THE TERM OF REPAYMENT
USUALLY INCLUDES FEMALE
STOCK AS INTEREST.

KAALISIMI
A LOAN OF A MILK ANIMAL
(CATTLE OR CAMEL) TO
THOSE IN NEED OF MILK.
THE ANIMAL IS USUALLY
KEPT FOR THREE OR MORE
SEASONS.

ERGA
A LOAN OF A CASTRATED
MALE CAMEL FOR MOVING
OR A BULL FOR BREEDING.

HALLAL
A GIFT OF PERSONAL
ANIMALS. THESE ANIMALS
ARE YOUR *ANDURR*, YOUR
UMBILICAL CORD. THEY ARE
GIVEN ONLY AMONG CLOSE
FAMILY MEMBERS AT TIMES
OF RITUAL CELEBRATION
SUCH AS BIRTH, CIRCUMCI-
SION, MARRIAGE, OR THE
KILLING OF AN ENEMY.

HIRB
A COMMUNITY GIFT OF
MANY ANIMALS TO THOSE
WHO HAVE SUFFERED
LOSSES DURING RAIDS,
DROUGHT, OR FLOODS.
CLOSE RELATIVES GIVE UP
TO TEN ANIMALS, OTHERS
ONE OR TWO.

AL BAKU
A TYPE OF CURSE FOR
REFUSING TO HELP OTHERS.
AMONG THE GABRA, A
FAMILY CAN CARRY THE
BURDEN OF THEIR FORE-
FATHERS' SELFISHNESS FOR
GENERATIONS.

entreaties of strangers – to say, as we so often do in affluent societies, that they have brought their misfortunes upon themselves? The Gabra consider it a grave sin not to help others by lending; but are there some Gabra who, like the early Dutch bankers, sin and get away with it? Katelo, for example, who is aspiring to be a chief, would not even make a gift to his younger brother until the entire community put pressure on him and forced him to give one camel. On another occasion, a visitor was shuttling water in to the Gabra at a time of severe drought. Katelo said the community wanted the pregnant goats watered first and insisted that this be done. In fact, the community had wanted nothing of the sort. It was Katelo who wanted it, since he had more than a dozen pregnant goats. The village was furious. But the fury would soon be forgotten and Katelo and his goats would thrive, would they not?

Gabra do not think so. A Gabra elder explained what happens to people who do not give in the Gabra way: they end up dying alone, under a tree. "Even the milk from our own animals," he added, "does not belong to us. We must give to those who need it, for a poor man shames us all."

It is not only the Gabra, however, in their austere surroundings, who behave in this way. Traditional societies in bountiful environments, indeed in those tropical paradises that so fascinated the early European explorers, also operate a moral economy; that is, an economy permeated by personal and moral considerations. In such a system, exchanges of goods in the "market" are not divorced from the personal relationships between those who exchange. On the contrary, the exchanges define those relationships. People who engage in such transactions select exchange partners who display integrity and reliability so that they can go back to them again and again. Even when cash enters such an economy, it does not automatically transform it. People still look for just prices, not bargain prices, and the system depends on trust, complementarity, and interdependence. In traditional societies the motto is "seller beware," for a person who gouges or shortchanges will become a moral outcast, excluded from social interaction with other people. He will end up dying alone under a tree.

We refer to traditional societies as traditional precisely because they are productive communities, much concerned with the social relations between their members, as opposed to marketplaces that are primarily concerned with the economic transactions between their members. The moral economy exists, as the name implies, for moral reasons. It is not a simple necessity for survival under adverse circumstances, and it is not intended to produce financial gain. By contrast, modern societies depend on an amoral economy, in which producers and consumers rarely meet face-to-face. The motto of this system is "buyer beware" (or, perhaps, P.T. Barnum's pithier adage, "There's a sucker born every minute"). It is a system in which economic rationality and profitability have replaced, or at least superseded, ideas of obligation and mutuality. The community of exchangers has been replaced by the mechanisms of an impersonal marketplace. Where traditional societies have complementarity, we have competition. Where they strive for stability, we seek dynamism. The news that the economy has not grown in the last quarter casts a pall over the breakfast tables of the modern world. Even those who do not understand the technical significance of the news, even those who hastily switch it off and turn to sports, know that such news is bad news. If a downturn continues for long, people will lose their jobs and may eventually end up on the streets.

Yet the dynamism that we sometimes disparage has transformed the world, and it is intimately related to the triumph of individualism. This glorification of the individual, this focus on the dignity and rights of the individual, this severing of the obligations to kin and community that support and constrain the individual in traditional societies, all this was the sociological equivalent of splitting the atom. It unleashed the human energy and creativity that enabled people to make extraordinary technical advances and to accumulate undreamed-of wealth. The very impersonality that traditional societies find weird or downright immoral in our arrangements was a condition of our material success. It is difficult, in fact, to see how else we could have gone beyond the limited range encompassed by the networks of traditional societies, transcended the parochialism of the Middle Ages, and expanded our horizons to encompass the huge political and economic systems of the twentieth century.

But we have paid a price for our success. The modern economy is a driven economy, one that survives by consuming the ever-expanding surplus it strives to produce. It must constantly generate surpluses and see to it that there is a need for them. Advertising, therefore, is revealed to be not an unfortunate and somewhat vulgar outgrowth of capitalism, as some of the more fastidious among us occasionally like to think. It is, as much as competition and individualism, an essential element of the system. An expanding economy has to create new needs so that people will consume more. Ideally, people should have unlimited needs so that the

INDIAN GIVER

Early settlers in America were puzzled by the Indians' insistence that all gifts be kept in circulation rather than become any one person's property. They coined the term "Indian giver" for someone uncouth enough to expect a gift to be returned to its original "owner." The Indians understood that the gift has more than use-value: it can also keep people in relationship with one another, passing from hand to hand, creating social bonds. The idea that reciprocity brought benefits to the group as a whole was foreign to the settlers, who treated gifts merely as possessions. Therefore, a settler who received a gift from an Indian effectively took that item out of circulation.

economy can expand forever, and advertising exists to convince them of just that.

The driven economy is accompanied by a restless and driven society. In the United States, for example, the educational system teaches children to be competitive and tries to instill in them the hunger for personal achievement. In our culture even team sports, which require a high degree of cooperation, are turned into arenas of individual competition. Drive is esteemed in American culture and required of business executives and even anthropologists if they want to be promoted. The system requires and rewards driven people. Other human capabilities – for kindness, generosity, patience, tolerance, cooperation, compassion – all the qualities one might wish for in one's family and friends, are literally undervalued: any job that requires such talents usually has poor pay and low prestige.

It is as if our cornucopia has, through its very abundance, robbed human beings of their human dimension. It has placed such emphasis on the economic roles people play that it has reduced them to a sum of the jobs they do plus the things they consume. This in turn acts as a spur, for what happens to a person without a job or one who cannot consume the right things in sufficient quantity to gain him some respect? Nor is joblessness the only terror. A dynamic economy presupposes, indeed plans for, obsolescence. Jobs disappear. Goods become obsolete. People are declared redundant.

The heart of the difference between the modern world and the traditional one is that in traditional societies people are a valuable resource and the interrelations between them are carefully tended; in modern society things are the valuables and people are all too often treated as disposable. We sense this whenever we pass the destitute and the homeless on the streets of our cities, but I suspect that we sense it with a feeling of helpless rage. Why is this happening to them? Why do I feel uncomfortable when there is so little I can do for them? I cannot, Gabra-like, give a camel or even a dollar to everyone I meet who is down on his luck. What responsibility do I have to these people anyway? This is the unanswered question of our times. In an age of competitive individualism, who am I responsible for and to whom do I have obligations?

Adam Smith, a Scottish philosopher, argued in the eighteenth century that if one left individuals free to pursue their own self-interest, this would tend to improve the general welfare. It followed that the community had no interests of its own that were separate from those of the individual. To the contrary, the community as a whole would benefit most when individuals were left alone to do what they felt was best for themselves. This view of society as little more than an aggregate of atomistic individuals, all acting selfishly, became exceedingly influential in the nineteenth century. It is still held today by those who argue that the best government is no government and the best communities are those that allow the greatest freedom for the people in them.

This outlook was fiercely opposed at the beginning of this century by a leading

French social theorist, Emile Durkheim. Durkheim founded sociology as a field of inquiry because he was convinced that social institutions had a life of their own. They could not be adequately explained in terms of individual intentions and actions. He was, furthermore, deeply concerned about the state of modern industrial society. While he understood and appreciated the scientific advances that made people so optimistic about the future at the end of the nineteenth century, he also felt that science had undermined people's faith and that industrial civilization had broken up their communities. The individual, deprived of social support, thus faced severe problems of alienation.

Earlier in the nineteenth century Karl Marx had focused on the problem of alienation in his grand critique of capitalism. He argued that when land and labor became commodities to be bought and sold this had drastic effects on individuals – at least on those individuals who were not doing the buying and selling. They were alienated from the products of their own labor, which someone else owned and disposed of; they were alienated from one another through competition; they were even, he suggested, alienated from themselves, unable to develop their own full capacities as human beings. The solution Marx advocated was socialism.

Durkheim, on the other hand, thought that the extreme division of labor in capitalism might itself hold the promise of a new interdependency. He spent his life trying to understand what it is that binds people together in moral communities, to understand the nature of what he called "social solidarity." He conducted an exhaustive study of tribal and traditional societies and concluded that they absorbed the individual in the community, providing social support at the cost of constraint. Modern society, on the other hand, liberated the individual but at the cost of doing away with the sense of community. Is there any way out of this dilemma?

The prospects at the end of the twentieth century do not look promising. The great Communist experiment has collapsed, repudiated for its despotism and inefficiency by all but its most diehard practitioners. The triumph of capitalism is proclaimed in the West, yet the mood of the "victors" is hardly triumphant. Ronald Reagan presided over the boom years of the 1980s in the United States, which he called the "age of the individual." They were years in which huge individual fortunes were made while the public sphere was impoverished. During the age of the individual, roads and bridges deteriorated, schools and hospitals scrambled for funds, cities were plagued by violent crime. The national debt grew unchecked, swollen by the government's willingness to allow private individuals to bankrupt institutions such as savings banks, which were then resuscitated with public money. Capitalism worked, it seemed, to keep profits private and socialize really big losses. Meanwhile, the gap between rich and poor – and that between the rich and the struggling not-so-rich – steadily widened. Citizens of one of the most affluent societies in the history of the world have to step around the homeless and the destitute as they make their way to work. Indeed, the new age of the individual has come to bear an uneasy resemblance to the old one, when capitalism was in its infancy. City streets have become unsafe after dark and the prosperous take shelter from the world around them by retreating into well-protected houses.

Adam Smith suggested that the hidden hand of the market would regulate the economy if men did not interfere with it. It seems, though, that the hidden hand does not work so well at regulating society. It is in this arena that human imagination and effort are required to maintain a livable world. We have in a sense always known this. That is why tribal societies invent ways of binding people to one another. That is why we, who live amid the affluence of modern societies, feel we must struggle to maintain human contact with others in what would otherwise be

WEALTH IN AMERICA

According to the U.S. Bureau of Census 1988, 1989:

Between 1980 and 1988 the income share taken by the upper 20 percent of American families rose from 41.6 percent to 44 percent of the total household incomes. This is the highest percentage since the Census Bureau began its measurements.

The lowest 20 percent of American families received 4.6 percent. Household income for these families has dropped more than 10 percent since 1969.

The top 1 percent of American families received 11 percent of the total income.

20 percent of American children are growing up in poverty. 44 percent of these children are black. 36 percent are Hispanic.

13 percent of American families live below the poverty line. More than one half of these families are households "with no father present."

According to the Federal Reserve Board's 1983 "Survey of Consumer Financing," 2 percent of U.S. families owned the following:

20 percent of all real estate;

50 percent of all privately held stocks;

39 percent of all taxable bonds;

70 percent of all nontaxable bonds;

33 percent of all business assets;

30 percent of all liquid assets.

an intolerably commercial world. We have our own kula systems, like the gifts we exchange at Christmastime. Our wakes may not be as spectacular as Sumbanese stone-draggings, but they serve a similar purpose, to gather people together and strengthen their ties to one another.

The problem is that our modern social systems have made it a struggle to be human, to connect with others. We are encouraged to be selfish and acquisitive. Our advertisers tell us remorselessly that if only we make it to the top, we can have it all. But there is no one like the Gabra elder to warn us of the terrible loneliness that afflicts the individualist, to tell us what we must do lest we die alone, under a tree.

STRANGE RELATIONS

Most young men dread meeting their prospective in-laws, and I was no exception. Fresh from college, with no job and no obvious "prospects," I expected to be received with skepticism. Pia's family were friendly enough, but their apprehension was obvious. In fact, it was only made worse by the one thing I thought I had going for me, my romantic determination to study the Indians of South America. This passion was beginning to define my life and that was precisely the problem. Pia's father would have treated it as an entertaining eccentricity if I had not intended to drag his daughter into it.

Her family's misgivings about our self-imposed mission were nothing compared to their horror years later when we proposed to return to the field with our baby son to live with the Xavante. By then both our families were used to our travelers' tales, but this was different. We could do what we liked with our own lives, they thought (and sometimes said), but did we feel no sense of responsibility toward our son? My parents as well as Pia's thought we were being foolhardy, especially since the Xavante were reputed to be hostile. Pia's father made the obvious suggestion: she should stay with her family in Denmark, where the child would be safe and she could look after him. Fortunately, Pia rejected the idea.

Perhaps we were lucky that we did not fully understand how our parents felt. We certainly do now that we have our own grandchildren. At the time, though, we could not be dissuaded. We wanted to stick together and that meant taking the baby with us. We tried to adopt an air of confidence to reassure our families. We had visited the Xerente; we knew the country; we knew what we were doing; everything would be fine. After all, the Xavante had babies too, did they not? Between ourselves we worried a great deal, so we took what precautions we could and all the medicines we could think of. We had no idea how the Xavante would greet us, but we felt that if we came as a family we would communicate our good intentions in a way that we could not put into words.

Yet, ironically, we had reason to believe that the Xavante family system was very unlike our own. We knew that the Xavante were divided into "moieties" and that social life for them was therefore likely to be a series of exchanges between the two halves of their society; but we had no idea how this would affect their families, or even how they would define their families. It may seem odd to talk about "defining the family," since most people imagine that families everywhere naturally consist of a father and mother and their immature children, but if that is the case, then why do not people everywhere "do what comes naturally"? Why do we find such a wide variety of family systems throughout the world? Are we perhaps mistaken about human nature, or does the naturalness of biological pairing tell us little about the cultural process of having a family?

The first person to study these questions systematically was Lewis Henry Morgan. He grew up in the early nineteenth century in upper New York State, where he spent much of his time with the Iroquois Indians. He admired them and was adopted into one of their clans. It was then he learned that their family system was quite different from that of the well-to-do white Americans from whom he was descended. The Iroquois, for example, reckoned descent in the female line, so that boys as well as girls considered themselves descended from their mothers and grandmothers. Furthermore, they grouped their relatives differently when they spoke about them. A man, for example, used the same term to refer to his father and his father's brothers. Could it be that among the Iroquois a man did not know who his actual father was? Or did he simply not care? But an Iroquois man would also use the same term to refer to his mother and his mother's sisters. Yet he must know who his actual mother was. What then was the sense of this way of classifying kin? Why did it differ in such important ways from our own?

The problem puzzled Morgan. He began to write to people all over the world to gather information about exotic family systems. It was then that he made an important discovery: a system of grouping and referring to relatives just like that of the Iroquois was reported to exist in southern India. Clearly these systems could not be historically related and must therefore have been invented independently in different parts of the world. Morgan had now established that, although family systems might differ from one another, they also showed regularities that could be studied scientifically. That was exactly what he set out to do.

Morgan pioneered the study of kinship systems, which became an important branch of anthropology. Anthropologists discovered that tribal peoples tend to see the world through the prism of kinship. Their mental world consists of various kinds of relatives, a view that sometimes extends to encompass all of society. In other words, if you are one of us you are addressed as a relative; if you are not addressed as a relative, you are not one of us. Kinship then is a kind of mental map, a map that differs sharply from one people to another. Morgan showed that you have to be able to read these maps in order to understand how other societies think and live.

Reading the map always involves understanding a society's views about marriage. In fact Claude Lévi-Strauss, the distinguished French anthropologist, has

A "tree of kinship" or *arbor consanguinitatis*. In the Middle Ages, "incest," defined as marriage between people related within seven degrees of kinship, was one of the few grounds for divorce accepted by the Christian Church. Aristocrats tended for reasons of property to marry within a small social circle – and in fact the Church often granted dispensations to the wealthy to marry their cousins. At the same time, nobles could use the technical prohibition to disentangle themselves from marriages which had become inconvenient or undesirable. After 1215, as a result of the general difficulty

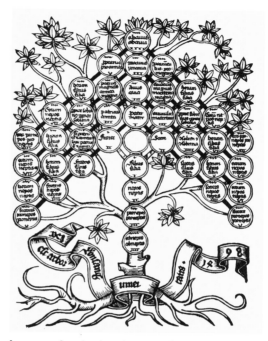

of finding spouses outside the seven degrees, the rules were relaxed to four degrees of kinship. In this 1498 diagram, the prospective bride or groom is represented by the empty circle in the center. The four degrees of forbidden kinship are traced both above and below the center.

From Anders Plitz, *The World of Medieval Learning,* translated by David Jones (Totowa, N.J.: Barnes & Noble, 1981).

argued that much of human evolution is related to changes in people's ideas about marriage. At the beginning of human history, he suggested, what most clearly distinguished human beings from animals was that humans prohibited incest. They did not do this because they feared the biological consequences of inbreeding. They might indeed have preferred to mate with their own kin, but this would have meant closing the small group in on itself. These isolated families would not have survived in competition with others that established wider networks by exchanging spouses. Faced with the choice of marrying out or dying out, human beings chose the former reluctantly, for it was a dangerous and scary business. Their solution was to control marriage and make sure that people did not marry too far afield by inventing systems in which people married their cousins (or those referred to as cousins). These systems left nothing to chance. A person knew what kind of cousin he or she must marry, though not which individual it would be, and each marriage therefore reinforced the social system by conforming to its preexisting pattern.

Such systems are, however, cautious by nature, and Lévi-Strauss suggested that a major change in human affairs came about when societies expanded their horizons and no longer insisted on everyone's marrying a certain kind of cousin. Once people were free, in theory, to marry whom they chose outside the immediate family, he argued, then marriage was no longer used to structure society.

It is true that many societies have, since time immemorial, organized themselves around cousin marriage. It is such an effective means of maintaining social systems that it is still found all over the world. But many societies that have given up (or never had) cousin marriage still regard marriage more as an affair of state than of the heart.

There is a famous passage in the *Analects* where Confucius writes: "Their persons being cultivated, their families were regulated. Their families being regulated, their states were rightly governed. Their states being rightly governed, the whole kingdom was made tranquil and happy." Well-regulated families are seen here as the cornerstone of society and of the state in China in the sixth century B.C. Confucius emphasized filial piety as the way to achieve stable families. If the father of the family is cultivated, if his wife is dutiful and his children respectful toward him, then harmony will prevail. Implicit in this idea is a belief that other societies make quite explicit: marriage is the foundation of the well-regulated family and cannot therefore be left to the passionate whims of immature young men and women.

This concern with marriage as the basis not only of the family but also of the society as a whole is both ancient and widespread. Most societies therefore make strenuous efforts to ensure that marriages will be stable. They recognize the power and the beauty of love, and they are keenly aware that love and sexual attraction are an explosive mixture when combined. So they take care to separate the serious business of marriage from the passionate business of romance. Such societies are amazed by the Western ideal of romantic love as the proper foundation for marriage. They consider it positively weird to allow – no, to insist – that something as important as marriage be based on a notoriously irrational and volatile passion. This kind of system, the traditionalists tell us, is likely to produce family instability and social chaos. But what are the alternatives? Marriage without love? Sex without passion? They are not very appealing. The problem is that love is ecstatic and personal, while marriage is sober and social. Individuals hanker after love. Societies need marriage.

The ancient Greeks certainly recognized and wrote movingly about the bittersweet attractions of love, but they considered it a violent and disruptive passion that should not be part of marriage. Sappho, one of the greatest of the early Greek poets, wrote powerfully of uncontrollable passion. She lived on the island of Lesbos in the sixth century B.C. and wrote poetry so beautiful that Plato called her "the tenth muse." Her poems evoke Eros, the god of violent desire, as in the following fragment:

> He seems as fortunate as the gods to me,
> the man who sits opposite you
> and listens nearby to your sweet voice
> and lovely laughter.
> Truly that sets my heart trembling
> in my breast.
> For when I look at you for a moment,
> then it is no longer possible for me to speak;
> my tongue has snapped,
> at once a subtle fire has stolen beneath my flesh,
> I see nothing with my eyes, my ears hum,
> sweat pours from me, a trembling seizes me all over,
> I am greener than grass,
> and it seems to me
> that I am little short of dying…

She is overwhelmed by Eros. Passion for her (as for Homer) was a divine interference, something beyond the constraints of human intent. We do not know much about the circumstances of Sappho's poems – whether they are lyrics referring to the erotic love of an older woman for a young girl or whether they were written as songs to accompany the processions or ritual dances of young girls. Most of them address beloved young women shortly before marriage, and they reflect the comparatively free and public life of girls in those early times. Later in antiquity no such poetry would be possible for women. What is remarkable, of course, about these great love poems is that they have nothing to do with the "attraction of the (opposite) sexes" that leads to marriage.

In Plato's time, erotic passion was associated not with marriage but with a great variety of other relationships. The prime impulse for marriage was not sexual but religious – to produce children to carry out burial rites and continue the family cult in perpetuity. Since girls in Athens were highly secluded, had little education, and were expected to speak, see, and hear little, and since the age gap between spouses was usually considerable, it is easy to see that a male citizen would find more attractive erotic interests among his worldly companions of the *polis* outside the household. Socrates asks a friend, "Is there anyone you know with whom you speak less than your wife?" and his friend answers, "Hardly anyone." Not that great love in marriage was out of the question; it is a vital theme of myth and tragedy, and Aristotle himself was very fond of his wife. It is only that sexuality – one should say, male sexuality – and romantic passion were better cultivated in other arenas, particularly those of the gymnasium, the symposium (the dinner meeting), and the salons of mistresses and courtesans. Homosexuality – in the form of passion between an older man and a younger man who played the part of the beloved – was culturally accepted, even idealized, at least in philosophical circles. Women were not supposed to have sex outside of marriage, whereas men were expected to. Indeed, powerful men could virtually have sex with whomever they pleased – woman, boy, or slave. Sexual gratification was considered similar to the satisfaction of any other appetite, to be indulged, preferably not to excess, by those who could with those who must.

The rise of Christianity radically altered Western views about sexuality. For the early Christians, sex was the key to human bondage; renunciation was therefore liberation. As a result of this intense focus on sexuality as the impediment to the "real life" of the soul – and not, as in the ancient city, as one of the cornerstones of civil life in the endless flow of generations – the nudity and eroticism of antiquity were suppressed. As time went on the community of the faithful grew larger, and the official apparatus of Christianity became more rigid. Renunciation of sex came to be practiced by ascetics but no longer by the lay community. Instead, the church inculcated a kind of prudery, confining sex within the boundaries of marriage and permitting only certain sexual practices believed to be consistent with God-given gender roles.

The Church's attempts to contain desire were not wholly successful. It found expression, for example, in southern France in the troubadours of the twelfth and thirteenth centuries. The troubadours were court poets and singers who developed a ritual and a mythology of love deeply rooted not only in chivalric Christian ideals but also in Jewish and Arabic mystical poetry. Love for them – often the adoration by a man of somewhat lowly position for a woman of higher station – became an art and a religion in itself. The rituals of love included the tempering of the will and of carnality through self-discipline (the lover must pass the supreme test of lying next to his naked lady without having sex with her), but physical satisfaction was possible if the lady was so inclined of her own free will. This whole world of love and poetry stood in opposition to that of the arranged marriages common at the time, where the lady was inevitably married to a less-than-sublime lord.

In the thirteenth century, the church placed marriage on its list of sacraments. Previously, marriage had been a matter of betrothal followed by sexual intercourse; now the church insisted that marriage was essentially a matter of vows taken in the presence of a priest. Medieval Europeans firmly believed that parents should arrange the marriages of their children, and in fact arranged marriages take place in parts of Europe to the present day. However, a countercurrent of opinion was forming that upheld the right of the individual to enter into a "love match" as he or she pleased. It may seem odd that the church itself encouraged

A troubadour and his lady.

love matches. It did so as part of its strategy to weaken the extended families of the landed elites and shake loose their property, which could then be left to the church.

The medieval struggle over the control of human passion is powerfully portrayed in the tragic story of Abelard and Héloïse. Peter Abelard was a distinguished twelfth-century philosopher whose teaching drew so many people to him that he is often regarded as the founder of the University of Paris. He was hired as a tutor to the beautiful Héloïse, niece of the canon of the cathedral of Notre-Dame. They fell in love and indeed made love every day until her uncle caught them at it and threw the philosopher-tutor out of his house. Later the uncle arranged for his wayward niece and her professorial lover to be married in secret, but they did not live happily ever after. The uncle's announcement of the marriage and this deeply conventional act had unexpected consequences. Abelard, the upright theologian, was shamed. Héloïse was mortified; she wanted to be Abelard's mistress, not his wife! She fled to a convent to escape the scandal.

HÉLOÏSE'S FIRST LETTER TO ABELARD

"YOU ALONE HAVE THE POWER TO MAKE ME SAD, TO BRING ME HAPPINESS OR COMFORT; YOU ALONE HAVE SO GREAT A DEBT TO REPAY ME, PARTICULARLY NOW WHEN I HAVE CARRIED OUT ALL YOUR ORDERS SO IMPLICITLY THAT WHEN I WAS POWERLESS TO OPPOSE YOU IN ANYTHING, I FOUND STRENGTH AT YOUR COMMAND TO DESTROY MYSELF. I DID MORE, STRANGE TO SAY – MY LOVE ROSE TO SUCH HEIGHTS OF MADNESS THAT IT ROBBED ITSELF OF WHAT IT MOST DESIRED BEYOND HOPE OF RECOVERY, WHEN IMMEDIATELY AT YOUR BIDDING I CHANGED MY CLOTHING ALONG WITH MY MIND, IN ORDER TO PROVE YOU THE SOLE POSSESSOR OF MY BODY AND MY WILL ALIKE. GOD KNOWS I NEVER SOUGHT ANYTHING IN YOU EXCEPT YOURSELF; I WANTED SIMPLY YOU, NOTHING OF YOURS.

I LOOKED FOR NO MARRIAGE BOND, NO MARRIAGE PORTION, AND IT WAS NOT MY OWN PLEASURES AND WISHES I SOUGHT TO GRATIFY, AS YOU WELL KNOW, BUT YOURS. THE NAME OF WIFE MAY SEEM MORE SACRED OR MORE BINDING, BUT SWEETER FOR ME WILL ALWAYS BE THE WORD MISTRESS, OR, IF YOU WILL PERMIT ME, THAT OF CONCUBINE OR WHORE."

From *The Letters of Abelard and Héloïse,* trans. Betty Radice, (London: Penguin Classics, 1974).
Original Latin manuscript in Bodleian Library, Oxford

maioz est tolendi cansa: maioza
sunt consolationis adhibenda reme
dia. Non utiqz ab alio q̄ a te ipso:
ut qui solus es in causa tolendi: sol9
sis in grā consolandi. Solus quippe
es q̄ me cōtristari. qui me letificare cōn
consolari uales. Et solus es qui pli
mū id m̄ debeas. Et nūc maxime ai
uniūsa que iusseris itā cōpleueri.
ut ai te in aliquo offende nō possē:
meipm̄ p iussū tuo pdē sustineremi.
Et qd manis est: dictuq̄ mirabile:
in tantū amuns mens uisus ē insaniā.
ut qd solū appetebat. si ipe sibi siue
spe reuocacois aufferret: ad tuam
statim iussione tū lp̄ai ipa q̄ aim in
mutari: ut tete tā corporis mei q̄ aimi
unicam possessore oñdem. Nichil
uncq̄ū deus scit in te nisi te requisiui:
te pure non tua cōcupistens. Non
matrimonii federe: nō dotes aliquas
expetam. Non deniqz meas uolup
tates ant uolūtates: sed tuas sicut
ipe nosti studui adimplex. Et si uxoris
nomi sanctius ac ualidius uidear:
dulcius semp michi extitit amice uo
cabulū. aut si nō indigneris: cōcubie
uĕscoza. ut quo me uidi pce aph̄i
humare. ampliore apud te cōseq r
grām. et sic t excelletie tue gl̄e minus
ledem. Quod t tu ipe tui grā peit̄
oblitus nō fiuli: tea q̄ supra menii
ad amicū epl̄a cōsolanois dnā. B
et rōnes nō nullas quib; te a cōiu
gio m̄o insautis q̄ his talentis re
uocare cōnabar: exponē nō es
dedignatus. Sed plisqz racis
quib; amoze tuito deu teste inuoca
si me augustus uniūso pīdens m̄o
matrimonii honore; dignaretur totii

q̄ orbem michi cōfirmarec ip̄etio
possidendū: carius michi et dignius
uidetur tua dici meretrix: q̄ illius ip̄e
imtrix. Non eo quo cuiusqz diciox siue
potēoix est: ideo t melioz. Fortune
illud: sj ūtutis. Hec se illa minime
uenalē estimet eē: q̄te libentius di
tioxi q̄ paupi nubit. et plus i marito
sua q̄ ip̄m cōcupisat. Certe q̄ticqz
ad nupcias hec cōcupiscēca ducit: m
ces ei pocius q̄ grā debetur. Cert9 est
quippe cam res ip̄as nō hoiem isequi.
et se si posset uelle p̄stituere ditioxi: sic
mouetio illa asp̄ñie phīe apud socis
eschine cū zeuofonte t uxore eius lp̄a
manifeste cōuicit. Qm̄ quid idnctio
ne eam predicta phīa ad recōciliādos
inuicem illos proposuisset: tali fine
ip̄m conclufit. Cum nisi hec pegerits.
ut necqz uir melioz necqz femina electi
or sit. p̄ceto semp id q̄ optimi puta
bits eē: uulto maxime requireus. ut
eē tu maritus q̄ optime. t sj q̄ optimo
marito nupta. Scqz p̄certo hec et plus
qm̄ phīca est sña: ipius pocius sophie
dicēdi. Sais hic eror t beata stullana
in cōiugatis: ut p̄stū dilectio illesa
custodiat matrimonii fedes. nō tā cor
por cōtinēcia. q̄ aīox pudiacia. q̄qz er
roz cetis: iucas michi m̄aifesta cōtu
lerat ai t ille iudez de suis estiarent
maritis. Hoc ergo de te t hic m̄o
uniūsus nō tā credet q̄ sciuet. ut tāto
iuioz in te mens amoz exist̄et: q̄to
ab errore longius assist̄et. Quis ui
regū aut pl̄oz tuā exegit famam
pocat? Que te regio aut ciuitas seu
uilla uide nō estuabat? Quis te uo
go i publicū procedēte respice nō
estimabat. aut discedētē collo erecto

Her uncle, thinking that Abelard had sent her away, had his men break into Abelard's room and castrate him. Abelard took this as just punishment for his sins. Convinced that he could not love God and woman at the same time, he became a wandering teacher, systematically avoiding Héloïse, who still loved him and wrote him beautiful and passionate love letters till the end of her life.

The relationship between love, sex, and marriage is clearly part of the human dilemma. The medieval church tried to harness private passion to the love of God and to separate it from sexual desire, which it condemned as base and sinful. It was not a solution that appealed to most of the faithful, who were forced to consider themselves sinners because they could not, and did not want to, curb their sexual desires. But even if sexual passion is not considered sinful, it is still hard to prevent it from being disruptive.

Many traditional societies recognize and value the kind of passion that our love stories are made of. They encourage it, but they contrive to keep it distinct from their formal marriage arrangements. They try to ensure that it does not destroy the lives of the lovesick or of those around them, and above all, they try to prevent personal passions from disturbing the social order.

The Wodaabe provide an excellent illustration. They are one of the Fulani peoples, about seven million strong, who live scattered through the nations of

LOVE SICKNESS

The medieval world considered passionate love to be a form of sickness. Knights became so distraught over their unrequited love that they often couldn't get out of bed. This was considered humiliating since it meant a man had become enslaved by a woman — his social inferior. Worse still, in the eyes of patriarchal courtly society, he even began to *act* in a feminine manner — passive, weak, helpless, emotional.

It wasn't until the eleventh century that anyone suggested a real cure. Constantine the African earned the gratitude of learned men all over Europe when he translated a series of Arab medical texts into Latin. His book was called *The Viaticum*, and in it Europeans read that love was a sickness just like insomnia, frenzy, drunkenness, and epilepsy. The cure for love was to let loose the humors that had been blocked up inside — let off some sexual steam, as it were. The afflicted lover was instructed to have hot baths, seek out conversation, music, even love poetry. One of the more highly recommended cures was sexual intercourse, but never with the loved one — this would merely sink one deeper into the obsession. The best recourse was to seek out a prostitute's service and get the love out of your system, once and for all.

Based on information in Mary Frances Wack, *Lovesickness in the Middle Ages* (Philadelphia: University of Pennsylvania Press, 1990).

West Africa. The Wodaabe are nomads and proud of it, and they look down on the sedentary Fulani whom they consider "Wodaabe who lost their way." The "Wodaabe way" takes them wandering through the scorching deserts of northern Niger, living off their camels and their flocks of cattle and goats. Yet in this harsh environment they cultivate an elaborate aesthetic sensibility that includes an important focus on personal relationships.

For the Wodaabe, personal relationships are the essence of being human, which is why they take them so seriously. They cherish them with a rich etiquette of intimacy and reserve. Men hold hands with their male friends as women do with their female friends. Yet men may not look each other in the eye when they meet, and a man and a woman (even a husband and wife) are never seen holding hands or otherwise displaying affection in public. Wodaabe believe that you should respect those you love and should not make public demonstrations of affection for those you respect. Reserve infuses even the most intimate areas of sexual behavior. Neither party is ever naked. The couple lies under a blanket; the woman lifts her skirt; the man lifts his robe; the woman covers her face with a shawl so as not to look at the man on top of her, and they make love. There is no mouth-to-mouth kissing, no groping toward the "Western" erogenous zones. Women say they prefer a man who does not take too much time.

And yet women talk a great deal among themselves about which men are the best lovers. A man may be known as a good lover because he is "as strong as a horse," but more importantly – and here perhaps is the key to Wodaabe notions of foreplay and the erotic impulse – because he is a beautiful *Yakke* dancer and he has lots of *togu* or "charm." It is togu that Wodaabe cultivate, not just physical beauty (which is called *bodem*), and it is this charm that attracts lovers and kindles romance. A man's togu is enhanced by *magani*, a potion or medicine, and most men go out to collect fresh magani for the Yakke dance, which is a well-known occasion for romantic liaisons.

Magani is a central aspect of Wodaabe life. They eat it, drink it, wear it, and rub it on their clothes. Men and women are always searching for various types of magani to cure their ills. Their ailments run the gamut from physical sickness – diarrhea, scorpion bites, broken limbs – to psychological complaints such as lovesickness, lack of charm, unpopularity, and so on. The Wodaabe do not consider magani any more magical than we do our medicines. As to whether magani works or not, well, of course it does, but not all the time. The Wodaabe are known throughout the neighboring West African countries as people with very powerful magani. When a Wodaabe man treats someone in Senegal, for example, he is not paid until his next visit and only then if the magani has been effective. While it seems like a fairy-tale potion to us, for a Wodaabe man it is the source of his seductive power.

Wodaabe philandering takes place within an elaborate set of rules that allows for romantic sexual passion while preserving the stability of the family. Within one's lineage – and there are fifteen separate lineages among the Wodaabe – a man may only marry one woman, and this marriage is arranged at childhood. It is called the *kobgal* marriage. Affairs are not outlawed within one's own lineage, but they can never lead to marriage. It is considered dangerous and disruptive to the entire lineage to carry on one of these affairs for too long, and while it is going on, it must be very discreet. Wodaabe etiquette says, "What the eyes do not see did not happen," which means that rumors and suspicions have to be ignored. Unless the couple is caught in the act, the affair is not reckoned to have taken place.

A far more common source of romantic adventures is the practice of wife-stealing between different lineages. This occurs throughout the year when lineages meet at marketplaces or common wells, but again the biggest opportunity is at the annual Geerewol celebrations, the great festival that includes the Yakke dance. This dance competition lasts for a week and may involve as many as a thousand young men who compete to be chosen as the most charming and beautiful. The competition is judged by three unmarried girls, also chosen for their beauty, but it is watched by everybody who can get to it. The men therefore perform before a critical and appreciative audience of women, with members of both sexes on the lookout for possible liaisons. A woman has to indicate her interest in a dancer very subtly. If he is interested, he will wink at her. At that she is supposed to lower her eyes demurely but, if he has not made a mistake and winked at the wrong person, she will not lower them all the way. She is now watching for him to indicate, by a slight twitch of the mouth, the bush behind which he wants to meet her.

A couple may meet each other for trysts, where they lie "invisible" under a blanket and make love. They may eventually decide to elope. What is extraordinary from the Western point of view is that the decision to run away together, made "from the heart" as they say, is often reached very quickly. A Wodaabe couple may arrange a meeting, sleep together once, and decide to marry. If they are already married to others, as is often the case, and her husband is anywhere near, he will give them chase. But this is a ritual, strictly for show. He usually accepts that if his wife wants to leave, there is no point in trying to stop her. His best bet is to go off and use his togu to persuade another woman to join him. The runaway wife goes to live with her new husband and his other wives. Why would a woman want to leave the formally sanctioned kobgal marriage within her own lineage to join another wife or wives in the foreign camp of another lineage? Such a union is considered a marriage all right – it is called a *teegal* marriage – but it is a secondary one. The kobgal wife is a man's principal spouse and takes precedence over teegal wives. She has the largest dowry of calabashes and animals. Above all, she stays with her children. A woman who runs away has to leave her children behind to be raised in her husband's lineage.

A woman who is a kobgal wife is unlikely to be deterred from leaving her

The Wodaabe believe that certain roots, leaves, grasses, and barks have magic powers. These are crushed and encased in small leather pouches that serve as talismans, which are worn in the hair, around the neck, and across the chest. Benefits to the wearer are thought to include increased beauty and charm, heightened virility, and protection against sorcerers, swords, and evil spirits. Talismans may even bestow invisibility upon a young lover on the prowl.

From Marion Van Offelen and Carol Beckwith, *Nomads of Niger* (New York: Harry N. Abrams, 1983).

marriage by material considerations. There is not a lot of material wealth among nomads anyway. One person may have a few more animals or calabashes than another, but the differences are insignificant. A man might be deterred from taking a teegal wife by the additional strain she will put on the resources of his camp. She will need her own milk cows, donkey, and goats. This, in addition to any feelings of personal jealousy that might arise, is the reason why a new teegal wife usually gets a frosty reception in her new husband's camp. He leaves her at some distance from his camp, where she sits under her blanket, socially "invisible," until the other women of his household are willing to accept her. The process may take a few days and cannot be pleasant for the newcomer.

In spite of the drawbacks, Wodaabe are regularly willing to take the plunge in teegal marriages. Accustomed to getting by with little and to sharing what little they have, they do not measure their comfort or success in terms of material possessions. What they do value, almost above all else, is personal relations. So men are constantly on the lookout for lovers, and women are often willing to leave the stability of their arranged marriages and go for love into the household of a man whose togu has charmed them. But life goes on, even if they do. Their children are not uprooted, and the orderly relations of Wodaabe society, which are built around the kobgal marriages, are unaffected. The Wodaabe have dealt effectively with the age-old problem of trying to reconcile marriage with passion by instituting these two kinds of marriage. The sensible kobgal marriages form the foundation of their social institutions while spontaneous teegal marriages allow a freer rein to passion and personal whim.

THE WAY OF THE WODAABE

"WE ARE LIKE BIRDS IN THE BUSH," SAID DJAJEEJO, "TRAVELING FROM ONE SPOT TO ANOTHER, BUILDING OUR CAMPS WITH TREE BRANCHES AND THORN BUSHES, NEVER STAYING TOO LONG IN ONE PLACE – THIS IS HOW WE STAY FREE, FOLLOWING THE WAY OF THE WODAABE."

A FEW THOUSAND STRONG, THE WODAABE CLANS LEAD THEIR NOMADIC EXISTENCE IN THE SUB-SAHARAN TERRAIN OF THE WEST AFRICAN COUNTRY OF NIGER. EVERY THREE OR FOUR DAYS THEY MOVE CAMP, FOREVER FOLLOWING THE GOOD PASTURE FOR THEIR FLOCKS OF SHEEP AND GOATS AND MAGNIFICENT HERDS OF LONG-HORNED ZEBU CATTLE. FOR ELEVEN MONTHS OF THE YEAR THE WODAABE LIVE IN NEAR-DROUGHT CONDITIONS UNTIL THE RAINS COME – THE TIME THEY CALL "FOLLOW THE CLOUDS."

FOR ONE MONTH, THE DESERT BLOOMS AND THE WODAABE HOLD THEIR ANNUAL FESTIVAL CALLED THE GEEREWOL. IT'S A TIME OF GREAT CELEBRATION, INCLUDING THE FAMOUS *YAKKE* DANCES WHERE THE MEN VIE WITH ONE ANOTHER IN MAKEUP AND BRILLIANT COSTUMES TO ATTRACT FEMALE ATTENTION. "ISN'T IT THE SAME WITH BIRDS?" DJAJEEJO, THE BEST DANCER, ASKED. "THE FEMALE ALWAYS CHOOSES THE MOST BEAUTIFUL MALE."

THE WODAABE ARE A POLYGYNOUS SOCIETY, WHERE ONE MAN CAN HAVE MANY WIVES. THERE ARE TWO TYPES OF MARRIAGES – ARRANGED ONES (*KOBGAL*) AND LOVE MARRIAGES (*TEEGAL*). EVERYBODY SEEMS FOREVER INVOLVED IN THE PLAY OF INTERPERSONAL RELATIONSHIPS, ALWAYS STRIVING FOR THE BALANCE BETWEEN INDIVIDUAL PASSION AND THE SECURITY OF FAMILY AND COMMITMENT.

DJAJEEJO ALREADY HAS TWO WIVES BUT HE WANTS A THIRD, EVEN A FOURTH. HIS CURRENT WIVES AREN'T HAPPY. THEY SEE HIM APPLYING *MAGANI* (LOVE POTION) OVER HIS BODY. THEY DISCUSS LEAVING HIM IF HE BRINGS IN A NEW WIFE. THEIR WORST FEARS ARE CONFIRMED. DJAJEEJO DANCES SO

BEAUTIFULLY AT THE YAKKE THAT A WOMAN NAMED FAJIMA, LIVING UNHAPPILY
IN AN ARRANGED MARRIAGE, CATCHES HIS EYE. THE TWO AGREE TO ELOPE. ALL IS
IN AN UPROAR. DJAJEEJO'S WIVES START PACKING UP TO LEAVE HIM (BUT THEY
DON'T), FAJIMA'S HUSBAND IS FURIOUS (BUT CAN DO LITTLE TO WIN HER BACK),
AND THE TWO LOVERS WHISPER SOFTLY TO EACH OTHER AT AN OASIS.

THOSE OF US OBSERVING THE DRAMA WONDERED WHY THE WODAABE SEEMED TO
RELISH ALL THIS ADDITIONAL EMOTIONAL HEAT IN A LIFE THAT SEEMED
DIFFICULT ENOUGH AT 120°F (45°C). FAJIMA, THE PERSON RISKING THE MOST IN
THIS DRAMA OF SEDUCTION AND ABDUCTION, OFFERED AN EXPLANATION
THAT HAD AN ODDLY MODERN RESONANCE: "IF YOU CANNOT BEAR THE SMOKE,
YOU WILL NEVER GET TO THE FIRE."

Wodaabe society seems to be male-dominated. Descent is in the male line, a man has authority over his family, and it is he who may have a number of wives. Yet Wodaabe women enjoy considerable freedom of action. They can leave their husbands without stigma and always have a place to go if they do – back to their own family's camp. They can enter into as many love marriages as they have the heart and the stamina for. The price they pay is that if they move from one marriage to another they must leave their children behind with their husband's lineage. That is how the Wodaabe ensure the stability of society while allowing individuals to pursue their romantic impulses.

In another society, half a world away from the Wodaabe, is a family system that appears to be the exact opposite of theirs. Among the Nyinba of Nepal, a woman is expected to have a number of husbands. The Nyinba are a Tibetan-speaking minority in a land where their neighbors speak Nepali. Nevertheless, the Nyinba have maintained their Tibetan traditions partly because they are devout Buddhists in an area surrounded by Hindus and polyandry (one woman having a number of husbands at the same time) is very much part of Tibetan culture.

The Nyinba value reserve and discourage strong and exclusive emotional attachments, which are thought to focus people's energies on this world and therefore to interfere with the pursuit of salvation. The Nyinba ideal is a kind of disinterested compassion for one's fellow human beings that is not selfishly charged with private passion. The ideal can only be fully realized in the practice of asceticism, which Nyinba admire. Nyinba realize, however, that most people cannot live this kind of life, so they condone the passions and the sexual involvements of ordinary people, while at the same time condemning excessive passion or promiscuity.

Nyinba do not consider sex defiling or sinful. Young people are expected to have sex with each other before marriage and are only criticized if their behavior is excessive – if, for example, they engage in several affairs simultaneously. When they marry, as they invariably do, it is normally an arrangement where a woman marries a group of brothers and moves into their household. The wife is then expected to treat all her husbands with equal consideration and affection. Passionate attachment to one of them is frowned upon, for it risks alienating the others and threatens to break up the family, and it is precisely to keep families together that the system was devised. It is the brothers who are thought to be the heart of the family. If there is only one son in a family, he marries and has a wife to himself, but Nyinba women say they prefer to have more than one husband since it gives them greater economic security. Another man can be brought into such a marriage, but this is rare, since the point of polyandry among the Nyinba is to keep the brothers together. Occasionally more than one woman is involved in Nyinba marriages, and in this case it is a group of sisters who marry a group of brothers.

Tibetan polyandry has frequently been explained as a special adaptation to a land where life is hard and resources are limited. It harnesses the contributions of a number of husbands to support the family, while simultaneously limiting family size by having only one (or only a few) wives to bear the children. But many societies, including the Hindu neighbors of the Nyinba, live in harsh environments and do not practice polyandry. In fact only about half the Nyinba do. It is, furthermore, the wealthier families that are more likely to practice it, in order to avoid having to divide their property. Poorer ones can have a wife for each man without worrying about how they will divide up the property because there is not much to divide anyway.

The Nyinba not only live side by side with Hindus who have marriage and family systems different from their own, but they also tolerate different marriage arrangements among themselves. They prefer polyandry but permit polygyny (a man married to more than one wife). There are also cases of what Nancy Levine – the foremost authority on the Nyinba and on polyandry – calls "conjoint marriage," where a man in a polyandrous marriage marries another woman on the side, so to speak. There have also been rare instances of a widower and his son marrying the same woman or a widow and her daughter marrying the same man. This tolerance and recognition of a variety of family arrangements contrasts with the passionate rejection of anything out of the mainstream that usually characterizes modern societies. Mormons practicing polygyny were persecuted by the police in the United States until recently. If they had chosen instead to let their men marry a number of wives one at a time, abandoning each former spouse with limited means of support, that would have been within the law.

The Nyinba themselves stress the material advantages of polyandry, but it seems clear that the system endures because of its cultural importance to them. The legends through which they define themselves and their past tell of ancestors who lived in polyandrous marriages. The institutions by which they live in the present extol the virtues of the household based on a group of brothers. Personal actions that lead to divisions within the family and eventually its partition and the division of its property are condemned. For this reason, Nyinba voice strong disapproval of extramarital affairs, yet they indulge in them quite frequently and for an unexpected reason, given the formal prescriptions of the system by which they live. The Nyinba are romantics. Young men and women search eagerly for lovers with whom they can be emotionally as well as physically close. The quest often continues, though more circumspectly, after marriage. It is newly married women who are most likely to have extramarital affairs. Men, particularly if they are the younger or less-favored husbands in large polyandrous groups, may continue to look for lovers long after marriage. The Nyinba understand this and do not truly condemn it, provided the liaison is discreet and does not interfere with the man's responsibilities to his household.

Occasionally a couple will put their own feelings ahead of their duty to the family and elope. This inevitably causes an uproar, but often people come to accept the situation and try to get the respective families to accept it, too. Still, the Nyinba do not take such affairs lightly and believe that they usually lead to family tragedy and personal sorrow, so they counsel young people to keep cool and avoid passionate and selfish attachments. They drive the point home with terrifying cautionary tales like this one, collected by Nancy Levine:

> Approximately thirty years ago a man and woman of the same village became involved in an adulterous relationship. They pledged to wed and sealed this pledge by consuming barley consecrated to a god, an act used to prove their commitment to one another. By so doing, the god was thought to become a witness to the pledge and a guarantor of its fulfillment. But the marriage proved impracticable. The man, Pama, was already married, polyandrously, to a virtuous and fertile wife. His brothers would not countenance an addition to the marriage. Moreover, the woman, Rinchen, had borne a son by her husbands. Still they continued the affair and Rinchen remained determined to marry Pama. One day she became so bold as to move into his home. She refused to leave and it took all the pleas and efforts of both households before she would return to her husbands. Then Rinchen became acutely ill. Her relationship with Pama had apparently deteriorated, for he failed to visit her, even in the final days of her life. Rinchen, deeply hurt, cursed him; she prayed that he too would fall sick and die – and join her in death, if not in life. Shortly thereafter, Pama did die; his death was followed by that of Rinchen's young son. The couple is now believed to have become ghosts, so consumed by their attachment that they are unable to release their hold on this life. Otherwise inexplicable deaths of children are still attributed to them and it is thought that they live together with the ghosts of these children. Separated in life, they have created a dreadful mockery of marriage and family in death.

Stories like this one frighten young lovers but do not deter them, and the Nyinba do not really expect them to. The Nyinba way is to warn the young and then devise a system that allows them some leeway for their romances while maintaining the stability of the family.

The stability of the family – this is the constant preoccupation of societies the world over. It does not result from any particular system; human beings can make all sorts of systems work. It comes rather from a society's determination, expressed in its values, taught in its precepts, and enshrined in its institutions, to make its family system work. One of the main problems that a family system has to solve is how to take care of the children, especially if their parents divorce and remarry. The Wodaabe and the Nyinba insist that the children stay with the father's family. Women who divorce and move away have to give up their children. This approach is the norm in societies where descent is reckoned through the male line and women marry into the man's lineage or family.

What about societies where descent is traced through females and it is the husband, not the wife, who is thought of as "marrying in" to the family or lineage? Anthropologists have suggested that such societies create special problems for themselves because they make the father into an outsider who either has little authority over his own children or must share that authority with the mother's brother. The children belong after all to their mother's clan and the mother's brother is the authority figure on that side. One people in southern India, the Nayar, are famous for having invented a logical solution to this problem. They abolished the father altogether. The Nayar were traditionally divided into matrilineal clans. When a girl reached a marriageable age she was formally married and formally divorced from her husband shortly thereafter. Henceforward she could take lovers (including her exhusband, if she liked him) but since she was not married to them, they would not be the fathers of her children. The children grew up in their mother's clan, where her brother played the role of father to them.

Few societies go to this extreme. The Hopi in the southwestern United States are a people who have lived where they now are for thousands of years and have fiercely defended their way of life against the Spanish, the Mexicans, the Americans, and even the neighboring Indians. Essential to that way of life, to being Hopi, is membership in a matrilineal clan. A Hopi household is therefore a piece of a clan. It is headed by a senior woman and may include her husband, her daughters and their husbands, and her unmarried children.

Hopi have a relaxed attitude toward sex. They expect young men and women to seek each other out as sexual partners before marriage. After marriage, a man moves into his wife's household and lives with "her people." If there is a divorce, the husband moves out, leaving the children with his wife in their clan, where they have been growing up all along. The Hopi do not go to the Nayar extreme of abolishing the role of the husband altogether in order to anchor the children in their mother's clan, but they succeed in doing this anyway. If the system "works," and it has persisted for thousands of years in the face of incredible pressures from the outside world, it is less because of the formal arrangements that the Hopi make than because of their deep-seated commitment to social harmony.

The modern family is different. It offers individual freedom and personal fulfillment, not constraint and responsibility. In the West we speak of young people growing up, leaving their parents, and "starting a family." To most of the world,

ZUMKET AND SONAM

Zumket stops harvesting the millet and laughs. "For me, polyandry is fine. If I had only one husband I would be very poor."

"It's as old as the Mahabharata," says Lopsang, the father of Zumket's husbands. The Nyinba practice fraternal polyandry, in which a woman marries all of the brothers in a family. Lopsang prides himself on having continued a seven-generation tradition in his family of never partitioning — that is, having brothers go their own way, marrying monogamously and causing the division of the family land and herds.

Not all Nyinba agree with Zumket, for other forms of marriage coexist with polyandry in these mountain villages. Some choose monogamy, others polygyny (many wives). Divorce is not uncommon. Zumket had been married to three brothers when she met Sonam, just as he and his four brothers were wed to another woman. Zumket and Sonam eloped and in a customary fashion took refuge far from their own villages until their respective divorces were settled by their families. Then Zumket moved in with Sonam and his brothers. With the youngest only eight years old and the second youngest studying to be a Buddhist lama, the marriage proved less strenuous for twenty-three-year-old Zumket than it might have been.

"You must treat them all equally and all well or they will go out and play with other women," she says. "What the heart feels, we are too shy to say to others. If you like one husband more than the others you have to be secret. You meet together in the middle of the night when the others are asleep."

The Nyinba have no word for "love." They call it "beautiful from the heart."

Hopi Reservation, Arizona. Hopi weddings still include a great number of traditional customs. For the four days leading up to the wedding the bride goes to her mother-in-law's house, where she grinds corn from dawn to dusk and is generally tested on her wifely abilities. On the day before the wedding, an unofficial war is declared by the groom's aunts against the bride's family. They believe that their favorite nephew is too good for the bride and set out to prove their point in a mud-slinging battle. The women arrive at the house where the bride-to-be is grinding her corn; they are met at the doorstep by the bride's aunts. All are armed with pails of slimy mud, and a wild melee breaks out. If the groom's father is unlucky enough to show up, he is promptly set upon by the bride's aunts, who proceed to have him stripped, covered with mud, and sheared of his hair. When the battle subsides, the groom's aunts go into the mud-encrusted house, where they receive gifts of food and drink. This mock battle is the one and *only* time in-law conflict is tolerated.

including parts of Europe, this notion seems strange. Individuals do not start families, they are born into them and stay in them until death or even beyond. In such societies you cannot leave your family without becoming a social misfit, a person of no account.

The modern family is ideally a creation of a loving couple who marry and produce children. Of course it includes grandparents and uncles and aunts. These are the people one meets on "family occasions," which in modern society are remarkable for being rare and stressful. Americans, for example, make a point of trying to be with their families at Thanksgiving, but they joke too about the strain of being together even briefly. The United States is a good place to look at the modern family, for it is perhaps the society that has most wholeheartedly embraced the values of freedom and individualism.

American society was created by people who were consciously trying to leave behind the hierarchies and constraints of Europe and set up a different way of life, where an individual could be himself, the captain of his soul, the master of his fate. Americans therefore think and try to act as if they were individual atoms, much better off if left alone. They search for community, tolerate society, and tend to consider the state to be at best a necessary evil and at worst something they want to "get off their backs." They do not, like the seventeenth-century English philosopher Thomas Hobbes, fear that such a society will lead to a war of all against all, producing, in his famous phrase, a life that is "solitary, poor, nasty, brutish, and short." On the contrary, they believe that individualism plus competition are the foundation of the American way of life, with its promise of material abundance together with the personal freedom to enjoy it. They do, however, see this way of life as undeniably stressful, and speak of it as a "rat race."

The family is seen as a refuge from this rat race – in the title of a well-known book, it provides a "haven in a heartless world." The problem is that the family is also part of the world from which it is supposed to provide an escape, subject to its pressures and guided by its values. If people are brought up to be individualistic and competitive, they are not likely to leave these traits at the door when they come home.

Meanwhile, a lot is demanded of the modern family. Couples expect to share each other's interests, to have fun in each other's company, to enjoy sex together frequently and exclusively, and to find room for personal growth in the sanctuary they have created. We have come a long way from Socrates's Athens, where men never expected to talk to their wives. Yet these high expectations can turn into

When you get married do not make an idol of the woman you marry; do not worship her. If you worship a woman she will insist upon greater and greater worship as time goes on. It may be that when you get married you will listen to the voice of your wife and you will refuse to go on the war-path. Why should you thus run the risk of being ridiculed? After a while you will not be allowed to go to a feast. In time even your sisters will not think anything of you. (You will become jealous) and after your jealousy has developed to its highest pitch your wife will run away. You have let her know by your actions that you worship a woman and one alone. As a result she will run away from you. If you think that a woman (your wife) is the only person you ought to love, you have humbled yourself. You have made the woman suffer and have made her feel unhappy. You will be known as a bad man and no one will want to marry you again. (Perhaps afterwards) when people go on the warpath you will join them because you will feel unhappy at your wife's desertion. You will then, however, simply be throwing your life away.

CRASHING THUNDER

From *Crashing Thunder: The Autobiography of an American Indian,* by Sam Blowsnake, edited by Paul Radin (Lincoln: University of Nebraska Press, 1983).

pressures, and they are far from the only ones. In the United States, the majority of young married couples both work outside the home, either because they want to or because they need the income. This introduces a kind of exhaustion into married life that is particularly hard on women. In an era when properly modern couples express their determination to share everything, it is still the wives who do the major part of the housework. It is still the wives who do more of the child rearing, which is especially difficult in the United States since there are not nearly enough daycare facilities. Women are made to feel guilty if they go to work and "neglect" their children and inadequate if they stay at home to look after them. Marriage is not much easier for men. They may be distanced from other men by competitiveness, alienated from the family by their work, and end up isolated emotionally.

If pressures overwhelm and expectations go unfulfilled, divorce is readily available and frequently chosen. Americans have the highest divorce rates in the world. There is no longer much social pressure to make a marriage work; there may even be a certain encouragement to get out of a marriage where things are not going well, expressed by friends who "wonder why she puts up with him" or he with her. But Americans also have very high marriage rates. People want to be married, and if they opt out of a marriage that they find unsatisfactory they more often than not remarry and start another fragile family. Anthropologists call this system serial monogamy, which means that people of both sexes have multiple spouses, but only one at a time. It is remarkable that if marriage is so stressful people keep plunging into it and coming back for more. Yet not everybody does. In fact, the marrying frenzy may be a trend that has peaked, a practice that is on the wane in American society. More and more people are choosing to live in "relationships" that may have considerable stability but are explicitly *not* marriages. They are relationships without the "commitment" that individuals dread, without the responsibilities that marriage entails. That is precisely the point of them. They are designed to provide solace and comfort for individuals with as few social implications as possible. While this is true of heterosexual relationships, many homosexual couples in America today are demanding the social recognition traditionally accorded only to heterosexual marriages. They are also insisting on the right to raise children and have them recognized as their offspring.

From serial monogamy – in successive marriages or "relationships" – to homosexual partnerships, Americans seem to be experimenting with various forms of companionship that lie outside the mainstream of their own culture. How would we try to make sense of this if we were anthropologists coming to America from one of the remote societies we have been discussing? First of all, we would have to consider the cultural context of the American family. We would note the enthusiastic individualism of Americans and their corresponding search for companionship as a shield against loneliness. We would also observe that this

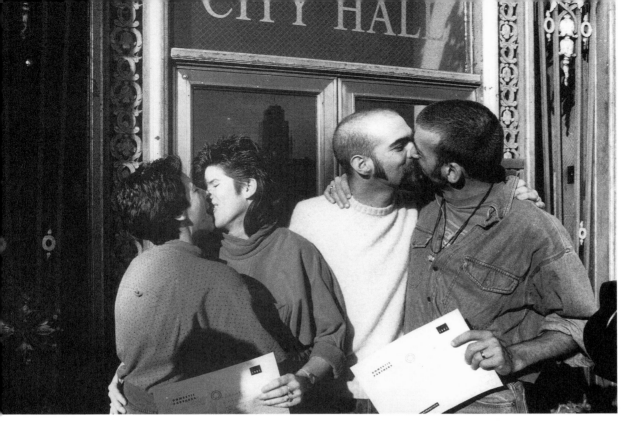

The first two couples to register as domestic partners in San Francisco celebrate after their registration.

Susan Berry and Martha Cody; Chris Minor and Richard Mulholland. In North America, homosexuality was,

until recently, illegal and even considered an illness by the medical establishment. Education and political

activism have largely reversed this conception. Now, in many constituencies, gay couples can legally cohabit

and raise children together.

individualism and the contractualism that goes with it are related to many of the unusual features of the American family system. Parents make contracts with their children about doing the household chores. Husbands and wives make contracts with each other about everything from division of property to who will do the dishes. Admittedly, when a wife took her husband to court in Boston for failing (as promised in their marriage contract) to take out the garbage, this was unusual enough to be reported in the newspapers. People laughed about it as part of the quirkiness of modern times...but family members go on making contracts with one another anyway.

As anthropologists from afar we would also remark that the "nuclear family" on which Americans pin such high hopes is terribly isolated. Other relatives are usually far away, physically or emotionally, and therefore cannot help. Nor are they really expected to. Meanwhile, the little family haven, which Americans are encouraged to think of as a love nest, can sometimes become a place of desperation. We would note with amazement the extraordinarily high frequency of incest in American families, almost always committed by fathers and stepfathers against their daughters, and of violence by husbands against wives and parents against children. We would recognize too that if a husband batters his wife or parents abuse their children, they are not often restrained by outraged relatives or concerned neighbors. Protected by the privacy that the society values so highly, they are tacitly permitted to continue until somebody is hurt badly enough to bring the family in to court.

We would already know that America is a violent society. We would have read the statistics and would hear Americans talking about it all the time, about the problem of crime, about where it is safe to go and about places where it is risky even to live. We might be surprised, though, by the extent to which violence has apparently infiltrated the American citadel and undermined the family dream. In this connection we would certainly be surprised to discover that American children spend as many hours watching television as they do at school and that television programs offer them a steady stream of violence, hour after hour, day after day, year after year.

We would also note that a standard theme of television thrillers concerns violence against women, usually lone women being stalked, brutalized, and raped, or threatened with rape. We might begin to wonder if this sort of thing happens all the time or, if it does not, why it figures so prominently in American fantasies. By now we might begin to wonder too whether Americans are not profoundly ambivalent about the position of women. American women are encouraged to "go it alone" but warned simultaneously, and none too subtly, of the dangers they face if they do. We would also note that women who try to "go it alone" after divorce are much worse off financially then their husbands. They and their children make

DOMESTIC VIOLENCE AGAINST WOMEN AND CHILDREN

Domestic violence is the single largest cause of injury to women in the U.S.; 20 percent of emergency room visits by women are for injuries caused by battering.

Three to four million women in the U.S. are beaten in their homes each year by their husbands, exhusbands, or male lovers.

One of every seven wives is the victim of marital rape.

Thirty-one percent of all female homicide victims in 1988 were killed by their husbands or boyfriends.

Twenty-five percent of abused women are battered during pregnancy.

Fifty-three percent of battering husbands also abuse their children.

Fifty-five percent of all female victims of domestic sexual abuse are children under the age of eleven.

These statistics are taken from *Ms.*, Sept.–Oct. 1990, p. 45.

up a substantial portion of those who live in poverty in an affluent society. Our visiting anthropologists would note therefore that this is a society that seems unable to persuade or oblige many of its fathers to provide for their children and has not developed other ways of taking care of them.

These observations might lead to speculation about the purpose of marriage and the family in America. In other societies these institutions are designed both to harness passion in the service of social stability and to provide for children. Americans, on the other hand, idealize passion, isolate the family from society, and insist less on the needs of children. When the American system works, it provides a marvelous release for individual creativity and emotion; when it does not, it causes a lot of personal pain and social stress. It is, characteristically, an optimistic system, hoping for and betting on the best. In contrast, traditional societies have settled for more cautious systems, designed to make life tolerable and to avoid the worst. Americans, in their version of the modern family, are free to be themselves at the risk of ultimate loneliness. In traditional family systems the individual may be suffocated but is never unsupported. Is there a middle way?

Human beings have been grappling with that question since the beginning of time, seeking the balance between individual desire and social responsibility. We want to be ourselves and yet we have to be dependent on others. So we find release from the dilemma in jokes about our in-laws, which are the only truly international form of humor.

BEAUTY AND THE BEAST

The story of Beauty and the Beast is one of Europe's and in fact the world's best-known fairy tales; variants of the story appear everywhere from Scandinavia to the Mediterranean. The oldest version, which combines Greek and Roman elements, involves Eros (or Cupid), originally the Greek god of desire, and Psyche, an incarnation of the feminine soul. In the story Psyche is a beautiful young girl fated by an oracle to marry death or a monster. Instead she is carried off by an invisible Eros and enters into a happy life in paradise. But Psyche's envious sisters find her, lure her away, and convince her that her husband, whom she never sees but only lies with in the dark, must be an awful monster and that she must expose and kill him. She looks on Eros while he is sleeping and discovers that he is beautiful, but accidentally scalds him with a drop of oil from her lamp. He wakes, and flees, and Psyche must undergo many trials before they are reunited. In most traditional versions of the tale, the drama centers not merely around the monstrous marriage but also around the conflict between the girl's loyalty to her own mother and sisters and her loyalty to the generous beast, her husband. In a seventeenth-century literary version from France, different preoccupations are exposed. Here the drama focuses on the tension between romance and marriage. Beauty is so disgusted by the Beast

that she takes a lover. In revenge, the Beast transforms the lover into a creature like himself, thus eliminating the attraction of lovers over husbands!

5

MISTAKEN IDENTITY

The women gathered the children around them on a broad platform bed in the darkness of the hut and motioned to Pia to join them. They hushed the children and sat there, expectant.

A few moments earlier they had all been chatting outside the hut. The men were away in the forest, and the sound of their singing had wafted through the village in the early morning sunlight. Suddenly, the women froze: Pia turned around to see a man in full ceremonial paint approaching them. He carried a club in one hand and walked with bent head and ceremonial gait. He gave no sign of recognition and spoke neither to her nor to the Xavante women. He wordlessly shepherded them all inside the hut, then went around the outside adjusting the thatch, so that there were no apertures left through which the women or children could peep out.

This, Pia knew, was the most important of all Xavante ceremonies, the *wai'a*, during which the men flaunt the paraphernalia of the spirits in the center of the village and make aggressive forays into the women's huts. Traditionally, a small number of women are then taken out into the male places in the forest to have sexual intercourse with the celebrants of the ritual. All of this happens during days of drama and tension as the men make contact with the spirits. At the climax of the ceremony, the spirits of death fire arrows into the village that are caught by the celebrants, by then working themselves up into a frenzy of aggression, which they pour into their dances.

Now, from within the hut, the women heard pounding feet and deep cries of "U, he, he, he..." coming from all directions. They felt they were engulfed by the sound as it ebbed this way and that. Suddenly they heard pounding on the thatch of their hut, followed by rustling and shaking. Somebody or something was clambering over the outside of the house. The women and children remained deathly still. Pia felt as though they were in the eye of the storm, surrounded by thunder, waiting for the lightning to strike. The thundering shouts began to fade. A little boy ventured outside to pee. His little sister, equally anxious to run around and relieve the tension, was not allowed out. She started to whine but came scurrying back to the bed when she heard more shouts outside. Soon the shouts died away, but now the little girl did not want to go outside. The women waited a long time before they breathed a sigh of relief and made some coffee.

The Xavante separate the sexes. The men spend their time in their meeting places in the center of the village or away in the forest; the houses are regarded as female places. The center of the village is where politics and ceremonial affairs, preeminently male activities, are conducted. The periphery is for domestic affairs. Women participate in some Xavante ceremonies, in log races (sometimes) and age-set rituals (but shyly and not in large numbers), but they are excluded from the most solemn ceremonies, confined within their houses and forbidden to watch the proceedings.

Separation of the sexes, exclusion of women from public affairs, ceremonial aggression against women, ceremonial sexual intercourse with women who are married and would not normally be available as sex partners, all of these are Xavante practice – and yet, shocked by what they see of the relations between the sexes in Brazilian cities, Xavante say that in their society there is respect for women. The drama of sexual antagonism is very much part of Xavante identity, and the apprehensive stillness of the women as the men surge around the hut is very real, but the drama is not a personal one. Male aggression against women only takes place here, at the ceremonial level. In everyday life, Xavante women are quite outspoken. Domestic violence against women and children is unheard of, and so is rape. It is the casual aggression against women in cities that shocks the Xavante, while the polarization of the sexes (which might shock us) is deeply part of the Xavante sense of self.

Gender is only one of the many components of our sense of personal identity, and for us now it is perhaps one of the most vexed and confusing parts. The beauty of the modern family, as we have just seen, is that it leaves you free to be yourself – at least in theory. But how do you know who you are? We have to go back to the very beginning of our lives, or perhaps before the beginning, to find clues to what makes up a human identity.

The problem was brought home to me the very first moment I started work as an anthropologist. Pia and I arrived by boat at a Xerente village, where we were to start the process (still mysterious to us at that time) of "doing fieldwork" and learning the language in preparation for our grand goal of visiting the Xavante. It was the dry season, and the huge Tocantins River was running strong but low between banks that towered twenty feet or more on each side. The Xerente helped us scramble with our gear up the slope and along a crooked path to the village. We sat in a big thatched hut, listening to the nasal bumble of their speech and wondering how to get started. Kwiromenkwa, the chief, sat opposite me on a stool, with a little girl standing between his knees. It seemed from the affectionate way he treated her that she was probably his daughter.

"What's her name?" I asked in Portuguese, selecting what I thought was the most innocent way to get acquainted. The chief looked nonplussed. Did I want to know the name of his daughter? By now I was embarrassed, but not knowing what else to do, I persevered. Yes, I did. Kwiromenkwa leaned back and called over to the next house. I did not understand what he said, but he was clearly asking a question. There followed a lively debate with his wives, while I sat there in the darkened hut aghast at what I had let myself in for. After all these years, I was among the Indians at last, and hoping to learn from them about their lives...but how could I do it if even the simplest question turned out to be so impossibly complex?

But it was not a simple question. Xerente babies are not named at birth. Indeed, they are not named for years. Toddlers run around quite happily, addressed by their kin as "daughter," "son," "niece," "nephew," and so on. They do not often meet people who are not kin and, when they do, the strangers call them quite simply "boy" or "girl." A society without any individual names? Not at all. Names are very important among the Xerente – too important to be casually bestowed on babies by parental whim. In fact, the Xerente feel that the burden of a name would be too much for a small child to bear. Young children are weak and might sicken and die if they were weighed down with a name, so they can only be named later when they are strong enough for it. A name is not a device for singling out an individual; it is a way of making an individual into a social being, of linking him with society, just as society is linked to the cosmos.

Little girls are named when they are about six or seven years old. They are led out in pairs to receive their names from the associations of mature men that are the mainstay of Xerente social life. Boys may be even older when they are named, for a boy's naming ceremony is, to the Xerente, a more important affair. A number of villages usually get together for the occasion. There are log races and feasting, and then the men of the two moieties line up opposite each other. A crier steps out from one moiety and a boy steps forward from the other. The crier than calls out the boy's name for all to hear. It takes quite a long time but, by the end of it, the moieties have named each other's sons.

A Xerente boy's name will thus tell you which clan and which lineage he belongs to. A Xerente girl's name will tell you which men's society named her. But they are not much help in identifying the individuals who bear them, for they are little used in conversation, and Xerente can know other Xerente quite well without actually knowing or remembering their names. A Xerente is thus tied into her world from the very beginning. She knows her relationship to every individual in it and soon learns her relationship to the groups that make up her society. It is from these that she acquires her sense of self.

In modern industrial society, by contrast, we expect a child to develop her own individual personality in a less structured context. We expect, or at least hope for, a kind of unfolding of the inner self or character of the child, without linking her too firmly with her surroundings. This places a considerable responsibility, even a burden, on the maturing individual, especially since society at large is deeply divided about the nature of children and how they should be brought up. Raising children seems to be a practical task, but it is imbued in every society with powerful moral overtones. It is not simply a matter of sleepless nights and wiping bottoms, or even of giving wise counsel to anguished teenagers (something that would make most parents take a vow of celibacy if they had any advance knowledge of what it would be like); it is essentially an effort to shape a good person. It requires, therefore, some firm conviction about what a good person is and how a child can be helped or trained to become one. It is the debate over such issues in modern societies that makes child rearing such an anxious business. Parents in America worried twenty years ago about whether they were too strict. Now there is a current of opinion that attributes the ills of American society to parental permissiveness. The passion that inflames these controversies swirls around the theme of values. What are the central values of our society? What should they be in a nation that encourages people of different races and nationalities and backgrounds to come to it from all over the world?

This is a problem that tribal societies do not have to face, at least not unless they find their way of life overwhelmed by the outside world. They normally get on with the business of bringing up children against a background of consensus about what should be done and how, which means that they can also be more relaxed about who does the bringing up. Children may spend as much time with other adults as they do with their parents, or, like the Xavante, they may wander around in a flock that is vaguely supervised by whichever adults happen to be nearby. As soon as Xavante babies are old enough to toddle and confident enough to wander away from home, they attach themselves to one of the eddies of children that come and go in the village. There they are socialized by their peers. The older kids keep an eye on the younger ones and teach them their place in the pecking order. Of course there are squabbles and scraps and one often sees a little child who has got the worst of it wobbling home and yelling furiously. What fascinated us was the reaction of the child's parents. They would never do what parents in our society often do – go out and remonstrate with the children in an attempt to impose some kind of adult justice on their interactions (often leaving the children with a burning sense of impotent unfairness as a result). Instead they would simply comfort the child and let her return to the fold as soon as her bruised knee or battered ego permitted. At the same time, we never saw anything approaching bullying among the Xavante children who were left to police themselves, and we watched them constantly for they were a kaleidoscope of activity and amusement for us during the long, hot days of our fieldwork.

They watched us, too, and everybody else. Xavante children, like village children the world over, are the eyes and ears of the community. There is very little one can do that escapes their notice, and their curiosity is insatiable. As soon as they see anyone going anywhere, they call out "Where to?" and we very soon learned to give them precise answers or they would follow us to see what we were doing. This could be embarrassing if we were going into the forest to relieve ourselves.

The Xavante system represents a kind of informal dilution of parents' everyday responsibilities toward their children. In many societies these responsibilities are formally transferred to other relatives. In the Pacific Islands, for example, it is quite common for children to be raised by their parents' kin. Among the Trobriand Islanders, whom we met earlier on their kula expeditions, this is seen as a useful thing to do for the child, for it expands his or her network of active kin relationships without severing ties to the biological parents. If children are unhappy, they can return to their true parents. If they are contented, they remain with their adoptive parents until adulthood. In fact, many societies are so uninterested in the genetic relationship between parents and their children that anthropologists have debated whether or not they were ignorant of the biological "facts of life." Australian Aborigines as well as Trobriand Islanders, for example, traditionally insisted that women became pregnant when spirits entered them. What puzzled Malinowski, who reported the Trobriand belief, was that the islanders nevertheless maintained that children bore a physical resemblance to their fathers. They explained this by saying that a father shaped his child through repeated intercourse with the mother during pregnancy and by providing the child with food in its earliest formative years. Trobrianders are now familiar with modern biology's account of what happens at conception, but they find it insuffi-

If one were asked to state briefly and succinctly what are the outstanding positive features of aboriginal civilizations, I, for one, would have no hesitation in answering that there are three: the respect for the individual, irrespective of age or sex; the amazing degree of social and political integration achieved by them; and the existence there of a concept of personal security which transcends all governmental forms and all tribal and group interests and conflicts.

TRIBAL RESPECT FOR THE INDIVIDUAL

Paul Radin, *The World of Primitive Man* (New York: Dutton, 1971).

The possibility of conceiving of an individual alone in a tribal sense is ridiculous.... the very complexity of tribal life and the interdependence of people on one another makes this conception improbable at best, a terrifying loss of identity at worst.

Vine Deloria quoted in Jamake Highwater, *The Primal Mind: Vision and Reality in Indian America* (New York: Meridian, 1981).

cient. They still believe that the whole process is set in motion by a spirit that enters the mother's womb. In their view, the substance of a child is blood, provided by the mother once she has been impregnated by a spirit. This belief fits in very well with the Trobriand rule of descent, which follows the female line.

Peoples whose rule of descent follows the male line often interpret pregnancy in a diametrically opposite way. They sometimes insist that the essence of babies is contained in the father's sperm. The mother, then, is merely a receptacle in which the sperm is nurtured until it has grown into a child. This view was common in medieval Europe, as can be seen from illustrations of the process drawn from medical books of the time that show a perfectly formed human being contained in a drop of sperm.

Clearly all human societies recognize that when a woman becomes pregnant, there is some kind of relationship between her, a man, and the child she will bear, but they define that relationship in myriad ways. One such definition has consequences that amazed European observers of so-called exotic peoples. The travelers noted that in some societies pregnant women went about their normal tasks virtually until the moment of delivery, gave birth (usually assisted by other women), and then, after a little rest, went back to their normal lives again. Meanwhile their husbands lay down for days, even simulated childbirth – or so the travelers thought – and generally acted as if they and not their wives were having the baby. The explanation of this curious behavior is that these societies believe that there is a strong mystical bond between a father and his child, so much so that whatever a father does has a direct physical effect on the child. The father therefore refrains from eating foods that would harm the child if he consumed them and also from all activities that could pose a threat to the child. This restraint is particularly important during periods like pregnancy and childbirth when the child is in a vulnerable state, but a man will observe similar restrictions if his child gets sick later in life.

Some of the Indian peoples of central Brazil believe that such a relationship exists between a child and any man who has had intercourse with its mother during pregnancy. As the time of birth draws near, a woman names any men who have slept with her recently in addition to her husband, and they all have to observe restrictions to protect the baby's health. Every society, it seems, puts its own construction on "the facts of life," which is why early explorers, even when they no longer expected to meet human freaks in their travels, still wondered about whether the biology of other peoples was the same as ours. Now we know that it is, but we also know that the social interpretations of the biological facts vary widely, so that different peoples have quite different perceptions – no, convictions – about what happens when babies are made.

In the United States there seems to be a general feeling that identity is encoded in a baby's genes, needing only nurturing and loving parents to bring it out like a

flower in bloom. How else can one interpret the fact that many Americans brought up by adoptive parents are impelled to seek out their "real parents" to find out who they "really are," as if it is only by getting to know their biological parents that they can peer into their true selves? Compared with other peoples, Americans are extremists in their biological view of individual identity. Other societies (and not only tribal ones) take a more social view. They believe that individual identity is constructed out of the various forces that shape a growing child, and the most important of these is instruction in the expectations concerning gender. Modern societies divide babies according to their sex at birth, or even before it, now that we can tell the sex of an unborn child through amniocentesis. Pink or blue layettes serve to remind the world at large, even before birth, of the baby's sex. We find it difficult to think or speak about a newborn without knowing his or her sex. Many tribal societies take this sexual dualism even further. They do not simply divide human beings into male and female; they extend this distinction to the entire cosmos, which is seen as being in a constant process of mixing and synthesizing these two basic principles.

This kind of thinking is very old. The ancient Egyptians believed that a totality must consist of the union of opposites. A similar premise, that the interaction between yin (the female principle) and yang (the male principle) underlies the workings of the universe, is at the heart of much Chinese thinking. The idea has been central to Taoist philosophy from the fourth century B.C. to the present day and is still embraced by many Chinese who are not Taoists. Nor is the idea confined to the Egyptians and the Chinese. Peoples all over the world, in Eurasia, Africa, and the Americas, have come to the conclusion that the cosmos is a combining of opposites and that one of the most important aspects of this dualism is the opposition between male and female.

These ideas find an interesting expression in the societies of present-day Indonesia, where the complementarity inherent in the scheme of things is expressed in a whole range of associated oppositions. So male is to female as light is to dark, day is to night, life is to death, even right is to left. They are essential to each other. One cannot exist without the other. The harmony of the world depends on the capacity of human beings to maintain a dynamic equilibrium between these opposing principles. Note, however, that while complementarity is fundamental to this philosophy, it tends to be unbalanced. There is an ambivalence about the character of the female pole. Death and decay as "female" attributes are certainly powerful – they are, perhaps, the ultimate power – but they carry a charge of tremendous fear and negativity. Of course the idea of *day* makes no sense without *night*, and life (in our experience, if not in our religious hopes) is defined by contrast with *death*, but most people still prefer *day* and *life* (with male associations) to *night* and *death* (with female ones). Even the less highly charged oppositions, between *sun* (male) and *moon* (female), and *right* (male) and *left* (female), privilege the male side. Our own associations with right and left make this clear. Right is associated with what is correct and morally justifiable; left is associated with the sinister and gauche.

Anthropologists and historians have been trying for a long time to understand and explain why even those societies that insist on the complementarity between male and female tend to be ambivalent about the female. A Swiss scholar named Johann Jakob Bachofen wrote a treatise entitled *Mother Right* in 1861, arguing that human society had moved (regressed, in his view) from a stage of matriarchy to one of patriarchy. Bachofen's theory, if correct, would have shed light on the problem of misogyny, for the patriarchs would have been interested in denigrating the female powers they had so recently overthrown. Bachofen was, however, opposed by contemporary patriarchs, or rather by scholars who argued that the evidence was against him and that there never had been a period of matriarchy. Patriarchal institutions, they insisted, were very old indeed and were likely to have been preceded, at best, by small-scale tribal societies in which neither tendency was strongly developed. The argument still continues. There are those who claim that the archaeological evidence for goddesses and fertility cults in early Mesopotamia supports the view that the female principle was more revered in ancient times; others who argue that the roles of men and women were complementary at the dawn of human history and that the tilt toward patriarchy occurred when warlike pastoralists overwhelmed the neolithic peoples of antiquity; and still others

The Yekuana, who live along the Orinoco River in Venezuela, believe that a successful life is one that continually integrates the visible, everyday world with the invisible world of the spirits. They express this visually in the patterns of the flat, round baskets that are used to serve food. Not only are the baskets designed, like Yekuana houses, according to a pattern of two concentric circles, characteristic of the dualism of Amazonian peoples (the inner circle of the house or settlement is the men's circle, the outer ring belongs to the women and the separate families), but each pattern can be read in two ways, with white or black as foreground or background. The movement back and forth between the two images encapsulates the reciprocity that is at the heart of Yekuana cosmology, a reciprocity between invisible power and visible world as well as between men and women. The baskets are also a kind of wedding ring or marriage crest: a Yekuana man will weave a special basket for his wife at marriage, and she must always serve food on a basket of that design, for to use any other would cause her to die.

YEKUANA BASKETS

There is nothing at all on this earth that is not paired. Everything must have its counterpart. The man and the woman are like the right hand and the left hand. The right hand is not worth much without the left hand. You must work hard to put everything in order, in balance. You must work especially hard to overcome one's debt to death and one's debt to life – for they too are a pair. We depend on the ancestors like swords hanging from a pole. We cannot do without them.

Back in the time "when the grass spoke and the earth talked," the people of Sumba, Indonesia, were head-hunters. The practice has stopped but stories are still told of the old raids on enemy villages. In the village of Tarung, a priest hangs some heads on a traditional skull tree. The heads are treated like brides – adorned with rich cloths and the red ribbon of weddings – because they bring fertility to the village. Only through death can one receive the gift of life, say the people of Sumba.

who argue that the evidence on these matters is inconclusive.

But how about the myths found in so many societies about a time when women ruled the world? Alas, they are just that – myths. Joan Bamberger, an anthropologist who studied such myths among South American Indians, points out that they portray the period of matriarchy as one of injustice, immorality, and the abuse of power, which was only brought to an end when men seized the sacred flutes or whatever else served as both the symbol and the instrument of control. Men thus established their rule over women and, incidentally, over the rituals surrounding the sacred instruments, from which women are strictly barred. These myths are clearly not history. Instead they are a rationalization and justification of the present male-dominated order. The peoples who tell these stories teach that women are potentially dangerous and immoral and that a stable and just order in this world depends on their being kept under the control of men.

It is interesting that woman appears most evil in societies where the solidarity of men is most important. In the South American tribes that tell the myths of matriarchy, men spend most of their time in one another's company, often in the men's house, while the women and children occupy the domestic area of the village. In highland New Guinea we find the same pattern. Men traditionally lived in communal houses, leaving the women in family dwellings with the children and the pigs that are their main form of wealth. Young men are nervous about sexual intercourse with women, for they have been taught by their elders that it draws off a man's limited store of vital energy. The polarization in the highlands is so extreme that, as Mervyn Meggitt, a veteran researcher on New Guinea, put it, men are either prudes – anxious about contamination by women – or lechers, determined to control the lot. The threat of female anarchy is for them a very real preoccupation.

Why should these malign influences be ascribed to women? Sherry Ortner has suggested that it is because women are generally perceived as being closer to nature than men. They menstruate, they bear and suckle their young like other mammals. Their physiology seems to chain them to their reproductive role, while men are left to roam free. So women are thought to derive certain powers from nature, but these powers have to be held in check and kept under control if human society is to flourish. Men therefore set themselves up as the guardians of culture and creators of society. Women, who – according to this view – cannot escape from nature, are considered only partly socialized, and their activities are confined to the domestic sphere for which their childbearing and child-rearing functions seem to have predestined them.

This ideology is not confined to tribal societies. On the contrary, echoes of it are found elsewhere. Even in modern societies that are attempting to legislate equality between the sexes, popular stereotypes persist that parallel the tribal distinctions. According to these, men are more rational, women more emotional.

The Hopi are a matrilineal society where the strongest ties are those between mothers and daughters, followed by those between sons and mothers' brothers. The father is a kind of guest or visitor in the household.

Menstruation and childcaring make women less reliable in their judgments and in their performance than men, and so on. But folk ideology in the United States also holds, for example, that men are less able to control their (natural) sexuality and that women, especially wives, have to "tame" them. So it all depends on how you look at it. "Nature" can be good (free) or bad (lawless, threatening); "culture" can be good (order) or bad (constraint). It is clear that tribal views of both women and men, just like the stereotypes held about men and women in modern societies, are ideological constructs that reveal more about the preoccupations of the societies that hold them than about any objective reality.

Some societies do hold quite different views about the "nature" of women and men. For example, Richard Huntington has reported an intriguingly balanced kind of complementarity in the ideology of male and female from Madagascar. The population of Madagascar is made up of people from the Indonesian Islands who sailed across the Indian Ocean more than a thousand years ago and mixed with people of Arab and Black African descent. Madagascan languages and cultures are, not surprisingly, strongly related to others in Indonesia. Huntington reports that the Bara of Madagascar, like their Indonesian cousins, make critical distinctions between male and female. Indonesian ideas of cosmic and sexual complementarity are expressed here as the opposition between semen and blood, bone and flesh. At the individual level, this means that a person gets her skeleton from her father's semen and her flesh from her mother's blood. At the cosmic level, the male principle is associated with enduring order, represented by the imperishable skeleton. The female principle is associated with change, growth, and decay, as represented by the all-too-perishable flesh. Note, however, that the contrast for Madagascans is not between male order and female disorder or anarchy, but rather between male structure and female vitality. The male principle is associated, for a change, with death and the female one with life.

Just as cosmic complementarity does not have to be tilted against the feminine, neither does social complementarity necessarily imply female subordination. There are really two questions here. The first concerns the kinds of *ideas* people hold about the nature and the proper ordering of the sexes. The second concerns the actual *status* of women and men in everyday life – in other words what kind of freedom and influence they have in society. The two things are related but not always equivalent. Even though male authority is often prevalent at the level of values and ideas, women in some societies possess tremendous power and personal autonomy. We have to know where to look, and what questions to ask, to discover what is not always apparent. A "yin and yang" view of the cosmos as the sum of

THE ASHANTI QUEEN-MOTHER

The Ashanti maintain that the queen-mother originated from the moon and as such she is the source of life....they say the sun originated from the moon. In support of this they point out that it is the moon which gives light in the presence of darkness....

The tribute of the Ashanti to the queen-mother can well be described by comparison with the life of the white ants or termites. The life of the ants is well known to the people. The queen ant is recognized as the origination of all lives within the ant society.... Every ant has its duty to perform to the queen-ant and so it was in the Ashanti community. Therefore all clan members regard themselves as children of one mother and consequently of one ancestress, the woman who gave life to their clan. Being the creator, in the beginning she ruled the state, assisted by a council of women; she was at the same time the supreme war leader (so indeed was the queen-mother of Ejisu, Yaa Asantewaa, A.D. 1900, whose bravery was renowned). Eventually she began to share her rule with kings, who took over many of her duties.

From H. Kullas and G. Ayer, *What the Elders of Ashanti Say* (Kumas, Ghana: University Press, 1967).

male and female principles can exist within a society that allows women little actual power or dignity. Conversely, a very sexist cosmology can flourish where sex roles are not hierarchical, but egalitarian and competitive. Then there are societies, like that of the Hopi Indians of the southwestern United States, that maintain a balance between male and female at both the cosmic and the social levels. The Hopi trace descent through females, as do many of the West African societies that are known for holding women in high esteem. In that part of the world, there are many societies where women are expected to be active – even dominant – in the economy or in ritual. Among the Ashanti of Ghana, for example, women are key figures. They are seen as the people who maintain continuity by linking generations; they are seen as the core of Ashanti settlements, which are formed around groups of related women. Men speak proudly of the wealth of their mothers when they want to praise their own lineages.

Societies that value women do not, however, necessarily trace descent through them. Women may be powerful heads of households even where descent is traced through men and even if those men can take more than one wife. In parts of Africa women may even, when left husbandless, decide to take other women as their "wives," not in the sexual sense but as helpers to share the burdens of the household or the business. The wives of successful women may take lovers and in this way can bear children for their female "husbands." These societies seem to be acting out the American joke that what a woman needs to be successful is a good wife.

One might ask how all this differs from what happens in modern industrial societies (apart from the businesslike marriages between wealthy women and younger wives, which one is not likely to encounter in London or Frankfurt). In fact there is a fundamental difference between female authority in a society that does not expect it and female authority in a society that does. The first believes in the preeminence of males and the contrast between male and female gender roles as clusters of personality characteristics that can be labeled "masculine" and "feminine." The second does not. So female power in the first tends to be seen as an anomaly or a threat; in the second as a legitimate resource.

In modern industrial societies, there is a push to try to institutionalize *equality* rather than *complementarity* between men and women. This effort is complicated by the fact that the same societies that work for this equality, albeit halfheartedly at times, nevertheless raise boys and girls differently. Girls in particular are given mixed signals: they are rewarded for being cooperative in societies that value competition, for showing empathy in societies that reward aggression. So it is not surprising that recent studies carried out by Carol Gilligan in the United States have shown that girls, who start out so full of bounce in a culture that encourages them to express themselves, undergo a crisis of confidence as they are about to enter their teens. It is then they start to realize that their own culture is ambivalent about women. They are encouraged to be feminine but are beginning to understand that "femininity" is a sure route to second-class citizenship.

If girls face the special problem of trying to find out what it means to grow up as a woman in the modern world, both boys and girls have to cope with the difficulties of growing up in societies that cannot decide exactly when maturity has arrived or should be acknowledged. Modern industrial societies are uncomfortably aware that individuals are physically old enough to produce children long before they leave home or school. Even graduation from high school does not, for many modern young people, mark the moment when they enter the adult world of work and responsibility. Western societies offer maturity piecemeal to their growing children – who are no longer children – and prolong a period of adolescence that seems to be as confusing and painful for the parents as it is for their offspring.

Such considerations do not complicate growing up in tribal societies, where the transition to maturity is made more cleanly and is marked with greater ceremony. These tribal initiation rites have always held a special interest for outside observers, who have been fascinated by their exotic, and especially by their sexual, aspects. It is the pain and terror of such initiations that make the deepest impression, and these are most frequently inflicted on boys, who are in the process of being taken out of the women's world and brought into that of the men. To this end, they are secluded and subject to privations and mortifications that may cause intense pain before they can emerge as men. Some Australian Aboriginal groups peel the penis like a banana and cut into the flesh beneath the foreskin. Some African groups cut the face and forehead of the initiate in such a way as to leave deep scars. Circumcision is, of course, the commonest of all initiation procedures. Its effect on the boy is, however, intensified in some places by an elaborate concern with his fortitude during the operation. The Maasai of East Africa, whose *moran* or warriors are world famous as epitomes of courage and bravado, closely watch a boy who is being circumcised for the slightest sign of cowardice. He is not supposed to so much as twitch during the operation. Even an involuntary twitch could make him an object of condemnation and scorn. So he sits, impassive, surrounded by a throng of family and friends who crowd around to watch – and to prevent others from pressing in on him so closely that he is thought to move or flinch. The boy's anxiety can be imagined.

Initiation rituals are intended to provoke anxiety. They act out the death and rebirth of the initiate, which is a stressful process. His old self dies and he is separated from his society. He is in limbo. While he is in this marginal state he learns the mysteries of his society, instruction that is enhanced by fear and deprivation, and by the atmosphere of awe that his teachers seek to create. In some societies that atmosphere is enhanced by the fact that the teachers are anonymous, masked figures, representing the spirits. The initiate, stripped of his previous identity and held in this shadow world of betwixt-and-between, is at his most susceptible. He

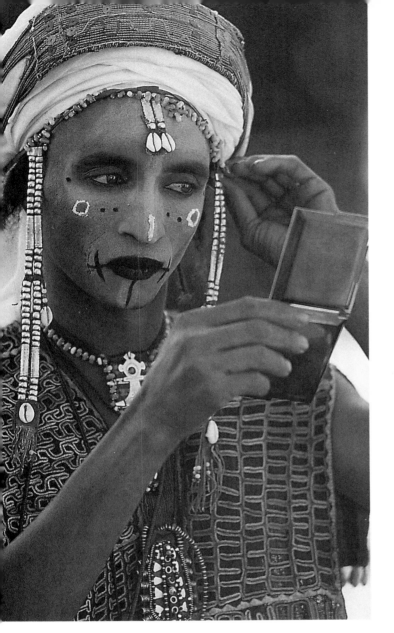

WODAABE MASCULINITY

Gender: the way in which sex (the designation of individuals within a species as either male or female) is used as a structuring principle in human culture and society. Gender refers either to symbolic constructions (ideologies) or to social relations. As such, unlike sex, gender is variable cross-culturally, intraculturally, and historically. What is described as "masculine" or "feminine" in a given society is culturally rather than biologically prescribed.

Male beauty is prized among the Wodaabe of Niger. It is considered among the most masculine of attributes. Wodaabe men take great care in preparing themselves for any public celebration of their beauty and masculinity. A *Yakke* dancer lightens his skin with a pale yellow powder, then darkens his eyes and lips with black kohl to bring out the whiteness of teeth and eyes. Jewelry and a hand-stitched dance costume complete the ensemble. A mirror is a treasured acquisition.

learns with all his being what he needs to know about his society, and the lesson is often inscribed unforgettably on his body as well as in his mind. Then, some time later (for the full cycle of ceremonies may last weeks or even months) he is reborn as an adult. The symbolism of this transition can on occasion by quite explicit. The initiate crawls between the legs of his sponsor to be reborn, but this time reborn of man into the world of men.

Girls' initiation ceremonies are as dramatically marked in some societies as those of boys. Audrey Richards's account of the *chisungu*, a month-long initiation ceremony for girls among the Bemba of Zambia, describes the complex way in which a girl becomes a woman, knowledgeable in the responsibilities of her sex and the values of her society. Like religious initiations, this ritual does not so much add to the girl's practical knowledge as inculcate certain attitudes – a respect for age, for senior women and senior men, for the mystical bonds between husband and wife, for what the Bemba believe to be the dangerous potentials of sex, fire, and blood. The initiate learns the secret names of things and the songs and dances known only to women. She is incorporated into the group of women who form her immediate community, since this is a society that traces descent in the female line and a husband moves to his wife's village at marriage. Western writers tend to assume that it is more important for boys to undergo a separation from their mothers as they mature than it is for girls. But the Bemba stress that mothers must surrender their daughters in the *chisungu* to the community at large (and the venerable mistress of ceremonies in particular) as part of a process through which they will eventually gain sons-in-law.

The ceremony Richards observed for the initiation of three girls included eighteen separate events, at least forty different pottery models (shaped for the occasion and destroyed immediately afterward), nearly a hundred songs, and numerous wall paintings and dances, all used to instruct the girls in their new status. The initiates had to pass through difficult and sometimes ridiculous ordeals, such as climbing a tree backward or drinking beer backward over the shoulder, leaping through hoops, and so on. They were not meant to fail these tests but to learn from them that they must now face new things and to see that they could indeed accomplish them.

All of this represents a large investment of time and resources. The Bemba take the initiation of girls very seriously. All important ceremonies, including major

AMERICAN MALES

Men are committing suicide at four times the rate of women.

Men between the ages of eighteen and twenty-nine suffer alcohol dependency at three times the rate of women of the same age group. More than two-thirds of all alcoholics are men, and 50 percent more men are regular users of illicit drugs.

Men account for more than 90 percent of arrests for alcohol- and drug-abuse violations.

Real wages for men under twenty-five have actually declined over the last twenty years.

60 percent of all high school dropouts are males.

More than 80 percent of America's homeless are men.

Men's life expectancy is 10 percent shorter than women's.

Andrew Kimbrell, "A time for men to pull together." *Utne Reader* May – June 1991, p. 66.

agricultural rituals and even the accession of a (male) chief, rest on the foundation of a properly performed chisungu. Even the relations of husband and wife, in a society in which they are pulled apart by loyalties to different clans, depend on the chisungu. The initiation gives girls a strong sense of the solidarity and powers of women in a society that also stresses male authority and female submissiveness. Richards's graphic description of how the "dirty, frightened, exhausted creatures" of the first days of the initiation are transformed into demure young brides by the end of it shows that the rite does, as Bemba women say, "grow the girl."

Ever since the influential work of Margaret Mead, there has been a tendency in the West to assume that, if growing up is less stressful in tribal societies, it is because they are less puritanical about sex. The modern world has, however, undergone a sexual revolution since Mead was writing in the 1930s and 1940s, and it does not seem to have made growing up in it all that much easier. I think that, in our preoccupation with sex, we miss the point. Take the case of tribal initiations. It is true that they normally make it clear to the initiates (and to the world at large) that they are now mature enough to have sex and to have children. But the important difference between these ceremonies and the customs of modern societies lies not in their sexual explicitness but in their clarity about what is happening. This clarity provides a sharp contrast to societies where families dither over their maturing and often resentful young, suggesting that they may be old enough but not yet mature enough, mature enough but not yet secure enough, and so on through an obstacle course that keeps being prolonged. Tribal initiations involve pain and stress for a time, but they enable the individual to move with a fair degree of certainty through clearly demarcated stages of life.

This is particularly true of societies like the Xavante where the position of an individual relative to everybody else is indicated by the age-set that he or she belongs to. A boy is brought into his age-set when the elders of the village decide that it is time for a new group to enter the bachelors' hut. They gather the boys who are between seven and twelve years old and, on an appointed day, take them all to build a new bachelors' hut, in which they will live, at one end of the village semicircle. When I first saw an age-set being formed in this way, the boys were a splendid sight, naked, painted scarlet from head to foot, and wearing broad ceremonial collars of white cotton. Each one sat before the hut, removed his collar, and gave it to the master of ceremonies. In return the boy received a tiny conical spiral of palm leaf. He pulled the foreskin of his penis forward, moistened the spiral with his tongue, and placed it on the tip of his penis. After that he entered the hut. From that moment on, he was no longer a child. He would never remove his penis sheath, except when it was physically necessary. The sheath "concealed" his penis, indicating his sexual potency and at the same time the social control to which otherwise dangerous sexual powers must be submitted.

He would spend about five years in the bachelors' hut, and most Xavante look

PAULO

MY CHILDHOOD NAME WAS WORANIPIWA. THE NAME WAS GIVEN TO
ME BY MY FATHER. NOT ALL INDIAN NAMES HAVE SPECIAL
SIGNIFICANCE, BECAUSE I HAVE NO IDEA WHAT MY NAME MEANS.
LATER ON, HOWEVER, WHEN I WAS INITIATED AND BECAME
A YOUNG MAN, I RECEIVED ANOTHER NAME FROM THE ELDERS,
WORADZUPÁ, WHICH MEANS "HE WHO KNOWS OUTSIDERS."
THIS NAME WAS GIVEN TO ME BECAUSE OUR ANCESTOR, APEWEN,
HAD HAD A DREAM IN WHICH HE SAW A YOUNG MAN AMONG
THE WHITE FOLK. SO APEWEN GAVE ME THAT NAME. I HAVE
ALWAYS BEEN SOUGHT OUT BY OUTSIDERS WHO HAVE COME TO
THE VILLAGE AND I SEEM TO GET ON VERY WELL WITH THEM,
SO I'M KNOWN EVERYWHERE BY THIS NAME. I'M VERY HAPPY WITH
THIS NAME AND MY ROLE.

A FEW YEARS AGO I WENT TO THE CITY TO LIVE AND WORK
AMONG OUTSIDERS. THAT'S WHERE I TOOK MY BRAZILIAN NAME,
PAULO. THE CITY'S A TOUGH AND DISORDERLY PLACE. YOU NEVER
KNOW WHAT'S GOING TO HAPPEN TO YOU. I COULD PROBABLY
MANAGE THERE BUT I'D BE A DIFFERENT PERSON. I MIGHT END UP
KILLING SOMEONE IN THE CITY JUST TO MAKE ENDS MEET.
I WANTED TO GO BACK TO THE VILLAGE WHERE THINGS ARE MORE
ORDERLY, WHERE I KNOW THE SYSTEM, AND WHERE I CAN
LIVE A DECENT LIFE.

IT'S TRUE THAT NOW I'M ONE OF THE MATURE MEN BUT I'M NOT
ONE OF THE ELDERS. THE ELDERS ARE STILL TEACHING US – ALL
OF THOSE MATURE MEN WHO ARE IN THE SAME AGE GROUP. LATER,
WHEN THE ELDERS HAVE PASSED ON, WE WILL BE THE ELDERS
AND WE WILL BE THE ONES WHO WILL DO THE TEACHING. BUT
WE'RE NOT READY FOR THAT YET. I'M STILL LEARNING, ALTHOUGH
I'M HELPING TO INITIATE THE YOUNGER ONES.

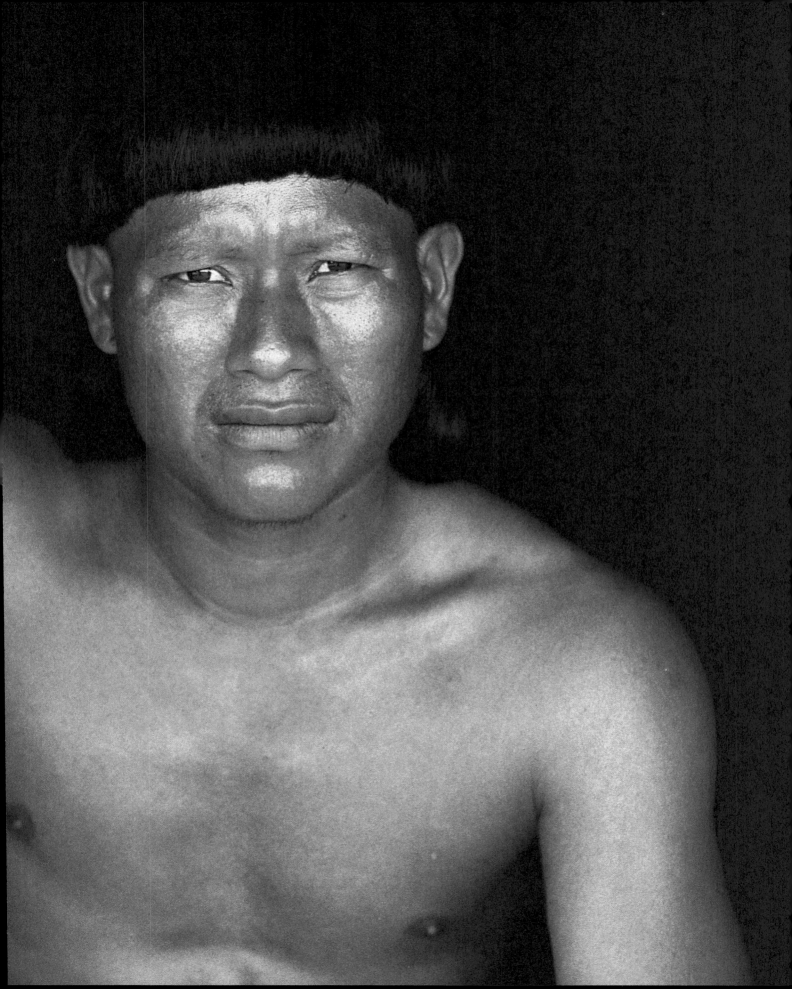

back on those as happy years. The boys live together, but they are not secluded. They can come and go as they please in the houses of their families, but now they have the status of bachelors, the young ones who sing round the village at night. The older men teach them how to survive in the jungles, how to hunt and to fish, but they need be neither assiduous nor successful at these pursuits because their families send food over to them anyway. Most of all, they learn the songs and rituals of their people and perhaps even begin having significant dreams themselves, for it is through their dreams that Xavante innovate and experiment with life.

After these five years in the bachelors' hut comes the six-month period of initiation. It starts when the bachelors have their ears pierced to insert the small, white wooden cylinders worn by adult Xavante. The symbolism of this practice is explicitly sexual, indicating that the young men are now mature enough to have sexual intercourse. They are not supposed to have done so up to that point and indeed do not have much opportunity for it, since Xavante men marry several wives, and their elders will have claimed most of the women in the community who are old enough for sex. An initiate who has had an affair with a married woman and is unlucky enough to be found out faces a double jeopardy – not only does he have to deal with her husband, older, senior, and probably irate, but he also faces the prospect of being shamed at initiation. If his sponsor thinks he has behaved with flagrant indiscretion, he will insist on piercing his ears long before the ceremony for his age-set. That way he will be publicly humiliated when his age-set undergoes the initiation, which now has no point for him.

Next come the privations. The boys are not only led out to sing round the village three or four times every night, but they are taken before dawn to the river. They have to immerse themselves in it and then jump up and down, thwacking the water with their hands each time they land. The older men sit around their fires and can hear by the splashing that the boys are still at it. From time to time the splashing dies down. The boys, by now chilled to the bone, have crept onto the bank to warm themselves at their own illicit fire. When their senior sponsors detect this, they run to the river, stamp out the fire, and chase their charges back into the water. The water ordeal is repeated at various times throughout the day for weeks. After that, the initiation moves from water to land. Once again the boys are led out by their sponsors many times during the day, but now they are brought ceremonially to the apex of the village horseshoe and required to dash repeatedly into the center. By the end even the strongest of them are aching and limping.

On the final day of initiation, all the age-sets run the dash, starting with the elders and working down through all of them till the bachelors have run yet again. Then the boys return to the bachelors' hut for the last time. The whole village gathers round to see all the initiates betrothed in a joint ceremony to the girls who have been chosen for them. Since the girls of their own age are already married, the ones who are brought to them are children, some little more than toddlers.

I saw tearful little girls, frightened by the solemn row of young men lying in all their ceremonial regalia in the darkened hut. They were half coaxed, half pulled into the hut and persuaded to lie down briefly next to their betrothed. Each young man turned his face away in shame at that moment, so the little girls found themselves facing the glistening and unresponsive backs of their future husbands. It was with understandable relief that they returned to their mothers. In fact, there was relief on both sides. I was of the sponsoring age-set in those days, so I got to know the initiates quite well. They were glad that their wives were not old enough for them yet for they wanted to savor a few years of freedom, now that they had attained the status of young men, before they moved into their wives' houses and had to deal with their in-laws.

The next day, the bachelors' hut was dismantled. People took away its thatch and used it to repair their own houses. The village felt quite naked without it, but not for long. A few days later the new bachelors were being gathered and directed to build their hut – which, according to the Xavante tradition of alternation in all things, had to be at the opposite end of the village from the old one. I was surprised to see Apewen, the elderly and esteemed chief of the village, helping the boys put up their hut. He was the only mature man doing so. Why? The explanation, as I learned, was simple. Apewen was in the same age-set as the new bachelors. The Xavante have eight age-sets. Each age-set moves through a progression, five years as bachelors, five years as warriors, then thirty years as mature men, moving up in seniority every five years as another group is initiated. Finally, if you live long enough, your age-set becomes the most senior one in the village. Then, after the next initiation, it goes back to the beginning of the cycle again. Apewen was the only man in the village left from the set of boys that had been initiated with him. It had felt pretty lonely, he told me, but now he had company. He was in a sense being reincarnated in the new group of bachelors who had joined his age-set.

I remembered Apewen when I returned to the Xavante as an elder myself last year. Another initiation was in progress and I discovered that my age-set was now the most senior in the village. At the close of the initiation, it would be reincarnated in the boys entering the bachelors' hut. But the running phase of the initiation had only just started and the ceremonies would not be completed for some weeks. I could not stay that long, and I suddenly regretted it bitterly. I badly wanted to be there, to see the children coming in to renew my age-set, to help them put up their hut, as I had seen Apewen doing before me. I felt then, but only briefly, something of the sense of connectedness in time and with people that provides Xavante with the framework of their lives; and I realized that perhaps we miss that in the hurly-burly of the modern scene.

The age-set system gives the Xavante the coordinates that orient individuals throughout their lives. It works that way for girls as well as for boys. Even though Xavante women do not have the intense social life with their age-mates that Xavante men do, they are nevertheless defined by their age-set, which helps to structure their identity. I have the feeling when I am with the Xavante that people have a strong sense of themselves. It comes from a set of defining institutions that I would find unbearably claustrophobic if I had to live my life within them, but it gives the Xavante a certain security that enables them to be as tough and outspoken as any rugged individualist from the American West.

These institutions give them security in death as well as life. Although the Xavante are not much given to metaphysical speculation about life and death, they seem to feel secure about where as individuals they fit in. People in other tribal societies derive a similar sense of confidence from their feeling that they are part of an unending flow that connects their ancestors with their descendants. Of course people are universally aware that they had forefathers and will have successors, but for many societies this is not an abstract piece of knowledge. On the contrary, they strive to keep in touch with the generations who are not physically present, especially the ancestors. They do not think of death as a great divide, but rather as another initiation.

It is this certainty about their position in this world and the next that probably, more than anything else, distinguishes the situation of the aged in tribal societies from that of the aged in our own. Modern society tends to be very much oriented toward this world and interested in who is producing what in it. It glories in change and admires the expertise of "movers and shakers." These are not comfortable emphases for the elderly, who find themselves once again caught up in the swirling ambivalence of their own civilization. They are urged to retire to "make way for the young," which makes them feel like obstacles rather than contributors. Yet when they do retire they are likely to hear that so many of them are living longer and longer that their retirement benefits are becoming an intolerable burden on society. With their productivity diminishing and their skills no longer in demand, they have to face the prospect of being considered superfluous. Modern societies do not, on the whole, value the wisdom of the old and do not need their knowledge. After all, the knowledge of even the most creative among us is quickly transferred to libraries and becomes common property. We do not need to seek out the old in order to acquire it. Deprived then of their usefulness and often reduced in their economic circumstances, the old fear "being a burden to their children." Where possible, they cultivate a fierce independence, determined at least to be cheerfully redundant to the end.

People in tribal societies are routinely shocked when they learn how the industrial world treats the aged. Probably the only other aspect of modern life that they find equally shocking is how we handle the relations between the sexes. Women in most tribal societies might seem to us to lead hard and subordinate lives, yet from their point of view modernization is a very mixed blessing. They are often deprived of their traditional rights in land as colonial and national governments, following legal codes that do not recognize tribal law, emphasize male ownership. Women also bear the brunt of labor migration. Left behind in the villages, they must now work even harder to provide their families with food, and often, as in New Guinea, the proceeds of cash-cropping belong to men. It is men, too, who have access to education and wage labor; women become dependent on men for goods and cash, while in many traditional economies they produced, managed, and inherited wealth independently from men. Modernization thus has the paradoxical effect of widening the gulf between men and women.

In modern industrial societies we are faced with a problem unfamiliar to traditional societies. Tribal societies, as we have seen, cast men and women in well-defined masculine and feminine identities, although their definitions of masculine and feminine may seem very strange to us. It is true that some groups allow women and men to reverse roles and dress up and behave like the other sex

THE BERDACHE

Among the North American Indians, androgynes (people or gods who combine male and female roles and attributes), mythical hermaphrodites (people or gods possessing both male and female sexual organs) as well as transvestites (cross-dressers) hold a recognized and in some cases respected position in native life and imagination. The "Trickster" figure so widespread in North American mythology not only disguises himself as a woman but also gives birth to children and keeps his detached phallus in a box. (To have intercourse, he simply sends it to the women he desires.) Wendy Doniger O'Flaherty calls him a "satire on human sexual integration." Among the Zuni, one of the most important creator figures is called "He-She" (Awonawilona). Awonawilona is unusual even in the Native American context in that her/his female attributes are as highly valued as her/his male characteristics. The portrait shown here is of Finds-Them-and-Kills-Them, the last Crow "Berdache" — a man who dresses as a woman and performs women's work. Among the Navajo these men are called *nadle*: they do not have children, and they mediate between women and men in cases of domestic conflict.

I remembered Apewen when I returned to the Xavante as an elder myself last year. Another initiation was in progress and I discovered that my age-set was now the most senior in the village. At the close of the initiation, it would be reincarnated in the boys entering the bachelors' hut. But the running phase of the initiation had only just started and the ceremonies would not be completed for some weeks. I could not stay that long, and I suddenly regretted it bitterly. I badly wanted to be there, to see the children coming in to renew my age-set, to help them put up their hut, as I had seen Apewen doing before me. I felt then, but only briefly, something of the sense of connectedness in time and with people that provides Xavante with the framework of their lives, and I realized that perhaps we miss that in the hurly-burly of the modern scene.

during festivals, and some have developed cross-sex or androgynous alternatives for individuals who find themselves at odds with their allocated roles. The majority of people are expected, nonetheless, to conform to a gender-divided universe. With us, things go in rather the opposite direction. In keeping with our desire to allow all people all roads to happiness, we increasingly reject the idea of separate socialization for girls and boys. While tremendous social and commercial pressures still push "boys to be boys" and "girls to be girls," we are becoming more and more perplexed by what this means and by what place sexual identity has or should have in our identity as individuals. So while we protest against the limitations of sexual stereotyping, we seek at the same time to find ourselves, often in "women's groups" and "men's groups" as women and men.

We have begun to discover that the facts of conception, birth, maturity, old age, and death do not by themselves produce human identity. Every society develops its own view of life and then attempts to create citizens in that image. However much we study male and female bodies, we will not find the essence of sexual difference in them, any more than we will find the Mona Lisa in a box of paints. Some people may be disappointed that the study of society cannot tell us what human beings "really" are, only that we exist in particular varieties. Others will see this as giving us the freedom to be what we have not yet been. Traditional societies offer us the insight that, if we are to find ourselves, most of us need more than a hint as to what we should be looking for.

THE ART OF LIVING

When at last we reached the Xavante, they took us into their village. We were lodged in a small hut in the village horseshoe, next door to the ceremonial end house occupied by chief Apewen and his family. It was late afternoon by the time we had moved ourselves and our meager stores into our new dwelling, slung our hammocks, and fed our baby son. Darkness fell like a curtain, as it does in the tropics, and we fell asleep exhausted. Hours (or was it minutes?) later we were awakened by what sounded like a platoon of men approaching our hut. We lay there with beating hearts, wondering what was happening. I rolled out of my hammock and searched desperately for a flashlight, then froze, for the Xavante were all about us now. We could hear them gathering right outside our hut. Then silence. We strained to hear what they were doing, but they made no sound. We heard a shuffling, then a rhythmic stamping, then singing. I crept outside and heard rather than saw the night shapes of a score of young men dancing and singing outside Apewen's hut.

After a few moments they stopped, formed up in single file, and walked along the village horseshoe before stopping outside another hut to repeat the dance. They sang and danced before various houses until they reached the far end of the village, from which the sounds of their gruff chorus came wafting faintly over to us.

When we visited the Xavante in later years, it was difficult to remember how startled and nervous we were the first time we heard the young men singing round the village, for this is a most reassuring sound to the Xavante and one we soon came to like, indeed to rely on. We would only half wake up as we heard the familiar songs, now coming closer, now fading away into the distance. Like watchmen calling the hours in a medieval city, Xavante age-sets sing and dance around their villages during the night, bringing a feeling of community and harmony to their drowsy fellow citizens. When Xavante want to praise a community (usually their own), they say, "There is a lot of singing." They mean by this that people get together, ceremonies are performed properly and frequently, and the young men are alert, wakeful, and in good voice during the night. It is a severe condemnation when they say of a community (invariably not their own) that it is "sleepy." That means that it is a community without much spirit and, of course, without much singing during the night.

The singing is important to the Xavante because it is tangible evidence of the harmony for which they strive. Xavante believe that the fundamental oppositions in human experience (such as life and death, day and night, male and female) are part of the whole tissue of oppositions that make up the cosmic scheme of things. Since the cosmos is made up of opposites, Xavante society must also be constructed that way. And so it is divided down the middle in complementary halves or moieties, as we saw in chapter 1. The Xavante are not content, however, with a single pair of moieties. After all, if each community were divided into two according to clans and political factions, then social life would be contentious and conflicts would escalate into local civil wars. They therefore assign people to different, overlapping pairs of moieties for different purposes. Two men who belong to the same political moiety are likely to find themselves opposing and complementing each other in the moieties that perform important ceremonies. They will find themselves lined up with yet another set of moiety mates for log races.

Log races! We had heard so much about them. I had read seventeenth-century accounts in Latin describing the tall savages of the interior of Brazil who apparently delighted in running through the wilds with tree trunks on their shoulders. Why would they do such a thing? No one could be sure. When twentieth-century observers witnessed log races in central Brazil, they were equally puzzled and concluded after the fashion of the time that the races must be trials of strength that young men had to undergo in order to show they were fit for marriage. If they saw women running with the logs (as we did), they forgot to mention it. At least one thing was clear to even the dimmest observer: all the Indians speaking languages of the Gê family in central Brazil just loved log-racing.

The Xavante were no exception. Whenever there was a ceremony of any importance, the climax had to include a log race. The mature men's council would decide to hold the race on the morrow and shout out the news to the community. Then the excitement was electric. Shouts of "Kai, kai, kai" from the meeting place of the young men. Laughter and yells of encouragement from the women gathered around the cooking fires before their huts.

The next day, men set out at dawn to cut down a palm tree and chop two logs from its trunk, each about four feet, one for each moiety that would run with it. Before noon the logs were ready and the runners began to arrive. They heaved the logs up on their shoulders and carried them from the marshy ground around the palm trees to the trail where the race would be run. More and more men (or women) arrived now, elaborately painted in scarlet and black and binding up their hair with long strips of grass as they walked. This was usually the time when I showed up with my tiny notebook, suitable for cramming into the pocket of my

A Xavante log race.

shorts. I asked which moieties were running with the logs that day and noted it
down. Then I lifted the end of each log off the ground (only an inch or two, since
they were pretty heavy) to see whether they were about the same weight. Then I
noted who was lining up with which log and how they were painted. The Xavante
noted my solemn absurdities with ribald amusement. "What for?" they asked,
laughing. I invariably answered with a joke, since I did not speak Xavante well
enough to give them a proper explanation of what I was trying to find out.

The time for note-taking was soon over. I took my place with my moiety and
then, at a given signal, three or four men heaved each log onto the shoulders of
the two lead runners. They set off along the trail at a shambling run. Their teammates trotted along behind them, except for those who went leaping like dervishes
through the bushes and around the trees by the side of the trail. As soon as the
runner began to tire (or sometimes beforehand, for his excited teammates could

SPORTS AND THE END OF PLAY

NOW, WITH THE INCREASING SYSTEMATIZATION AND REGIMENTATION OF SPORT, SOMETHING OF THE PURE PLAY-QUALITY IS INEVITABLY LOST. WE SEE THIS VERY CLEARLY IN THE OFFICIAL DISTINCTION BETWEEN AMATEURS AND PROFESSIONALS. ... THE SPIRIT OF THE PROFESSIONAL IS NO LONGER THE TRUE PLAY-SPIRIT; IT IS LACKING IN SPONTANEITY AND CARELESSNESS. THIS AFFECTS THE AMATEUR TOO, WHO BEGINS TO SUFFER FROM AN INFERIORITY COMPLEX. BETWEEN THEM THEY PUSH SPORT FURTHER AND FURTHER AWAY FROM THE PLAY-SPHERE PROPER UNTIL IT BECOMES A THING *SUI GENERIS*: NEITHER PLAY NOR EARNEST.

IN MODERN SOCIAL LIFE, SPORT OCCUPIES A PLACE ALONGSIDE AND APART FROM THE CULTURAL PROCESS. THE GREAT COMPETITIONS IN ARCHAIC CULTURES HAD ALWAYS FORMED PART OF THE SACRED FESTIVALS AND WERE INDISPENSABLE AS HEALTH AND HAPPINESS-BRINGING ACTIVITIES. THIS RITUAL TIE HAS NOW BEEN COMPLETELY SEVERED; SPORT HAS BECOME PROFANE, "UNHOLY" IN EVERY WAY AND HAS NO ORGANIC CONNECTION WHATEVER WITH THE STRUCTURE OF SOCIETY, LEAST OF ALL WHEN PRESCRIBED BY THE GOVERNMENT.

THE ABILITY OF MODERN SOCIAL TECHNIQUES TO STAGE MASS DEMONSTRATIONS WITH THE MAXIMUM OF OUTWARD SHOW IN THE FIELD OF ATHLETICS DOES NOT ALTER THE FACT THAT NEITHER THE OLYMPIADS NOR THE ORGANIZED SPORTS OF AMERICAN UNIVERSITIES NOR THE LOUDLY TRUMPETED INTERNATIONAL CONTESTS HAVE, IN THE SMALLEST DEGREE, RAISED SPORT TO THE LEVEL OF A CULTURE-CREATING ACTIVITY. HOWEVER IMPORTANT IT MAY BE FOR THE PLAYERS OR SPECTATORS, IT REMAINS STERILE. THE OLD PLAY-FACTOR HAS UNDERGONE ALMOST COMPLETE ATROPHY.

From Johan Huizenga, *Homo Ludens* (Boston: Beacon Press, 1955).

SQUAWS PLAYING
BALL ON THE
PRAIRIE.
SETH EASTMAN.
c. 1849.

not wait to carry the log) another man presented his shoulder. The log was rolled from runner to runner and the fresh log-bearer would dash into the next stage of the relay. The Xavante expected me to take my turn. They showed me how to carry the log, angled so it rested on the pad of flesh where the neck meets the back so it would not bounce up and down and chip the bones in my shoulder. They also showed me how to transfer it without dropping it and breaking somebody's leg. They were usually kind enough to relieve me pretty quickly so that I could join the others who were crashing through the undergrowth and urging on the log-bearers. The race went on for a few miles before the village came into view. Here the runners put on an extra spurt. Both teams streamed into the village with the élan of a cavalry charge. The logs were run to the mature men's meeting place and flung down with cataclysmic thuds.

Now the senior runners launched into speeches. Half a dozen of them orated at once, while other men stood around panting and children scampered about and danced with excitement on the fresh logs. I was fascinated by the postmortems. There were elaborate discussions of who had run well, though the people who came in for most praise were not those who had carried the log farthest or fastest. I was asked over and over again if I thought the race was beautiful. "It was beautiful," I answered, bewildered, puzzled by the ethos of it all.

I was even more puzzled by the fact that the Xavante did not seem to mind if one log was heavier than the other. At first I thought this was accidental. But one day I noticed at the beginning of the race that one log was obviously *much* heavier than the other. I pointed this out and asked if they wanted to trim it. Now it was the Xavantes' turn to be puzzled. "What for?" they asked. I tried to explain that the team with the lighter log was bound to win. The Xavante simply did not understand my concern. We raced off anyway with the mismatched logs and, sure enough, the team with the heavier log fell farther and farther behind. I was loping along happily with the lighter log when I noticed that men from my moiety were dropping back to help the team that was behind. Soon the others had so many people on their team that they were shifting the log to a new runner every thirty yards or so. They began to catch up and were right behind us as we burst through the ring of huts and made for the central plaza in a cloud of dust.

The village went wild. Dogs barked. Children ran beside us. Women raced up and offered their shoulders for our log. We let them have it and in that way held off the challengers. But only just. The two logs arrived in a virtual dead heat. Pandemonium. Everybody seemed to be speechifying or shouting or just yelling with glee. It was by common consent the most beautiful log race that had been celebrated for a long time. It was then that I understood. It was not a race at all, at least not in our sense. It was a ceremony, an aesthetic event. Xavante meant it when they asked if it was beautiful. They were as nonplussed by notions of winning and losing as we might be if a Xavante turned to us at the ballet, after watching the principal dancers leap athletically off the stage, and asked, "Who won?"

The logs are cut in the forest and run into the village, thus linking the realm of nature with the realm of human culture. They are carried by two teams, representing the oppositions that Xavante believe go to make up the universe. The running of the logs expresses the dynamic tension between opposing principles. The purpose of the ceremony is to stress that these antitheses need not tear the world apart. If one is careful, oppositions can be controlled, they can complement each other and create equilibrium and harmony. And what better symbol of equilibrium than two teams that exert themselves to the utmost and finish in a dead heat? At last I understood that this was the ideal, the most beautiful outcome of a log-running, for it established the perfect synthesis. I remembered the accounts I had read of communities of North American Indians playing lacrosse against each other for days at a time and ending the game only when they had achieved a tie.

At last I felt I was beginning to understand the Xavante view of life. It is expressed in their sweeping, curvilinear villages with the men's meeting places in the center and the women's houses at the edge – women's because a man goes to live in his wife's house after marriage. At the end of the line of houses there is a small gap and then the bachelors' hut, where teenagers go to live preceding initiation. (It is this set of boys, of course, that is called out at night by older men from a senior age-set to sing around the village.) When the hut is dismantled after their initiation, the new one for the next crop of teenagers is built at the opposite end of the village. Every activity of any importance is carried out by moieties, by opposites interacting with each other. Life is a constant series of oppositions that the Xavante reconcile through alternation, seeking harmony through complementarity. It is a cosmic and social design that Xavante learn as they grow up and into which each individual is woven. They do not lose their individuality in the process: Xavante tend to be assertive and outspoken. But anybody who has experienced the enveloping mesh of relationships in a Xavante village and the regular ebb and flow of Xavante life can understand why Xavante who go away to big cities often come back, longing to be woven back into the pattern of their people.

Xavante aesthetics are concerned with this whole pattern of living. The beautiful things they produce – the mats, the baskets, the songs and dances – are merely contributions to their major art form, which is life itself. Art is in fact embedded in life in most tribal societies, unlike modern societies, in which we tend to separate art from the worlds of work, business, or politics, contrasting the aesthetic side of our lives with the practical. In this view, art is seen as something more like play than work of any importance. Even when we accord art a lofty status, viewing it as the expression of the best that is in us, we still tend to see it as something set apart from our lives, a province of specialists, enshrined in (or perhaps relegated to) museums and concert halls.

It was not always so. Our word *art* derives from the Latin *artem*, meaning "skill."

The "seven arts" of the medieval university curriculum were grammar, logic, rhetoric, arithmetic, geometry, music, and astronomy. In the sixteenth century, the word *artist* was usually applied to astronomers, but it also covered practitioners of other skills, including those inspired by the "seven muses" of history, poetry, comedy, tragedy, music, dancing, and astronomy. Skills like painting, drawing, sculpture, and engraving only came later to be considered as *arts*, but eventually these monopolized our notion of what properly constitutes art. It was not until the nineteenth century that *art* came to refer to certain kinds of creative and imaginative activities associated with aesthetics and distinguished from *science*. Science and art had previously been thought of as closely related if not actually identical pursuits, but in the nineteenth century they were contrasted with each other. Art came to refer to the fine arts, which cultivated the aesthetic side of life in the quest for beauty. Science now denoted the useful or industrial arts, which concerned themselves with the utilitarian (and by implication unaesthetic) aspect of life.

Such distinctions would have been meaningless to the hundreds of people who worked to build each of the great medieval cathedrals. We now consider them works of art par excellence, perhaps the most beautiful achievements of the Middle Ages, yet they were also remarkable feats of design, mathematics, and engineering. At the time, people did not attach much importance to distinctions between artists and artisans, between aesthetics and engineering. They worked, sometimes for an entire lifetime, on constructions they would never see completed, confident that their enterprise represented the best of what human beings could do for the greater glory of God. They were confident, too, that those who were not involved in the task would nevertheless understand it: whether they came from hovels or from baronial castles, they would look on the cathedral and recognize its meaning and its beauty. Michelangelo shared this assurance. He lived amid the political and social upheavals of what we now refer to (thanks to him and to others like him) as the early Renaissance. He felt, indeed he *knew*, that his art was revolutionary, that it was transforming the entire way in which people would look at and think about things in the future. He took to signing his works, in irritated response to his patron, Pope Julius II, who believed that some of them had not in fact been done by Michelangelo of Florence but by Roman artists. Michelangelo's signature became the stamp of an art that was personal, individual in a way that would have surprised the cathedral builders. Yet even in the depths of the melancholy that afflicted him for most of his life, he expected people to understand and to respond intuitively to his paintings and sculptures.

I had a dream about Michelangelo after my last visit to the Vatican. I looked up and saw him painting the ceiling of the Sistine Chapel. He was lying there, high up in the air on a little platform that looked for all the world like one of those we use to crank workmen up and down the outsides of tall buildings. Naturally I

An allegorical representation of the seven medieval arts: grammar, logic, rhetoric, arithmetic, geometry, music, and astronomy.

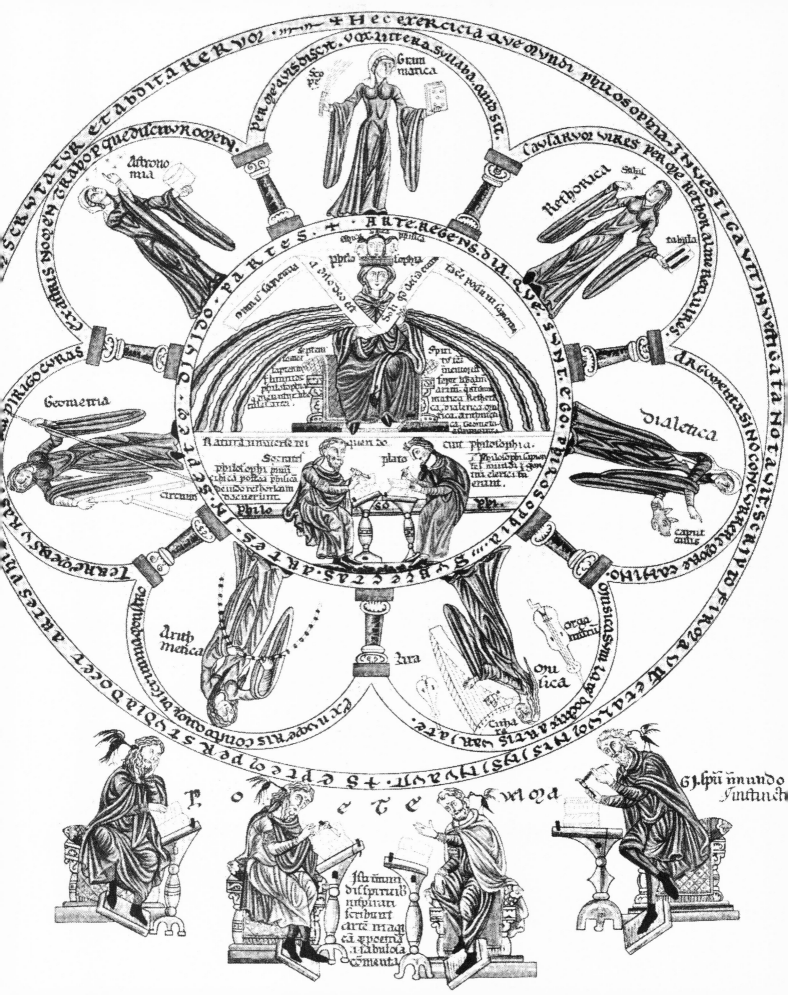

INTRINSIC VALUE OF ITEMS IN TRADITIONAL SOCIETIES

Native American writer Jamake Highwater explains, "The objects of Indians are expressive and not decorative because they are alive, living in our experience of them. When the Indian potter collects clay, she asks the consent of the river-bed and sings its praises for having made something as beautiful as clay. When she fires her pottery, to this day, she still offers songs to the fire so it will not discolour or burst her wares. And, finally, when she paints her pottery, she imprints it with the images that give it life and power — because for an Indian, pottery is something significant, not just a utility but a 'being' for which there is as much of a natural order as there is for persons or foxes or trees. So reverent is the Indian conception of the 'power' within things, especially the objects created by traditional craftspeople, that among many Indians, the pottery interred with the dead has a small perforation, a 'kill-hole,' made in the center in order to release the orenda — 'the spiritual power' — before it is buried."

From Jamake Highwater, *The Primal Mind: Vision and Reality in Indian America* (New York: Meridian, 1981), pp. 77-78.

thought he *was* a workman, engaged on the much discussed renovation of the famous ceiling. But then I noticed that the ceiling was unfinished. He was actually painting it. The authority of his brush strokes and the brilliance of his colors left me in no doubt that it was Michelangelo himself I was observing. Then, to my horror, he started to rub out his own creation. The powerful, tormented frescoes vanished before my eyes. I was horrified. I tried to call out to him, to beg him to stop. But he could not hear me. At last I shouted so loudly that I surprised myself. Michelangelo stopped and turned to me. In the voice one uses to reassure a small child, he said: "But they are not meant to last forever."

I woke from my nightmare with Michelangelo's words still weighing on my heart. He had spoken them as if stating the obvious. If they were true, however, then it was a truth that I wanted passionately to deny. Of course his frescoes were going to last, if not forever, at least as long as human ingenuity could preserve them. Was that not the point of them? They were now more than the work of his brooding genius: they were Great Art, Masterpieces of Western Civilization, and, therefore, timeless.

I was uneasily aware that not everyone shared my feelings. My bad dream had been inspired by looking at Michelangelo's ceiling and thinking about the furious controversy that was raging about whether or not it should have been restored, about whether its postrestoration colors were garish and untrue to the artist's original intention or whether they were brilliant and close to what he had composed. What if we just allowed the frescoes to fade away? The thought was too painful to take seriously as I looked up at that spectacular ceiling and imagined the years of torment that Michelangelo had endured in order to paint it. Still, I knew that in many parts of the world artists erase their works on completion.

Navajo artists, for example, create exquisitely beautiful sand paintings that they rub out as soon as they finish them. A cynic might say that few Navajo artists have the genius of Michelangelo, but that misses the point. Few artists anywhere rival Michelangelo, yet we feel that works of art should last, while in many other cultures people feel that works of art should be constantly created. Art for such people is not so much the finished product as the act of creation. And, among the Navajo at least, many more people take part in these acts of creation than in the industrial civilization that applies itself to restoring Michelangelo. The Navajo sand painters are not specialists marginalized from everyday life by their extraordinary talents. On the contrary, most Navajo men have participated in the creation of sand paintings, though some are much better at it than others. More important than the paintings themselves, however, is the context in which they are created. They are contributions to the harmony that is the Navajo idea of beauty.

Gary Witherspoon, an anthropologist who has devoted his life to the study of the Navajo, points out that the Navajo word *hozho*, usually translated as "beauty," actually means more than that. It refers to a total environment (*ho*) that includes

B E A U T Y W A Y

Beauty will come in the dawn

And beauty will come with the sunlight.

Beauty will come to us from everywhere,

Where the heaven ends, where the sky ends.

Beauty will surround us. We walk in beauty.

Billy Yellow

Navajo Medicine Man

Monument Valley, Utah

beauty, harmony, happiness, and everything that is positive. Life for the Navajo therefore consists of constantly taking steps to enhance hozho, to live in hozho, and to die in due course of old age and be incorporated into the hozho that permeates the universe. Navajo culture is a way of life that requires the individual not merely to create beauty sporadically but to think it, act it, and live in it constantly. This is clear in the prayer that Navajos recite daily:

> With beauty before me, I walk
> With beauty behind me, I walk
> With beauty above me, I walk
> With beauty below me, I walk
> From the East beauty has been restored
> From the South beauty has been restored
> From the West beauty has been restored
> From the North beauty has been restored
> From the zenith in the sky beauty has been restored
> From the nadir of the earth beauty has been restored
> From all around me beauty has been restored.

Creating sand paintings, then, is part of life, part of the constant striving for hozho. Obliterating them makes sense because the Navajo value the dynamics of their creation and recreation more than the contemplation of the finished products.

Jackson Pollock, the American painter who is probably second only to Picasso in his influence on modern art, took much of his inspiration from the Navajo. He was particularly impressed by the dynamism and the sense of motion expressed in Navajo weavings and sand paintings, all contained within an overall scheme of balance and harmony. Pollock explained that he wanted to be "in" his paintings like the Indian sand painters. That is why he spread his unstretched canvases on the floor, walked around them, tackled them from all sides. He wanted his paintings to convey a feeling of continuity with the general order of the universe. The difference between Pollock and the Navajo artists he admired is that the Navajo worked within their own tradition, whereas Pollock rejected the artistic conventions of his society, indeed rejected the society itself. He felt that modern industrial society diminished human beings, reducing them to mere producers and consumers. He sought another way of thinking about the world and living in it, a way that would enable him to see it whole and participate in it more fully, a worldview in fact closer to that of the Navajo than to that of Modern Man or Woman.

It is not only the Navajo who try to perceive the world as a whole and whose idea of the good life is to be in harmony with the scheme of things. Such thinking is characteristic of many tribal societies. The Wodaabe, for example, whom we met in chapter 4, are as preoccupied with the idea of beauty as the Navajo are. Here is

American painter Jackson Pollock. Impressed by the way Navajo sand painters integrate art and life, Pollock tried to include himself in his work. He strapped his canvases to the floor and walked around and on top of them as he painted. He sought an artful worldview that resembled the all-embracing Navajo concept of *hozho*.

Navajo healer and sand painter Billy Yellow. Yellow prepares the *Red Antway* sand painting in an effort to cure his sick grandson. By creating the sand painting and healing his grandson Billy is contributing to the harmony that every Navajo strives toward.

a people who could be forgiven if they had a dour and dogged view of life. After all, they wander across the parched grasslands just south of the Sahara Desert, husbanding their camels and their cattle through the endless dry seasons when their world turns yellow in the torrid haze. Each year they are rescued from the burning heat by storms and violent rains that briefly revive the grasses and the leaves before the drought sets in again. Life for the Wodaabe is hard and, for the most part, short, but they do not live like people who are struggling to survive. Instead they cultivate an aesthetic sensibility that brings great beauty to their lives.

Wodaabe strive consciously and without embarrassment to be beautiful and to create beauty around them. They are proud of their world, which they consider superior to that of other peoples, and they defend it fiercely against outsiders who are forever trying to get them to stop roaming and to settle down into the dreary routines of the agriculturalists whom the Wodaabe despise.

Creature comforts are in short supply in the Wodaabe world. Nevertheless, it is a world of bright colors and lovely things. Men treasure their finely worked saddlebags and handsome saddles bought from the neighboring Tuaregs, their brilliant blankets, the decorated leather pouches that hold their charms. Women glory in the shiny wraps, shot through with gold and silver thread, that they wear around their heads, and the lovely saronglike garments that set off their lissome figures. Most of all, a woman treasures her collection of exquisitely carved and painted calabashes, which are at once her most prized possessions and the expression of her individuality.

The Wodaabe surround themselves with beautiful things, but most of all they strive to be beautiful people. The phrase has acquired a vacuous connotation in modern society because of its association with plastic surgery and celebrities and the pursuit of an image of glamour that trivializes, rather than deepens, the rest of life. The Wodaabe preoccupation with beauty is, by contrast, part of an aesthetic approach to life that enhances the relations between people, in everyday circumstances as well as on ceremonial occasions. Wodaabe decorate themselves like artists. They massage the heads of babies to give them the most pleasing shape. Their faces are tattooed in symmetrical but individual patterns, and both sexes apply elaborate makeup on the occasion of important dances. Men are fastidious about their finery – their swords and spears, their beadwork, and the conical hats they wear at the climactic dances. Women commission metalworkers of the Hausa tribe to make them brass leggings to order, and they dress up on important occasions in dramatic outfits, their bright, flowing robes set off by cascades of jewelry and accentuated by the dozen or so earrings that a mature woman will wear in each ear.

Beauty for the Wodaabe is more than physical, more even than the combination of good looks and beautiful clothes. These are called *bodem* and are mere adjuncts to the most important quality of all, *togu*, which can be translated as "charm."

Togu is a social virtue, indicating the ability to captivate and interact with other people. Togu is the spice of life, but in the Wodaabe view of the world it should go hand in hand with *munyal*, with its connotations of patience and loyalty, and *sentende*, meaning "reserve," especially toward those one loves and therefore respects the most.

When the Wodaabe come together in the rainy season for the festivals that highlight their year, flocks of women stroll around the encampment, wearing all their finery. They admire the displays of one another's possessions and break into song and dance to honor displays they find peculiarly artistic. It is of course at the annual Geerewol celebration that Wodaabe thoughts are especially and collectively focused on beauty. This is the time, as we saw in chapter 4, when hundreds of young men dance for a full week, vying with one another in charm and beauty, and being admired by all the women who can possibly get there. The Wodaabe consider the festival to be the focus of their aesthetic expression, part of the legacy of beauty that has come down to them from their ancestors Adam and Adama.

Wodaabe have no "artists" in our specialized sense of the word because Wodaabe aesthetic activities are also social activities, in which everyone is expected to take part. Their aesthetic, like that of the Navajo or the Xavante, is an aesthetic of involvement, whereas the aesthetic in modern societies seems to be one of detachment. In fact the whole process of industrialization and modernization can be seen as one that detached the individual from the world around him and encouraged him to view that world as an object. Furthermore, as that world became more varied and complex, it became increasingly difficult for anyone, even the most gifted artist, to "see it clearly and see it whole." Our artists, therefore, face the challenge of interpreting a fractured world to a fragmented society.

By contrast, the way in which tribal art, in its passionate spontaneity, is woven into the fabric of society is rooted in something that the modern world has lost, a cosmic confidence in ourselves and in the whole scheme of things. It is this confidence that enables tribal societies to resolve the conflicts and contradictions that are an inevitable part of life itself, to play with oppositions that would otherwise tear their worlds apart. Tribal art thus becomes a means of reconciling what is otherwise irreconcilable, of making the painful crises of life manageable – even of overcoming the ultimate disjunction, between life and death.

This reconciliation is one that we in the modern world contrive to avoid. We have made it possible for most people to avoid the sight of the dying and to avoid coming to terms with death. In our fragmented and specialized world, death, like art, has become a matter for specialists. By contrast, traditional societies tend to make the relationship between life and death accessible and familiar through song, story, and dance – the arts of myth and ritual.

The Dogon of West Africa are such a society. They are a people who live in the

NOMADIC ART

THE WODAABE ARE THE AESTHETES OF THE DESERT. DURING THE ANNUAL
GEEREWOL CELEBRATIONS OF THE WODAABE THERE IS A PERIOD OF THREE DAYS,
CALLED THE *WORSO*, WHEN WOMEN DISPLAY THEIR PRIZED CALABASHES. THE
DISPLAYS ARE ELABORATELY DECORATED CALABASHES MIXED IN WITH "OBJETS
TROUVÉS." THERE IS A GREAT SENSE OF ARTISTIC CREATION IN THE INSTALLATIONS –
ALMOST LIKE SCULPTURES, REALLY – AS WELL AS A STRONG SENSE OF FEMALE
PRIDE. THE CALABASH IS THE WOMAN'S MAIN WORK TOOL IN THAT SHE USES IT TO
COLLECT MILK FROM HER COWS AND TO MIX MILLET FOR THE DAILY MEALS.
BUT THESE SPECIAL CALABASHES ARE NEVER USED IN DAILY LIFE. THEY HAVE NO
UTILITARIAN FUNCTION. AFTER THE THREE-DAY DISPLAY THEY ARE
PACKED UP FOR THE REST OF A LONG NOMADIC YEAR.

JARO, A YOUNG WODAABE WOMAN OF FIFTEEN, EXPRESSES HER OWN AESTHETIC
SENSIBILITY: "EVERYONE MUST HAVE CHARM AND BEAUTY. MEN SHOW THEIR BEAUTY
IN THE DANCES. WOMEN SHOW THEIR BEAUTY BY THEIR DISPLAYS OF CALABASHES
AND THE MANY BEAUTIFUL THINGS THEY PUT ON THEM. WE SEEK BEAUTY
EVERYWHERE. IT IS THE WODAABE WAY – GRACE AND ELEGANCE IN ALL THINGS."

spectacular cliffs of the narrow central neck of the Republic of Mali, about a thousand miles west of the Wodaabe. They retreated into this rocky terrain in the fifteenth century, constructing their villages on high ground to provide a defense against the slave raiders that were the scourge of western Africa. When the French took control of this part of Africa in the late nineteenth century and abolished slave trading, the Dogon were free to venture out from their cliffs and begin building villages on the plains. However, the majority of the three hundred thousand Dogon still live in a scattering of tight little villages in the escarpment of the Dogon heartland.

The Dogon are skilled artists and craftsmen, world renowned for their intricately carved masks and the dramatic ceremonies in which their masked dancers perform. These masks are worn by men during all dances, but especially those held to mark funerals. Curiously enough, the actual disposal of the dead is not a central feature of Dogon funerals. That is done soon after death, when the body is taken up and placed in caves in the cliffside reserved for the purpose. The masked funeral dances are great communal rituals that are as much about life as they are about death. If an old man dies during the dry season, there may be a personal dance held in his honor soon afterward. Normally, though, annual funerals are held in January for all those who died during the year. Every twelve years or so the *dama* dance is held to induce the souls of the recently dead to leave the village and go to join the ancestors. Finally, about every sixty years the Dogon celebrate the most important funeral rite of all, the *Sigi*. This ritual involves all Dogon villages and takes about six years to perform in its entirety. It commemorates the death of the first human and initiates a new generation of men into the secrets of Dogon culture.

Dogon dancers are men. It is a solemn moment when they come into the village, masked bearers of the mysterious power that vitalizes Dogon society. They come from the bush, from the wild place that contrasts with the civility of their communities. The bush is the source of power and wisdom, the place from which Dogon acquired the special language that they use on ritual occasions. It is from the bush that shamans and blacksmiths, the official loners of Dogon society, derive their special powers. It is from the bush that Dogon get their masks. Like Xavante logs, the masks serve to link the untamed power of the wilds with the civilized order of Dogon communities. The masks arrive in complete silence. Then the village explodes into a dazzling feast of noise and dancing and theatrical display. The celebrations, although they commemorate funerals, are anything but somber. They are a form of theater, in which the masks represent all aspects of Dogon life and the dancers mime their often satirical commentaries on that life. The masks can represent anything and everything. Animals, trees, and spirits are all impersonated, and so are characters from the social world of the Dogon. The neighboring Fulani and Mossi peoples are often satirized, as are various categories of white man, who tend to be represented by brick red masks each with a hooked nose, fluffy beard, and lank hair. These white men do not dance. Instead they walk stiffly about. Sometimes the mask represents a colonial administrator, who carries a paper and pencil. He writes on the paper, hands it to an onlooker, and demands money (taxes). When he gets his coin, he salutes and then lumbers away. Then there is the "anthropologist" mask favored by the Dogon who live near Sanga, which used to be the headquarters of Marcel Griaule, the first anthropologist seriously to "study" Dogon society. The wearer of this mask seats himself imperiously on a chair, waves his notebook to attract attention and then asks incredibly silly questions. Or the white-man mask may represent a tourist, identifiable by the contraption he holds in his hands. This is the "camera" that the tourist uses to photograph the most ridiculous things, pushing and shoving people out of the way to get a clear view. The Dogon are particularly scornful of the "tourist," for he understands nothing yet fights to record everything. "What is the point?" the Dogon ask. "Do they not have any stories of their own?" It is a good question.

These masked "funeral dances," as we call them, give the participants the chance to assert their vitality in the face of death. They are Dogon epics, dealing with the human comedy and, like the human comedy itself, intended to be lived rather than simply observed. These rituals are performed ostensibly to please the dead and speed them on their way, but they also serve to instruct the living and to incorporate them into the cosmic flow of Dogon being. So, when the Dogon see the tourists photographing so busily and so ignorantly, they wonder about us. Do we not have our own epics to make sense of the world for us?

In fact, the Dogon fascinate us because we lack a strongly integrated cosmology ourselves. The Dogon were made internationally famous by the work of Griaule, a Frenchman who published a series of books about them in the 1930s and 1940s. In the course of his work Griaule came to the conclusion that the Dogon were skilled and systematic cosmologists whose philosophical acumen was equal to anything the West had to offer. As the years went by, his work on Dogon cosmology centered more and more on his discussions with a learned Dogon by the name of Ogotommeli. In fact, the book that made Griaule and the Dogon internationally famous was entitled *Dieu d'Eau: Entretiens avec Ogotommeli* (Water God: Conversations with Ogotommeli). The book describes how Ogotommeli initiated Griaule into the Dogon world, where an all-encompassing creation myth permeates every aspect of life, giving both structure and meaning to activities as disparate as cultivating the fields, building granaries, carving masks, and celebrating the dead. There is a large problem with this account, however. Subsequent research, carried out largely by Dutch scholars, indicates that the coherent and all-encompassing system described by Griaule and Ogotommeli is not recognized by other Dogon people.

THE DAMA DANCE

The Dogon response to the pain and disruption of death is to hold elaborate funerals that give the living an opportunity to grieve yet also to assert their own vitality in the face of death. Dougalou had lost his uncle Abo, the last of his dead father's brothers. His death coincided with the end of several years' preparation for a dama dance which honors the spirits of all those who died during the past twelve years. The dama dance gives the dead one last glimpse of the pageant of Dogon life and invites the living to celebrate their own lives.

What happened? Is this just a case (one more case, the skeptics will say) of an anthropologist getting it all wrong? If so, how can we trust what we are told by anthropologists, those exotic investigators who come back from the remoter areas of our planet with their complex and often startling accounts of how other peoples live and think? These, I suggest, are the wrong questions. The moral of the story of Marcel Griaule and Ogotommeli is rather different. As Walter van Beek, a Dutch anthropologist who is a contemporary authority on the Dogon, describes it, this is a tale of two philosophies.

Marcel Griaule was fascinated by the sophistication of Dogon art and Dogon thought. After his research teams had documented the art and the everyday life of the Dogon, Griaule took it as his mission to acquaint the outside world with the richness of their ideas. With this end in mind, he apprenticed himself to Ogotommeli, but it was a curious apprenticeship. Because the disciple was a strong-minded man with close ties to the colonial authorities, he was in a position of power over his mentor. The Dogon remember Griaule as being impatient, always in a hurry. This forceful man felt that fieldwork was a matter of cracking the code of another culture and discovering the coherence in it that might have eluded even the natives themselves. He therefore pressed his teacher hard, or rather his teachers, for there was soon a cadre of Dogon whom he consulted who were, as far as he was concerned, the recognized experts on Dogon culture.

Griaule would refer to his copious notes and point out contradictions to his teachers. To explain the Dogon response, it is necessary to point out that they come from a culture that loves debate but detests confrontation. Harmony to them is all-important, and people are expected to reach agreement before they part company. At the same time, they are very respectful of authority. Older and more senior men are not contradicted. Van Beek describes this as a "courtesy bias" toward high-ranking people, which results in a tendency to tell them what they want to hear. In short, Griaule was convinced there must be a coherent philosophical system underlying Dogon culture. The more he pressed his informants on the topic, the more they gave him answers that confirmed his presupposition. Eventually, they ended up creating such a system for him out of bits and pieces of Dogon lore.

Griaule bullied his Dogon teachers only because he respected their sophistication and wanted to understand the complexities of their philosophy. He may have got the philosophy wrong, but, ironically, he got the Dogon right. They proved themselves to be every bit as sophisticated as he believed. Ogotommeli and the other informants came through years of cross-examination and, without benefit of notes or other memory aids, created an elaborate philosophical system that had a beauty and a coherence that fascinated scholars all over the world. It just did not happen to be the system the Dogon lived by.

Griaule's error does not call anthropology generally into question. He and his

Perhaps America's most eloquent advocate of the art of living was the nineteenth-century poet Walt Whitman. Whitman's poems celebrate a life lived with the senses wide open, keenly seeking out every possible experience, both joyous and painful.

WALT WHITMAN

Give me the pay I have served for,
Give me to sing the songs of the great Idea, take all the rest,
I have loved the earth, sun, animals, I have despised riches,
I have given alms to every one that ask'd, stood up for the
stupid and crazy, devoted my income and labour to others,
Hated tyrants, argued not concerning God, had patience and
indulgence toward the people, taken off my hat to nothing
known or unknown,
Gone freely with powerful uneducated persons and with the
young, and with the mothers of families,
Read these leaves to myself in the open air, tried them by
trees, stars, rivers,
Dismiss'd whatever insulted my own soul or defiled my
body,
Claim'd nothing to myself which I have not carefully
claim'd for others on the same terms,
Sped to the camps, and comrades found and accepted from
every State,
(Upon this breast has many a dying soldier lean'd to breathe
his last,
This arm, this hand, this voice, have nourish'd, rais'd,
restored,
To life recalling many a prostrate form;)
I am willing to wait to be understood by the growth of the
taste of myself
Rejecting none, permitting all.

From "By Blue Ontario's Shore," in *Walt Whitman: The Complete Poems* (London: Penguin, 1986).

colleagues did much work among the Dogon that has been confirmed by subsequent research, and his misconception is likewise being corrected and the reasons for it understood by anthropologists who tried to corroborate his findings. The story of Griaule and the Dogon is really about two styles of philosophy. Griaule thought he had to present the Dogon as systematic philosophers if they (and by extension other African peoples) were to gain the respect of the West. The Dogon, for their part, showed themselves quite capable of system-building, but they did it as a kind of academic exercise, elaborating a hypothetical cosmology much as a professor might do in a seminar, but in much more circumstantial detail.

Griaule was trying to pin down the Dogon system, to present it like a specimen to his Western audience. The Dogon, however, have an oral culture. Without writing, they have developed a different kind of system, one that is far more flexible than the literate systems we are accustomed to. Knowledge that is orally transmitted and employed is far more subject to individual inflexion and invention, far less confined by orthodoxy than is "literate" knowledge. Such a system relies on the tremendous memories of its specialists. Since there are no texts to compare, there is less concern with minor inconsistency and perhaps a richer sense of tradition. Jack Goody, an English anthropologist who has written about oral cultures in Africa and elsewhere in the world, goes so far as to suggest that many of the peculiarities of Western civilization come from our preoccupation with grids and lists, derived from the way we keep our records. After all, the earliest written documents we have uncovered were shopping lists!

There is more to modern civilization than literate gridlock, however. Modern societies are highly diversified and typically proud of allowing as much freedom as possible to individuals and subcultures within them. This means that artists in these societies are released from the constraints of tradition, but they may also be cut adrift from their audience. Alternatively, they may find a mass audience brought together largely by the feelings of isolation they all experience. Yet there have been times, and recent times at that, when artists have succeeded in expressing the yearnings of even modern and variegated societies, at odds with themselves. Many Russians feel it was their writers and poets who sustained them through the darkest days of their dictatorship. Czechs, thinking of their imprisoned playwright-turned-president, Vaclav Havel, may feel something similar. Mexicans may remind us of the magnificent murals of José Orozco and Diego Rivera that so movingly express the spirit of their revolution. These are (or were) societies under enormous stress, however. Does the modern world, then, only need its artists in times of crisis? Artists are meant to express our innermost concerns, to remind us of the values that lie beneath, or perhaps beyond, our everyday activities. Yet in ordinary times their work may seem remote from the everyday lives of the general public.

But there is at least one art form in modern society that is anything but remote, namely popular music. To the contrary, it sweeps the world, eliciting passionate engagement from players and listeners alike. It speaks to the heart of the young, offering them a spontaneity and sensuality to which millions enthusiastically respond. Yet there is ambivalence here too. While many seek a kind of community through the music or at the concerts given by its most famous players and singers, the music itself often voices the alienation that so many of its listeners feel. The rage and violence and nihilism of some popular music is notorious, but they are uncharacteristic, fringe phenomena. The dominant mood is sensual, seeking to express the deepest yearnings of the individual, and to assuage loneliness through ecstasy.

Loneliness and the struggle to overcome it are elements of the human condition, but they seem to be particularly powerful in modern societies. The art of

AZTEC SONG

Here through art I shall live for ever.
Who will take me, who will go with me?
Here I stand, my friends.
A singer, from my heart I strew my songs,
my fragrant songs before the face of others.
I carve a great stone, I paint thick wood
my song is in them.
It will be spoken of when I have gone.
I shall leave my song-image on earth.
My heart shall live, it will come back,
my memory will live and my fame.
I cry as I speak and discourse with my heart.
Let me see the root of song,
let me implant it here on earth so it may be realized.
My heart shall live, it will come back,
my memory will live and my fame.
The Prince Flower gently breathes his aroma,
our flowers are uniting.
My song is heard and it flourishes.
My implanted word is sprouting,
our flowers stand up in the rain.
The Cocoa flower gently opens his aroma,
the gentle Peyote falls like rain.
My song is heard and flourishes.
My implanted word is sprouting,
our flowers stand up in the rain.

From Gordon Brotherston, *Image of the New World: The American Continent Portrayed in Native Texts* (London: Thames and Hudson, 1979).

living in these societies is a difficult one to cultivate, for we cannot rely on shared assumptions either in art or in any other sphere of life. If, as Shakespeare said, "All the world's a stage, and all the men and women merely players," then it helps if the players know the play. Individuals in the modern world are all too likely to resemble the title characters in Tom Stoppard's reflection on *Hamlet*, entitled *Rosencrantz and Guildenstern Are Dead*, where two minor figures from the original play wander through each act, without ever discovering what the play is about.

The separation of art from life in modern societies is not a trivial matter, for how can we define the good life and live it with grace if we leave aesthetics to specialists? We can neither abolish nor ignore the confusion, anxiety, and loneliness of our times – and we cannot recapture the unitary vision of tribal societies. We simply do not live like that anymore. Living gracefully does not require that we attempt the impossible, however. What it does require is a determination that the aesthetic not be reduced to a commodity and ourselves to passive consumers of it, as well as a conviction that creativity and imagination are essential to our lives. It requires us to break the vicious cycle of compartmentalization that obliges us to live and work in a functional world that leaves little room for an aesthetic response. It requires us above all to understand that modern society separates: not only art from life, but life from death and all three from meaning. It is up to us to connect.

7

INVENTING REALITY

The Andes are dark mountains, jutting into the sky in a fierce tableau of sheer slopes and barren peaks. They make the majestic Himalayas seem lush, almost gentle, by comparison. Peruvian Indians have tattooed their fields onto these Andean inclines, creating a skyscape that bears witness to centuries of backbreaking toil. Just moving about in these mountains takes unusual effort. The Indians must come down from the high, treeless *puna*, through the endless terraces of potato fields and into the shadowed valleys, then climb all the way back up into high country again in order to go anywhere at all. Small wonder that, where possible, they used to string bridges over the narrower gorges. These catwalks were woven of reeds and oziers, fitted with slats to walk on and handrails of jungle vines. Even the slimmest and most circumspect of travelers would bounce with the give of the bridge, and many, I suspect, even among the Indians, did not like to look down into the void beneath them as they crossed. Still, it was better than slithering all the way down the mountain, perhaps crossing a torrent in the valley, and then climbing laboriously up the other side again. Better, that is, if the bridge was well constructed and not too worn.

In 1714 the finest rope bridge in all Peru snapped and the five people who were crossing it at the time hurtled to their deaths below. The tragedy inspired Thornton Wilder to write his moving novel *The Bridge of San Luis Rey* in which he describes how a gentle Franciscan friar, Brother Juniper, feels that the accident will provide him with experimental proof of divine providence. If Brother Juniper can only find out why the Lord chose to cut short the lives of those particular people (out of the hundreds who crossed the bridge every day, for it was on the main route from Lima to Cuzco) at that particular time, then he will understand the workings of the divine providence in which he so firmly believes.

In Wilder's novel, Brother Juniper's demonstration is unsuccessful. But the question is one most people would like to have answered. "Why me?" they ask. "Why could this misfortune not have fallen on someone else?" Science does not help us here. The most thorough understanding of the tensile strength of rope bridges, the stresses they can bear, and the point at which they will snap cannot tell us why it was those particular five people who plunged to their deaths outside Lima on that hot June day in 1714.

Edward Evans-Pritchard, a well-known British anthropologist, used a similar example to help us understand African ideas about witchcraft. He was writing about the Azande in central Africa. They, like many African peoples, build granaries on stilts to protect their grain from animals and insects. These granaries provide welcome shade from the fierce, equatorial sun so the Azande like to take their ease underneath them. They are careful, of course, to see that the stilts are kept in good repair. Occasionally, however, an accident happens. Termites gnaw unperceived through the supports, and a granary comes crashing down. If anybody is sitting underneath it, he is likely to be killed. Now, Azande know all about termites and they understand the physical reasons for the collapse of a granary, but these reasons do not interest them. If a man is killed under a granary, the Azande want to know why it collapsed then and why it fell on that particular person. They normally attribute it to witchcraft for they believe that people can project spite and envy in unseen ways to cause misfortune to others, so they set in motion their usual procedures for discovering who bewitched the victim of the "accident" and seeing that he is punished.

There is no room in scientific thinking for witchcraft, nor for divine providence, at least not of the demonstrable kind that Brother Juniper sought. So science cannot tell us why the granary fell when someone was underneath it, and not earlier when he was out in his fields. The scientific answer to that question is "coincidence," which is another way of saying "We don't know." If we have a properly scientific attitude, we will not waste time trying to find out either. Most people want to know the answer to such questions, however, and tribal societies have devoted much energy and imagination to answering them.

As a result, it became fashionable in the nineteenth century for people in modern societies not only to disparage the unscientific worldview of tribal peoples, but also to question their very capacity for rational thought. James Frazer, whose mammoth book *The Golden Bough* was obligatory reading for educated people in the early years of this century, argued that human societies passed through stages in which their thinking progressed from magical to religious to scientific. He soft-pedaled the final phase, for he was a Fellow of Trinity College, Cambridge – Isaac Newton's old college – and Fellows in his day were expected to be practicing members of the Anglican Church. For this reason, most readers of *The Golden Bough* come away with a stronger impression of the savagery of magic than they do of the final defeat of religion by science.

Evans-Pritchard, writing from Oxford half a century later, was much more open-minded. He pointed out that it was not *irrational* to believe in magic or witchcraft, it was simply *unscientific*. When he lived among the Azande and studied their way of thinking, he decided to test whether it "worked" in the pragmatic sense we favor in the West. So, he consulted Azande oracles and diviners and arranged his comings and goings and the activities of his household according to their advice. He discovered (and this should not surprise us) that he could get on with his life just as well when he planned it according to the oracles as when he arranged it according to his own rational and presumably scientific lights. Of course, skeptics will immediately object that it is not clear what an anthropologist in the field does anyway, and that it surely makes little difference whether he does it this way or that way, today or tomorrow, or perhaps even whether he does it at all. Still, millions of pragmatists in the busy, workaday world of our modern societies allow their actions to be guided by horoscopes and fortune-tellers. Ronald Reagan, when he was president of the United States, even allowed the White House schedule to be organized in conformity with suggestions made by an astrologer, and nobody seemed to be able to tell the difference.

Science cannot and does not try to tell you whether this will be your lucky day, whether you are going to meet a handsome stranger, or whether a granary is going to fall on your head, but when people do try to find out about these things, their reasoning may be (for the most part) eminently scientific. Evans-Pritchard pointed the way to this conclusion. He showed that the Azande, for example, thought in an exceedingly logical way about the projection of hostility through witchcraft. They would have been quite at home swapping stories with our best homicide detectives. The only difference between their thought and Evans-Pritchard's – and it is a big one – was that he did not accept their first premise that it is possible to harm somebody physically at a distance by supernatural means. The Azande, then, reason very much the way we do, but they reason from different assumptions.

Claude Lévi-Strauss took this argument further in a remarkable book, *La Pensée Sauvage*, published in 1962. This great study of "savage" thinking begins with a consideration of totemism, a phenomenon that appears to erect a barrier between the thought of "civilized" people and that of those they are inclined to disdain as "primitives." Totemism, the widespread system of belief in which a person or a group of people is associated with some material thing or animal species in the natural world, had long puzzled anthropologists. What does it mean when an Australian Aborigine says "I am an eaglehawk" or "The wallaby is my brother"? Lévi-Strauss contended that the Australian who says such things is neither feeble-minded nor confused and certainly knows a good deal about wallabies. He is making a symbolic statement that locates him and his people within a cosmic system of classification. Many Australian societies are, like the Xavante, divided into two halves or moieties. In such societies one moiety may have an eaglehawk as its totem, the other a crow. This is because the contrast between eaglehawk (hunter) and crow (scavenger) is a powerful symbol of opposition. A person who says "I am an eaglehawk" is therefore saying, in effect, "My moiety is

THE FOG THAT BROUGHT THE SICKNESS

An epidemic in the mountains of central Mexico has taken the lives of sixty Huichol Indians. Medical authorities describe the disease as a mutant strain of measles causing death by secondary respiratory infection. But Western doctors cannot explain why this disease occurred at this time, in this place, to these people.

Juan Bautista, a powerful shaman of the area, has an explanation. "Knowing the cause is essential to the cure. Over the last year there was much disagreement in the community about offerings and sacrifices to the gods. Too much attention was given to the eastern direction – Our Father Sun – and not enough to the forces in the west coming from Our Mother Ocean. The forces from the west brought fog from great waves in the ocean into our mountains. The coldness in the fog brought the sickness. We need to reestablish harmony with the gods and agreement in the community. Then the dying will stop. We must make many offerings and we must be in unison."

Juan Bautista appreciates the power of Western medicine to help heal the symptoms of a disease but it is his task, as a shaman, to remedy the cause. In contrast to the Western medical model, shamanic cures look to establish cosmic balance, then social harmony, and finally physical health. In this photograph, Juan Bautista applies paint to his sick son Juventin to receive the blessing of Father Sun. His son survived.

to the other moiety as eaglehawk is to crow, opposite but complementary." Similarly a person who says "I am a wallaby" is saying that his clan is to other clans as wallabies are to other species, distinct, but belonging to a single set of interacting categories. Such statements not only place the individual in a system of classification, but they also express the connectedness of things and species *and humans* within the universe, in much the same way as the Makuna, whom we met in chapter 2.

Lévi-Strauss was struck by something that anthropologists and others have reported over and over again, namely that human beings make very careful observations of their natural environment. This propensity for the study and classification of the elements of the physical world can be seen as the key to human thinking. After all, humankind made the great discoveries of the neolithic revolution – agriculture, weaving, pottery, metallurgy, and so on – on the basis of this kind of observation and classification, long before the advent of scientific thinking as we know it. Furthermore, Lévi-Strauss went on to argue, relatively isolated tribal societies continue to engage in this kind of speculative inquiry right down to the present day.

It was this intellectual approach that Lévi-Strauss called "savage thought," and he presented detailed evidence to show that it is as logical and systematic as scientific thought. Why, then, does it often reach different conclusions? Lévi-Strauss explained that savage thought starts from different premises and refuses to accept a vacuum. Where science accepts "don't know" as its horizon, savage thought presses on and establishes connections that science refuses to accept. It will not rest until it has constructed a total system of connectedness in which human beings and their thoughts are embedded. Classification is such an important element of this kind of thinking because it links natural history to cosmology without stopping at natural science.

The series of intricate demonstrations that Lévi-Strauss culled from the anthropological literature prove beyond a doubt that he is right about the logical and systematic thinking of tribal peoples. As he wrote:

> To transform a weed into a cultivated plant, a wild beast into a domestic animal, to produce, in either of these, nutritious or technologically useful properties which were originally completely absent or could only be guessed at; to make stout, water-tight pottery out of clay which is friable and unstable, liable to pulverize or crack (which, however, is possible only if from a large number of organic and inorganic materials, the one most suitable for refining it is selected, and also the appropriate fuel, the temperature and duration of firing and the effective degree of oxidation); to work out techniques, often

long and complex, which permit cultivation without soil or alternatively without water; to change toxic roots or seeds into foodstuffs or again to use their poison for hunting, war or ritual – there is no doubt that all these achievements required a genuinely scientific attitude, sustained and watchful interest and a desire for knowledge for its own sake. For only a small proportion of observations and experiments (which must be assumed to have been primarily inspired by a desire for knowledge) could have yielded practical and immediately useful results.

All this was accomplished by "prescientific" thinkers. Coming upon this passage, however, the reader is made uneasily aware that when Lévi-Strauss talks about "savage thought," he is not referring only to the thinking of people we might be tempted to label as savages but about us as well. He is, in fact, talking about the way most people think most of the time. If we pay attention to our horoscopes, since there is no scientific evidence to show any connections between our birthdays, our stars, and our lives, we are thinking savagely, positing connections where science sees none. If we act on superstition, we are thinking savagely. The professional athlete who wears his shirt inside out or puts his socks on in a certain order to bring him luck is a savage thinker, and so, of course, is anyone who offers up prayers for anything at all – particularly those prayers that take the form of vows. A prayer, for example, in which the supplicant offers to do penance or make some costly sacrifice in the hope that it will cure a child's illness demonstrates a far-from-scientific belief in connections between one person's actions and another's disease, mediated by supernatural forces within the universe. There is an important difference, however, between our "savage" thinking and that of tribal societies. We indulge in it to make connections that our science tells us are illusory, so we do not test our superstitions. In tribal societies, the search for the widest system of connections is carried out, as Lévi-Strauss remarked, in a genuinely scientific spirit.

Even though all of us think savagely some of the time, and it takes considerable effort for any of us to think scientifically any of the time, it is still not clear why some societies have relied exclusively on savage thought while others have developed the alternative approach that resulted in theoretical and abstract science. Scientific thinking, in which the modern world takes such pride, arose quite recently in the West, and was not, at the beginning, a purely secular inquiry into the laws of nature. On the contrary, it was solidly rooted in the spiritual and magical experiments of the European alchemists of the sixteenth century.

The word *alchemy* itself takes us on an interesting journey. It is medieval Latin from the Arabic *al-kimiya'*, which in turn derives from the Greek word *chemeia*,

DOGON FOX DIVINATION

Divination involves looking at the natural world in a special way: oracles function through a combination of natural "signs" and codes of human interpretation which depend on the premise that what happens in the natural world (the mysterious chain of causation which is constantly in process around us) is connected in an orderly way to human fate.

The Dogon fox divination pictured here rests on the assumption that, as a native of the bush, the desert fox possesses far greater knowledge than do village-dwelling beings. The fox is therefore consulted on matters of importance by diviners who, in the late afternoon, will begin the divination process by drawing three rectangles, each divided in half, in the sand. The rectangles represent the three aspects of the world — the celestial, the terrestrial, and the subterranean zone of death. The fox is expected to tread on the drawing during the night, and his footprints are read the next morning. Should the answers on successive nights seem contradictory, a sacrifice of a chicken may be made on a nearby altar to encourage the fox to tell the truth.

meaning "black," which referred to Egypt (the "black land"). Two other possible derivations of *kimiya'* add further drama: the Greek *chumeia*, which was a metal-lurgical term having to do with pouring, and a similar-sounding Chinese word that meant "sperm of gold." What this etymology suggests is that alchemy drew on combined traditions from ancient Egypt and Greece as well as from Arabic (Hebrew) and possibly Chinese philosophy.

In the ancient world alchemy was referred to simply as "the sacred art." It flourished in the first three centuries A.D. in Alexandria, where it was the com-bined product of glass and metal technology, a Hellenistic philosophy of the unity of all things through the four elements (earth, air, water, fire), and "occult" religion and astrology. How the technology of coloring glass and goldsmithing – kept secret in certain families – became involved with esoteric philosophy is a long story. The essential principle was that all things, both animate and inanim-ate, were permeated by spirit, and that the substances of the lower world could, through a synthesis of chemical operations and imaginative reasoning, be trans-muted into higher things of the spiritual world – things not subject to decay. Gold, of course, was the metaphor for this immortal substance, but alchemy was not just the "broiling of metals" or a primitive chemistry. It was above all meant to develop the wisdom and the spirit of the practitioner.

During the Renaissance the so-called Hermetic arts – named after the Greek god Hermes who served as a messenger between gods and humans – gained new life through the rediscovery of the classical arts and sciences. The occult philosophies of Alexandria were systematized and developed and became both more daring and more experimental in the hands of the people like the Swiss physician Paracelsus and the Italian philosopher-priest Giordano Bruno. The characteristic feature of the Hermetic worldview was the active posture it adopted with respect to nature. Hermetic magic provided methods by which nature could be manipulated, so it provoked a deeply experimental spirit in its practitioners. Those in Europe saw themselves as assisting in God's work by controlling the world for the common good of Christendom, but theirs was a heretical Christian-ity for which many of them would eventually pay with their lives. The church would not tolerate Bruno's view that the earth and its inhabitants were not at the center of the universe, much less his conviction that an infinite universe was alive with divine power.

Isaac Newton himself believed that alchemy might enable human beings to shape and control the world by understanding and participating in its God-given vitality. He conducted alchemical experiments with great secrecy at Trinity College, Cambridge, working alone, even building his own furnaces without the aid of a bricklayer. He made a pact with the chemist John Boyle not to communi-cate their shared alchemical knowledge to others, because the "subtle" and "noble" powers of matter and the means of controlling them should be kept secret

Sol and Luna

One of the fundamental tenets of alchemy was that the will of the Creator could be determined by discovering the laws of the heavens and of earth, thereby serving as a guide for personal conduct. As both a science and technology, alchemy drew upon astrology, astronomy, metallurgy, and medicine. Many alchemical drawings employed esoteric imagery to depict the complex relationship between the heavens and earth. Among a host of more specific meanings, this engraving by Matthaus Merian (circa early seventeenth century), depicts a more general mystical union between sun and moon, earth and sky, matter and spirit.

Phœnix

by those chosen by God to be entrusted with them. Newton's writings on optics, mechanics, and mathematics were the public aspects of his work. At the same time, he was working on his alchemical experiments and writing them up in more than a million words that were never published during his lifetime.

Clearly the Hermetic conception of a universe permeated by divine forces and manipulable by those who were in tune with them prepared the way for the emergence in the seventeenth century of a system of *mechanical* laws and a scientific method. In connecting the sensible world with the divine world in an orderly arrangement of substances and images joined by "sympathies," the alchemists provided the seventeenth-century imagination with the rudiments of a new science. The mathematician and inventor of calculus, Leibniz, called his system an "innocent magic" or "true Cabala." Francis Bacon and Descartes as well as Newton drew heavily upon earlier alchemical theory and practice.

The divine, the magical, and what we would nowadays call the scientific existed in a state of tension in the worldview of the alchemists. The practitioner of the occult sought to achieve both union with God through enlightened participation in his universe and practical results in the mundane world. His goal was always harmony and balance, which was quite consistent with the organic cosmology of the feudal world, but the rise of capitalism and the industrial revolution tipped the scales in favor of the practical at the expense of the cosmological. Science emerged as a kind of magic, stripped of its divine connections and cosmic implications, that now focused on understanding and controlling the physical world.

Before this separation of the cosmic from the scientific, the sixteenth-century philosophers of nature had assumed that the investigation of the world and its processes was a spiritual quest. The legends of the search for the Holy Grail, especially the most famous of them dealing with King Arthur and his Knights of the Round Table, represent the journey of the soul toward enlightenment in story form. In Europe these ideas about knowledge as a quest that brings the seeker into harmony with the universe and with God were derived from the Hermetic tradition, but similar ideas have existed and continue to exist in other parts of the world, notably in the thinking of people who put their trust in shamans. The word *shaman* comes to us from the Russians, who got it from the Tungus of Siberia. Siberian shamans, as often women as men, intercede with or try to manipulate the spirits on behalf of humankind. They usually sing and dance and beat a drum to induce a trance during which the soul of the shaman travels to the spirits or a spirit comes to the shaman and possesses him or her. Anthropologists use the word shaman in a general sense to refer to people who act as mediators between the mundane world around them and the cosmic world beyond. While the Makuna shamans I discussed in chapter 2 behave very differently from Siberian shamans, they are both mediators, working to ensure that there is no disharmony between the human world and the cosmos.

The function of shamans becomes very clear when we see them trying to cure the sick, as they are often called upon to do. A shaman working to cure a patient does not simply intercede with the spirits (though he may do that): he tries to rectify the disharmony that the sickness represents. He seeks to reestablish the balance not only of the sick body but also of the society to which the patient belongs – and of the cosmic order that contains it.

People in the modern world are inclined to be condescending toward the kind of treatment that a shaman offers – that is, until they themselves are seriously ill and realize that Western medicine may not be able to cure them. My wife and I learned this lesson the hard way, when we revisited the Xavante after many years' absence. We had planned to return to them accompanied by our son Biorn, whom they had known as a toddler. He and his wife would join us as research assistants in what we looked forward to as a reunion with old Xavante friends. But it was not to be. On the eve of our departure from Brasilia, Biorn was diagnosed as having cancer. He underwent an emergency operation in Brasilia and returned to the United States for further treatment. We did not know what to do. It had taken us literally years to prepare for our return. We were in Brasilia, ready to leave, with our permits in order, a vehicle to get us into the backlands, a photographer to accompany us, our gear and our presents for the Xavante gathered and packed. Should we cancel our expedition and go home with Biorn? What could we do for him if we did? He would not be going back alone. His wife was with him and his brother would meet him when he got back to Boston. It was Biorn who finally made the decision for us. We should go to the Xavante.

It was not the kind of return we had imagined. It had been decades since our previous visit and things had changed in central Brazil. The Xavante were no longer beyond the frontier. Cattle ranchers and rice farmers had come pouring into the lands over which they used to roam, so we could now reach "our" village by road, or at least by trail…if we could find it. Our friends had moved the village away from the Rio das Mortes and succeeded in chasing away any ranchers and squatters who tried to come too close to it. We made our way toward their new home by guesswork, picking our way through the maze of trails that meandered through the scrub, dipping in and out of patches of jungle, and skirting spectacular buttes and mesas. Just before nightfall we came over the crest of a hill and, peering through a gap in the trees, saw far below the sweeping semicircle of Pimental Barbosa, laid out like our memories before us.

We stopped first to announce our arrival at the squalid houses of the Indian agency, and there was Sibupa. He launched at once into a ceremonial speech of welcome and then asked after our son, his namesake. He led us to the village, where we were greeted by the chief. Old Apewen was dead and his eldest son, Waarodi, had taken over his role. Then we made the expected round of the village, being greeted again and again, each time having to explain where our own Sibupa

Drawing of a Yakut
shaman. Siberia.
1813.

Drawing of a Tungus
shaman. Siberia.
1813.

Drawing of Tatar
shamans. Siberia.
Eighteenth century.

Fig. B.

The Yakut shamans are the best known in Siberia. Their costume, covered with feathers, symbolizes the shaman's transformation into a bird as he or she travels to the different worlds to collect the *kut,* or soul, of the ailing person from the spirits. As the shaman travels to see the spirits, he or she must first pass through various stops along the way and converse with the protector spirits, who allow the shaman to pass to the next level. When a shaman travels to the lower world, in the Yakut tradition it is considered to be the swooping down of the loon into the "ocean of death." Once the sick person's soul is retrieved from the spirits the shaman places it in her or his ear in order to carry it back through the same trajectory to return it.

Photo of a Yakut shaman. Siberia. circa 1925.

Photo of a female Yakut shaman. Siberia. circa 1920.

Fig. A.

g. C.

was and why he was not with us. Women who had known us back in the old days sat with us and wept. Their weeping was a customary form of greeting, expressing the sadness of absence and mourning for those who had died while we were away. We wept, too.

A few days later the elders drew their mats into a tight circle in the center of the men's council. In low, whispering tones they decided that they would hold one of the most solemn of all Xavante ceremonies. Waarodi, the chief, was sick. Our son had not come back to them because he was sick. The whole community must therefore take part in a curing ceremony. The men spent all the next day in the forest, singing and painting themselves in preparation for the night. By midafternoon they were finished. Each man wore glistening white cylinders in his ears and a fresh cotton necklet decorated at the nape with an eagle feather. Their bodies were painted scarlet and black, and they wore wristlets and anklets of palm bark that had been kept meticulously white and free of smears from the paint they had to apply with their own hands. Each lead singer smoothed his long hair with palm oil and bound it into a chignon around a length of balsa wood into which macaw feathers were inserted. As they stood there in their spreading headdresses, it struck me that they looked no different than their parents had when we lived with them a generation ago – save that now they completed their ceremonial regalia with scarlet shorts.

It had been thundering ominously all afternoon. I went back to the village and took my place with the elders. The singing in the forest stopped and a great hush fell over the community. The senatorial elders stopped talking. The women and children were quiet. Even the dogs seemed to sense the solemnity of the moment. Then the men came, walking slowly and in single file. There were about seventy of them, from middle-aged men to striplings in their teens. With their eyes fixed on the ground in front of them, they stepped slowly around the great horseshoe of their world. They completed the circuit of the village and then formed a tight semicircle before Waarodi's house. Waarodi appeared and lay down on a sleeping mat. All this took place in a silence broken only by the rolling thunder.

Then the singing started. Lightning flashes illuminated the vermilion clouds of sunset. The deep chorus with its familiar rhythms washed over the community while the dancers twisted and turned, now looking left, now right, their movements measured, emphatic. I could see my old hunting partner and "younger brother," Surupredu. He was the lead dancer at the end of the line, and his headdress soared and swooped as he bowed and swayed in the dance. He marked the beat with two white wands in a graceful motion quite unlike the usual, thumping Xavante dances.

Night fell, but the singing and dancing went on. It was just a surge of sound now, ebbing and flowing in the darkness. An occasional flash of lightning held the whole scene for a split second and left us again in the dark, listening to the thunder and the voice of the community. The singers grew hoarse as the chill of the central Brazilian plateau crept in around us. The song would die to a quiet croaking until some singer with rested throat took it up again and the chorus swelled forth anew. There was no moon and few stars to be seen. We lost all track of time. Eventually Pia and I, exhausted by our activities, crept away to our hammocks. We lay there feeling the energy of the whole village focused on Waarodi, on us, on our son, willing the sickness to go away. The singing by now seemed to be a force of nature, mingling with the thunder and the surreal night to do battle with disease. The Xavante wanted to make sure we understood. Shadowy figures sought us out at intervals to remind us, "It is for Sibupa too. We sing for Sibupa. Your son will be cured." At sunrise they were still singing and Waarodi, at least, was feeling much better.

Our son recovered, but Waarodi, alas, did not. Neither the curing ceremony nor the Western medical care he received in Goiânia could save him. He died of cancer the following year. Although neither form of treatment was able to save his life, I am convinced it was the ceremony that prolonged it. So I am not surprised when I hear of cancer patients in modern society seeking forms of treatment other than those offered by conventional medicine. Cancer is for us the epitome of an incurable disease, although many forms of it can in fact be cured nowadays. Nevertheless, people do die of cancer, and when it is diagnosed the patient and his friends and relatives find themselves confronting uncertainty in a powerful and painful way. Science cannot help them, for it does not deal with uncertainty, but there are traditions of knowledge and healing that do. Shamanism does, which explains why the tradition continues to flourish today. Most of us, if we have ever heard of shamans at all, tend to disparage them as no better than "witch doctors." That was the attitude that Stalin adopted toward the Siberian shamans, and under his regime the traditional shamans were considered either hysterics or actually insane. They were harried and persecuted for obscurantist thinking and for defrauding their clients. In the West we do not go that far. We pay lip service to the idea that there are forms of healing other than those practiced by mainstream medicine, but we marginalize them. We may sympathize with cancer patients who are willing to look beyond Western medicine for a cure, but I suspect that many of us (especially if we are hale and hearty and do not face imminent death) think they are clutching at straws.

Yet we know that a person's state of mind affects his physical well-being, and not just to the extent of whether he crawls or jumps out of bed in the morning. It is not unreasonable to believe that an alteration of one's mental state is capable of affecting the body sufficiently to cure some cancers. In fact, this view is held by some orthodox medical practitioners. Dr. Alistair Cunningham is one such practitioner. Professor of biophysics at the University of Toronto and now a senior researcher in Canada's largest cancer research institute, he took his first doctorate

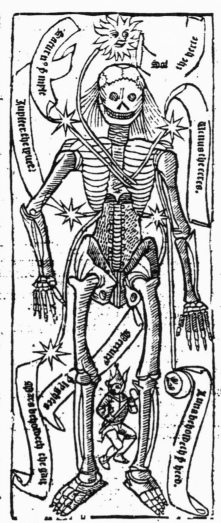

BODY AS COSMOS

Prior to the scientific revolution, Europeans felt a direct connection to the universe and its workings through the composition of their bodies. Throughout the Middle Ages, scientists and theologians alike considered the human body to be a microcosm — a micro-cosmos. Each portion of the body corresponded to other parts of the universe. This reflected the belief that since human beings were created in God's image, their bodies were models of the universe itself. Thus, characteristics of the planets and signs of the zodiac corresponded to the behaviour of particular organs. The sun ruled the heart, Mars the gall bladder; Aries, being hot, fiery and choleric accorded these characteristics to the head, while Pisces ruled the feet, the final sign of the zodiac calendar. Indeed, the body's cosmic unity was offered as the reason why dissecting corpses for medicine was forbidden — to dismember the body would be to mutilate the universe itself.

From S. K. Heninger, "The Human Microcosm." *The Cosmographical Glass* (San Marino, CA: Huntington Library, 1977). David le Breton, "Dualism and Renaissance." *Diogenes,* Summer 1988, p. 56.

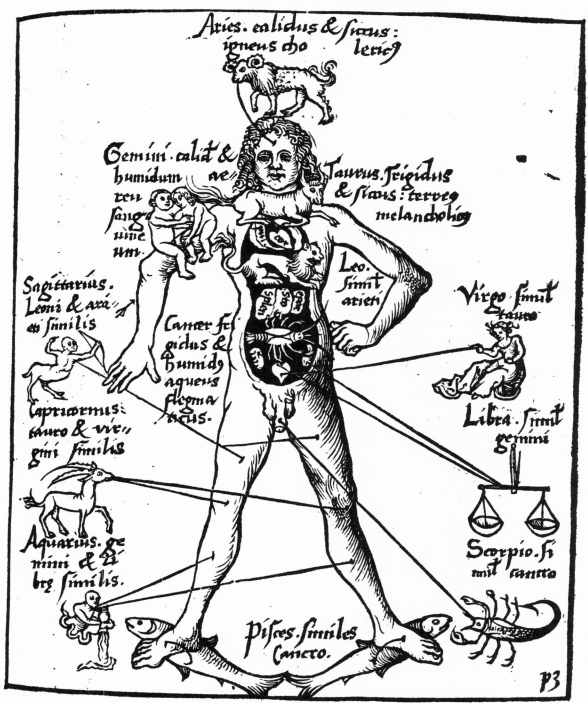

in cell biology and worked for twenty years studying the human immune system. In the course of his research he discovered that mental states do indeed affect the immune system, so he took a second doctorate in clinical psychology and now offers psychotherapy to cancer patients. He hopes in this way, as he puts it, to "awaken the inner healer" within the patient and thus to stimulate the immune system to do battle with and (we hope) defeat the cancer.

Of course Cunningham's therapy, when it succeeds, has a clear physical "explanation." He has demonstrated how the alteration of the patient's frame of mind leads to the production of endomorphines that in turn help the immune system to battle the cancerous cells. It is only the starting point that causes difficulty. How can one make (or help the patient to make) the right mental adjustment? Indeed, what exactly is the right mental adjustment? Finally Cunningham's treatments provoke a larger question. If they work and their means of working can be "explained" in terms of ordinary Western medicine, why does Western medicine not invest more money and energy in developing them?

I suspect the answer has something to do with the great divide in our thinking between the scientific, which we value, and the nonscientific, which we undervalue. We try to make a science of everything, including healing. There is much to be said for such an approach, especially when we consider the "miracle cures" of modern medicine. The problem is that this approach fails to recognize its own limitations. "What science cannot cure," we seem to say, "nothing can," and we sometimes follow that up by adding "and no one should be allowed to try." Meanwhile, modern medicine is becoming increasingly analytic and specialized. Its most prestigious fields are those that deal with specific diseases or parts of the body. Doctors who try to deal with patients synthetically, as whole people whose organs are connected to their limbs, with all of them influenced by their minds, are called "general practitioners." Though patients love them, they are harder and harder to find and have less and less time to practice their kind of healing.

It is as if science, which has been so successful that we regard it as the characteristic feature of our age, of our thinking, of ourselves, has carved the world up into little pieces to understand it better...and then forgotten to put it back together again. As a result, we feel disconnected within ourselves, among ourselves, both from the physical world that we claim to dominate and even more so from the cosmic world. We know we are part of the cosmos, but most of us do not know how we fit in or why we are here. Even stranger than our dismissive shrug in response to these questions is our air of superiority toward other peoples who take them seriously.

Perhaps this attitude will change – is changing – now that a small group we respect finds itself dealing with the issues of cosmic connectedness that have traditionally fascinated all of humankind. I am referring of course to physicists, who discovered early in this century that the traditional laws of Newtonian mechanics do not apply in the microworld of atoms and subatomic particles. They therefore developed quantum mechanics to describe systems where Newtonian mechanics breaks down. The new theory, developed in the 1920s, has been spectacularly productive, not only theoretically but also practically, making possible among other things the invention of the electron microscope, the laser, and the transistor. But it has also posed some difficult and as yet unsolved problems about the nature of the universe.

Quantum physicists discovered, for example, that two photons (the most elementary units of light) traveling in opposite directions at the speed of light nevertheless appear to be connected with each other in some way. The experimenter measures one of them and by the very act of measuring it changes its position and momentum slightly. When this is done the *other* photon also changes in the same way, as though the first had communicated with the second. Yet there cannot be any communication between the photons, for any message passing from one to the other would have to travel faster than the speed of light, which is impossible according to Albert Einstein's theory of relativity.

They also discovered that a photon was capable of behaving either like a wave or like a particle. If the experimenter measured its wavelike properties, it would behave like a wave; if he measured its particlelike properties, it would behave like a particle. Which was it really? Niels Bohr, the Danish physicist, dealt with this question in 1927 with his famous complementarity principle, which states that it is the form of measurement itself that determines whether an object will behave like a wave or like a particle. The wave-particle duality refers therefore to complementary aspects of the behavior of quantum objects. They were truly complementary, Bohr argued, because no experiment would show that these distinct behaviors ever conflicted with each other. Werner Heisenberg formulated the equally famous uncertainty principle in the same year. According to Heisenberg's principle, it is impossible to measure the position and momentum of a particle simultaneously.

These two principles indicate a curious indeterminacy in quantum objects. They cannot be described precisely in Newtonian terms. Their behavior is ambiguous. It is not clear what their real nature is, or even – some physicists concluded – whether they exist at all when they are not being measured. This view is similar to one put forward in the eighteenth century by the Irish philosopher George Berkeley, who maintained that material objects do not exist at all when they are not being looked at or at least thought about – a strangely idealist conviction to be held by physicists intent on describing the real world. In fact, Bohr insisted that it was meaningless to ask what the *real* nature of quantum objects was. Experiments showed them to be unstable, and that was all we could know about them. The rest was potential, not actuality.

This point of view allowed for a level of indeterminacy in quantum phenomena,

SCHRODINGER'S CAT-THOUGHT EXPERIMENT

Erwin Schrodinger, one of the founders of quantum mechanics, developed a famous thought experiment in 1935. It was a way of illustrating the superpositional (or "limbo") state in which matter exists at the subatomic level — hovering between expression as waves or particles. In order to carry out the experiment, one needs to imagine a sealed and insulated box (A) containing a radioactive source (B). The source has a fifty-fifty chance of activating the Geiger counter (C) during the experiment, which triggers a mechanism (D), which causes a hammer to smash a bottle of prussic acid (E), which kills the cat (F). We must then imagine that an observer opens the box in order to measure the state of the system — to find out what is going on inside. When he does so, he reduces the system's possibilities from many (the bottle may or may not be broken, the cat may or may not be alive) to one (the cat is either, upon inspection, dead or alive). To "collapse" something into a "state" is to bring it into what we call "concrete" reality — we determine, by measuring, if this thing is a particle or a wave.

The cat experiment is a macroscopic analogy that explains what happens at the quantum level. At the quantum level, a coexistence of states (between waves and particles) is implied and a true explanation is probabilistic. However, we cannot stop there. The *total* system includes not only the quantum indeterminacy but also the intervention of the observer, which creates, in a sense, one state or another, and the definitely dead or alive cat at the level of the nonquantum, everyday world. Both descriptions must coexist to achieve a consistent picture of the quantum realm.

and therefore in the world, that Einstein found repugnant. He dismissed it with the often quoted comment, "God does not play dice with the universe." His own conception of the nature of reality was that the indeterminacy of quantum phenomena was only apparent. He believed that they were actually determined by a deeper level of forces than physicists had yet uncovered. These forces, he thought, would turn out to have the precision and certainty of the old Newtonian scheme that had been superseded by quantum mechanics.

Despite their differences, Einstein and Bohr both stressed the incompleteness of quantum theory. The microworld of quantum objects and processes is either determined by a whole new level of yet-to-be-discovered principles (Einstein), or it is indeterminate, possessing no reality of its own, with a potential that only becomes actual when it interacts with the macroworld (Bohr). In short, the real world in which most of us think we live, the world of discrete objects and predictable cause and effect, turns out to be a sort of optical illusion, a partial glimpse of a deeper level of reality.

This conviction has, for quite different reasons, been shared by much of humankind for most of human history. Some quantum physicists pointed out the parallels between their conceptions of cosmic interconnectedness and those to be found in Oriental religions such as Buddhism and Taoism. What the physicists did not know, or at any rate did not mention, is that the ideas contained in quantum theory have interesting similarities to the worldview of Australian Aborigines, right down to the space-time continuum of relativity theory.

The Aborigines believe that their universe has two aspects. There is the ordinary, physical world in which they live and another, connected world from which it is derived. This other world, called the Dreamtime or the Dreaming, is the major focus of Aboriginal thought, because the principles and powers emanating from it determine what happens in this world. The Dreamtime is the aspect of Aboriginal culture that has proved most puzzling to outsiders. Most students of Aboriginal thought have, after all, been steeped in a Newtonian view of the world. Besides, the Aborigines have such a simple technology that, until quite recently, it was supposed that their ideas about the world would be equally simple, if not simpleminded. It is hardly surprising, then, that a well-known Aboriginal artist, Bunduk Marika, said recently and most emphatically that white people would *never* understand the Dreaming.

Part of the problem is the word *dreaming* itself. Modern society does not take dreams very seriously and tends to contrast them with reality. So when we refer in English to Aboriginal ideas about the Dreaming, our own translation of their word implies that we are dealing with a figment of their imagination, something not real. This immediately establishes a barrier between our thought and theirs, for the Dreaming is the very foundation of their reality. It is even harder for us to understand the Dreaming if we refer to it by its other common name, the *Dream-*

PADDY AND FRANS

Paddy Roe is an elder of the Njik'ina group in western Australia. Frans Hoogland is a Dutchman who has lived for fifteen years among the Aborigines. He has been initiated by Paddy into the secrets of the Dreaming, ritual knowledge that is traditionally passed from generation to generation within a kin group responsible for the care of a certain territory and its associated animals and songs. Young Aborigines are under pressure to move to the towns and to acquire the skills and style of white Australians, and turn their backs on the old ways. Paddy says, "Young fellas are gone cranky," meaning they're overburdened. "They can only look after their share. That's about all they can do." So Paddy accepted this young European as his pupil "to help the country."

Frans, for his part, had not planned to follow the Aboriginal way. He was dissatisfied with life in Amsterdam ("I was missing without knowing it the connection to nature") and began to travel. He arrived in Australia, and soon began his apprenticeship in the Dreamtime, the "Law," or as Paddy says it in his own language, "Bugaragara."

Frans is an exception, a white man who takes the Law seriously and has lived long enough in the country to learn something about it. He explains the Dreaming in his own words:

We start with nothing – a total emptiness – a void. Then we have some singing and dancing. We start by forming – the singing creates the sound and the vibration forms a shape, and the dancing helps solidify it. The dancing is making the form stand out as a tree, a bird, as land. The process, the Dreaming itself, becomes a reality, something we can work with and see.

Normally we follow roads that are already there. But that's the wrong way. When you walk you have to send the landscape and the road out of yourself.

In order to help this form, we carry on the ritual singing and dancing. This cultivates the form. It's not done through digging in the ground or watering and planting. It's done through the mind and the singing and dancing. And the songs have been handed over from the first Creator-Beings who produced them in their journey of making the landscape.

Everything on earth is kept together by the Songlines. The Dreamtime is an ongoing process that can create form and hold it for a while. To pay respect to the country, you will, as you walk along, say hello to the places through the song and dancing. That's the cultivation process: that's how you maintain it and look after it, instead of taking the ground and putting a fence around it. There's no need of that.

time, for Dreamtime bears little resemblance to our ordinary notions of time. For the Australians, the Dreamtime is not only the period when the original Ancestors created the world, but it is also parallel to and sometimes coincident with the everyday time in which ordinary people live. Before Einstein and quantum physics, people in the Western world were not much inclined to pay serious attention to anyone who talked about the simultaneity of different kinds of time. Even today, I suspect, there are few people beyond a handful of scientists who have a real understanding of what that means. But that is precisely why the Aborigines settled on the word *Dreamtime* to describe their ideas to pragmatic outsiders. They know that we are aware that in dreams the ordinary laws of time, space, and motion do not apply. One can be in two places at once. Past, present, and future fold into each other, and time and space are in flux. We have experienced this in our dreams. Aborigines live it in their reality.

The Aborigines believe that the Ancestors created everything in the universe at the time when the earth and sky separated from each other. Through their dreams, thoughts, songs, and actions the Ancestors created everything there is. Imagine an Ancestor breaking through the crust of the earth and emerging in the desert. Around him is a featureless plain. He lies down to sleep and begins to dream. In this dream he imagines the actions of the next day – sees a plain full of kangaroos issuing from himself, who is ancestor, human being, and kangaroo, all at the same time. When he wakes, the Ancestor finds the kangaroos, who have crawled out of his armpit while he slept, or he will proceed to give birth to them. So the dream and the actuality are, like sleeping and waking, merely different states of the same reality.

At the beginning of the Dreamtime is the original Ancestor, an extraordinary source of creative power that produces and reproduces till the world is filled with Ancestors and the human beings, animals, plants, and inanimate objects they have brought forth. The Ancestors walk through the land and sing it into existence, chanting stories that give form to it. The stories *are* the land, just as the land is a story. The songline or dreaming track of an Ancestor is the path that he or she took in forming the land. That path is part of the Ancestor. When an Aborigine walks that songline and sings that song, he is part of that Ancestor and part of the continuing creation of the land that both exists and is being created. All this is what Aborigines mean when they refer to their land as sacred and explains why they are serious when they say they die when the land is taken from them.

Aborigines believe that human beings emanate directly from the Ancestors, for it is they who enter women and make them pregnant. All humans derive from and have a continuing role in the world of the Ancestors, the Dreamtime, to which they have occasional access in sacred ceremonies. Traditional Aborigines devote their lives to learning about and obeying the rules of the Dreaming. This entails learning level after level of interpretation of the songs and stories, whose effects

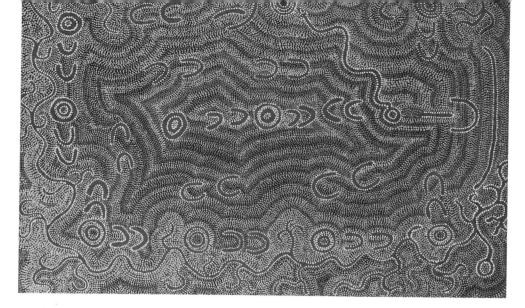

on the contours of the land become more evident as one's knowledge increases. The land itself is the primary text through which Aborigines are educated. It is encoded with information about every dimension of existence, so to learn the secrets of the land is to learn everything worth knowing. Since the Aborigines believe that the land actually participates in the actions and adventures of the Ancestors, they have dissolved the distinctions between culture and nature, between the human world and the cosmos.

The songs and the songlines are so important because they are the musical embodiment of the properties of reality. They are at once the equations that describe it and the forces that make it work. Human beings do not compose the songs. If they did, the songs would not have the power to hold the external world together and bind it to the Dreamtime. The songs come from the Ancestors, handed down through generations and replenished through dreams. They are, in effect, the cosmic rhythms and melodies that give the everyday world its form.

The Aboriginal view of reality appears strange to us because we are accustomed to thinking in Newtonian terms. In our system, objects are separated from one another and only become connected when force is applied to them. The Aboriginal system rejects our separation of the visible world into discrete objects, just as it denies that matter is the primary level of reality. Ironically, it is in the pursuit of the ultimate building blocks of matter that our scientists have encountered a world that exhibits traits found in Aboriginal epistemology. The quantum world suggests that objects are somehow interrelated without any force acting on them or any communication between them. Moreover, it appears that, in experimental situations at least, "matter" relies on an observing consciousness to dictate where it should materialize. A proton in an otherwise empty box has the potential of being everywhere or anywhere in that box until someone takes a look at it. Only then does it occupy a specific position.

These mysteries have led some physicists like David Bohm to argue that there is an overarching order responsible for the manifested order that we observe. Bohm, in his notion of the enfolded order, suggests that on one level of reality everything is attached to everything else, whereas on our plane objects appear dispersed and autonomous. Thus, the phenomenal world, which we take to be so firm and real, is actually unstable and is always changing, spending most of its time as potential. Bohm's is a theory of reality as continual fluctuation, where particular material properties are never as important as the overall system that includes all the possibilities, all the connections. In many respects, this theory sounds like a paraphrase of the Dreaming. Aborigines seek to define identity in terms of the connectedness of the disparate features of their world. The people, animals, rocks, and trees that fill the landscape are all subordinate to the power of the Dreaming that, while constant, is unstable – for it must be cared for and maintained if the phenomenal world is to endure. The observation made by both Bohr and Heisenberg that one cannot draw a dividing line between the observer and the observed is fully endorsed by the Aborigines. They imagine a world that was sung into existence by Ancestors and continues to need this maintenance. But in their identification with the land, they are at once objects and subjects, the singers and the song.

In his treatise on savage thinking, Lévi-Strauss paid particular attention to the Australian Aborigines. They represented for him a good example of what he called "cold societies," societies that see the world as part of a grand and essentially unchanging cosmic scheme (though one that needs constant renewal). By contrast, he suggested, people in "hot societies" see their world as being in a state of flux. They try to explain it and themselves in historical terms, an attempt that leads to the development of scientific thinking divorced from cosmology.

It is the hot societies, empowered by their sciences, that have taken over the world and now presume to label the cold societies as primitive, backward, and incapable of rational thought. The consequences of such labeling are drastic, for the societies so categorized are expected either to evaporate socially or to face the prospect of being eliminated physically. Yet it has now been proved beyond the shadow of a doubt that all human societies, not only the advanced industrial ones, are capable of remarkable feats of speculative thought. The modern world defines itself by the scientific advantage it holds over the other nations of the earth, but its claim to intellectual superiority over other peoples is difficult to sustain – and its claim to moral superiority even more so.

We can no longer assume, if we are fortunate enough to live in one of the "developed" countries, that our way of life represents the most advanced stage of progress and that other societies have simply been less successful than ours in attaining it. Instead we now know that other societies have made other choices, followed different paths in search of different destinies. This knowledge opens up new vistas on the richness and variety of what it means to be human. The challenge we all face is how to come to terms with these differences, how to live with the variety, now that we have discovered that there are more things in heaven and earth than were dreamt of in our philosophy.

TOUCHING THE TIMELESS

The sun dance, the most important ceremony for the Indians of the western plains, was banned by the United States government in 1904. The ban was ostensibly imposed to prevent the Indians from torturing themselves, for some celebrants, not content with dancing for days on end without food or water in the broiling sun, would pierce themselves with skewers or hang themselves from hooks inserted in the flesh of their chests as they sought their visions. Although not all Plains peoples mortified themselves in this way, all sun dances were prohibited nevertheless, and the ban was not lifted until 1935. It was not only the self-torture that bothered the authorities. The idea of whole peoples coming together to dance and fast and pray and mortify themselves until they see visions is somehow troubling to the official mind. The Plains Indians had, after all, been redoubtable warriors and the bitterness of their defeat by the whites was still poignantly fresh in their minds at the turn of the century. Better, then, that they should be discouraged from such ecstatic gatherings....

The Indians of central Brazil, however, still performed their own versions of the sun dance, or so we had heard. Yet by the time Pia and I reached the Xerente, it did not seem that they were any longer given to the visionary ceremonies of their traditional past. Or so we thought until an epidemic struck the village and babies began to die. It was a nervous time for us: we had not been with the Xerente long and our meager supplies of aspirin and other first-aid remedies were no match for the creeping sickness. It slowly dawned on us that we were suspected of causing it in some way, and these suspicions were allayed only when Pia herself got sick.

By this time Sizapi, the shaman, was dreaming intensively, traveling through space and time to track down the cause of the disease. Each day he marshaled the villagers, men, women, and children, and they danced to combat the plague. Each night I danced with them till I lost all notion of time and space and felt myself wheeling and reeling with the starlit sky. This went on for days – how many I do not remember – until the cold night, thinning into morning, when the dancing stopped. The dancers squatted down around their fires. Nobody spoke. They sat motionless and I was surprised, for Xerente are usually casual and conversational even in the middle of important ceremonies. We sat there for hours or minutes, I could not tell. The fires stopped crackling and glowed like wounds in the night. The Xerente waited. At last a sighing movement ruffled through the lines of men. My companion nudged me.

"Listen!" he said. "Can you hear it?"

"Hear what?"

"The souls of the dead. They are whistling all around us."

At this point Sizapi jumped to his feet and shook his dance rattle toward the heavens. Suddenly the tired dancers were leaping and bellowing, their energy and confidence restored by their epiphany.

I did not, myself, hear the whistling of the souls of the dead, although I had danced along with my companions to prepare for their visit. I have not been trained by my society to expect to meet spirits, and I have not been taught to recognize them. The spirit traditions of Europe are waning. A hundred years ago, country people used still to talk of many different kinds of spirit beings that lived in fields or groves or springs. They rarely, and then very self-consciously, acknowledge them now. Most of us assume that this is because science – Western technology – has provided other interpretations of natural events, and disease, and other misfortunes and mysteries, so that we no longer need these animate figures in our explanations.

"In short religion, regarded as an explanation of nature, is displaced by science." That, at least, is what James Frazer wrote in 1890 in the conclusion to his massive study of the world's myths and rituals, *The Golden Bough*. Frazer was probably the most famous anthropologist of his time. We no longer take his work seriously as anthropological study in the modern sense, because he worked entirely from second-hand sources and took bits and pieces out of context from very different societies to construct dubious, but very popular, evolutionary arguments. Still, Frazer had a deep interest in non-Western cultures at a time when this was considered rather perverse. Even more unusual was his uncertainty, despite the prejudices of his time, that modern Europe had finally discovered reality. If he wrote that science had eclipsed religion, he also wrote that magic, science, and religion are themselves nothing more than "theories of thought" about "phantom entities." He believed that the universe is a shadow play and we know nothing about what lies behind the screen, and he expected that some entirely different way of looking at phenomena would replace in its turn the material image of his own times.

Frazer's predictions have not been borne out. Religion has not disappeared, nor has science really triumphed as a superior form of explanation (or as a final solution to human ills). We continue to live with great uncertainties, and there are some strange facts which suggest that a material world is not sufficient for a great many modern souls. Forty percent of Americans, according to one survey, have had some kind of non-drug-induced mystical experience. Young people who live otherwise ordinary, practical lives have turned to Eastern religions, to pantheism, polytheism, tarot, "channeling," and astrology for insight.

Personal mystical experience is not necessarily uplifting, however. Hitler, Rasputin, Charles Manson, and a number of infamous serial killers were guided, according to their own testimony, by "mystical experiences," as, too, were the prophets of many world religions – and so are ordinary people like the Xerente who follow the traditional religious practices of their ancestors. What religion does, then, is encompass this individual desire for another kind of consciousness within an ethical frame that tells us how we must try to lead our lives. It confirms our suspicion that there is something in reality which always escapes description. It goes beyond magic and science which, in their different ways, provide us with explanations, and reaches out to the inexplicable. Religion enables the faithful to come to terms with the mysterious and to understand their place in the scheme of things, which is why religious symbols have so much power.

Religion is as vast, as all-pervasive, and as difficult to define as the Dreaming of the Australian Aborigines. The word itself works well enough when we apply it to societies in which "religion" appears more or less neatly cordoned off as a particular department of life (separated from politics, economics, and so on). Even then, however, religion seems to serve so many different intellectual and social functions that it is difficult to isolate. When we come to tribal cultures, the situation is even more complex, because here we find religion is everywhere at once, and as soon as we have begun to talk about it, we have to talk about every aspect of society. One solution is to avoid the word entirely and simply talk about cosmology and ritual and various other beliefs and activities that are learned in the course of tribal social life.

Tribal societies share the sensual world with unseen beings – spirits, gods, or ancestors. The spirit world is often dangerous, but there is no absolute barrier between it and the human world. People learn what this other realm looks like and how it should be approached through the stories or myths that describe it and through rituals in which things are offered to it. Yet indigenous peoples are keenly aware that it is not enough for society to teach about such profoundly important moral matters in an academic or abstract way. A personal experience of spirit reality is recognized as vital, and methods have been developed to induce and shape these experiences. Fasting, meditation, dancing, chanting, drugs, and the infliction of pain or extreme pleasure have all been used to bring on waking visions, dreams, and hallucinations.

Knowing all this, we were at first nonplussed when we reached the Xavante. They seemed to be little given to mysticism, and we began to wonder if we had chanced upon a people so practical that they made no effort to see beyond the airy vistas of the open steppes. They used no substances to alter consciousness. They brewed no alcoholic beverage, used no drugs, and did not even smoke tobacco as so many indigenous peoples did traditionally in the Americas. We learned however that they did open themselves to their dreams, which were of enormous importance to them. In fact Xavante men said that their guardian spirits sometimes came to them in their sleep and led them away along the trails that lead to the village of the dead. I never met anyone, though, who claimed to have been there and back. The distance, Xavante told me, is much too great. A man begins to fear that he will never get home again, and always turns back long before he has reached the beautiful place at the "beginning of the sky," where life is easy, food plentiful, and the spirits of the dead spend their time singing and dancing. In fact, wicked people never reach the village of the dead at all, even after they die. They are destroyed on the way or kidnapped by the malevolent opponents of the (benevolent) spirits of the dead. Dreams were nevertheless welcomed as opportunities for pilgrimages of the soul and even more so because it was from their dreams that Xavante derived their songs.

Xavante sang and danced constantly, not only "around the village" in the way we came to like and rely on, but also in their major ceremonies, where people danced themselves virtually into a coma. This was especially true of their most important ceremony, the *wai'a*, which I described from Pia's point of view in chapter 5. I saw it for the first time many years ago in connection with the initiation of a set of boys about to become young men. My age-set was formally sponsoring the ceremony, and it seemed as if we had been dancing for weeks. We danced at dawn and at dusk every day and were expected to go over to the boys' hut two or three times every night and get them out to sing around the village. The teenagers moaned and groaned when they heard the deep flutes that announced our arrival. Some of them had to be prodded awake and coaxed by their age-mates out into the cold night, but they always came, and the singing and dancing soon revived them. By day the boys ran races and the older men congregated in the forest preparing their regalia for the final ceremonies. Women and children were strictly forbidden to go to the men's clearing, but day after day they could hear the singing wafting over from it as the ceremonies built toward their climax.

The climax came suddenly. One night the elders drew their mats together in the middle of the men's council and conversed in low tones. The younger men remained at the fringes, but they knew what was happening. The next day we celebrated the wai'a. Long before dawn the men were up and chanting in the center of the village. It was still dark when they all trooped off to a forest clearing close by, from which their singing could still be heard throughout the community. At daybreak heralds went to each house and made sure that all door and window openings were properly sealed with thatch. Women and children had to stay indoors so as not to see what was to come. Pia, as described in chapter 5, was shut in there with them. All day the men were coming and going in full regalia, solemn as proconsuls, and the tension in the village was rising by the minute. My age-mates painted me for the ceremony, and one of them made white bark wristlets and anklets for Pia to wear, too. Every so often we heard a mournful hooting coming from the depths of the forest. It was the voice of the spirits. A hush settled over the village in the afternoon haze.

Then the men erupted. They poured into the village, painted scarlet and black and running like mad. They danced around the village, only this time the dancing was very different from the cozy night dances we had grown used to. The men were in limbo, between our world and another, and their dancing reflected that. It was furious, possessed. The dancers pounded on the thatch of the houses as they stormed by, while the women and children were quiet as mice inside.

The men entered three of the huts and led a woman out from each of them. I noticed that each of the women was wearing white bark ornaments like those given to Pia. Pia had removed hers, which was just as well because the women were led into the forest to have ceremonial sexual intercourse with the initiates. That night these women danced with the men in the middle of the village. The others were still confined indoors. All night the singing went on, while Apewen, the chief, sat still as a statue in the center, pondering the forces of life and death and the spirits that conveyed these powers to men.

At dawn the initiates assembled in the middle of the village. An arrow, decorated with snakeskin and human hair, came arching over the huts and the men broke into deep cries of "U, he, he, he" as the initiates ran to catch it. One of them barely had time to seize it when two black-painted "spirits" came racing into the village and danced at him. The young man stood with downcast eyes as the spirits thundered and snarled at him, twisting their faces into masks of aggression, lifting their knees to their chins and stamping the earth like berserks. Soon, arrows were swishing in from all sides. The initiates caught them and were danced at till the village seethed with the furious onslaught of the spirits. In the midst of it all Sibupa, my "brother," came at me snorting and stamping, his face twisted with fury, and I realized he was dancing at me. He worked himself into a frenzy, grunting in my face and almost knocking me backward with his flailing elbows. He stamped on my toe, then seized my head between both hands and bit me on both cheeks.

Apewen now stood up and made a speech in the repetitive style Xavante use on formal occasions. I was now a true wai'a celebrant, he informed me, a true wai'a celebrant. They sent for a pair of scissors and a woman came over to tonsure my hair Xavante style. They painted the crown of my head red just as the blood began trickling down my cheek. I was admitted to the Xavante universe, though I did not fully understand it. But I had been given a glimpse of how they saw the world – of the two cosmic principles of generation and destruction that created the framework of their lives, and how they could be as men possessed when these powers

Mandan *Okeepa* Ceremony

The *Okeepa*, practiced until the end of the nineteenth century by the Mandan Indians in what is now North Dakota, was a physically and psychologically demanding ceremony. It was similar in many ways to the Sioux Sun Dance. In this 1832 painting by George Catlin, the first white man to witness the rite in its entirety, young Mandan are hoisted and hung by skewers pierced through the flesh on their chests and backs. To add to their agony they are prodded with spears by elders and weighed down by buffalo skulls tied to their arms and legs. Further tortures awaited them after they were let down. Men who endured the four-day ceremony bravely would often go on to become tribal leaders. Their stoic silence during the tortures was repaid by strength received from the Great Spirit.

came together in them. We had been wrong about the Xavante. We thought they were an eminently social people, more interested in politics than in cosmology. Yet the apparently practical Xavante allowed for – no, insisted on – ceremonial pauses during which they danced themselves into states of near trance to commune with the spiritual forces of their universe. In many other societies, by contrast, the contact between people and the spirit world permeates every aspect of their lives.

Nowhere is this more evident than among the Hopi of Arizona, perhaps the most written about of all North American aboriginal peoples. Many tasks that are considered mundane by other cultures are, among the Hopi, accompanied by rituals which are seen as an integral part of their way of life. In addition, their spectacular ceremonies have been drawing curious spectators from the outside world for almost a century. In fact, Hopi hospitality has been so abused over the years that they no longer allow their sacred rituals to be photographed, although outsiders may still be invited to attend the performances in person. What is especially noteworthy about the Hopi is the tremendous amount of effort and time they invest in preparing for their ceremonials, which enliven each month and may last from a few days to two or more weeks.

The Hopi universe is divided into the upper world of the earth's surface, where people and animals live, and the lower world below the earth, which is the realm of the spirits. Hopi are preoccupied with the separateness of these two levels, though they are seen as complementary rather than opposing domains. A special system of rituals and symbols is therefore considered necessary to facilitate communication between the two realms. The primary notion underlying this interaction is reciprocity, the idea that proper behavior consists in respecting the ceremonial obligations that people have toward the spirit world and vice versa. Ceremonies correctly performed put the spirits under an obligation to keep their part of the bargain, to bring rain, for example, or protect people from disease. The relationship between spirits and humans is thus one of mutual responsibility.

The link between the ordinary world and the spirit world is made for the Hopi by their Kachinas. These are not gods, nor are they the spirits of the dead. They are messengers who listen to the prayers of the priests and the elders and convey them to the gods. Kachinas have human forms and distinctive personalities and are, on the whole, benevolent toward humankind if they are treated with proper respect. They may withdraw their protection, however, if they feel neglected. In fact, Hopi myth tells us that the Kachinas appeared on earth along with the Hopi themselves, but they were eventually killed off by enemy intruders or, in another version, they felt slighted by Hopi indifference and simply withdrew. They had taught the sacred dances to a group of young men however and these became the first Hopi priests.

The Kachina ritual season begins after the winter solstice rites of December

Hopi clowns appear unexpectedly. They are famous for their displays of obscenity and gluttony, and for their satirical performances of Kachina dances. Because they are endowed with supernatural powers, clowns can get away with doing things forbidden to others.

and continues for nearly half a year. Groups of Hopi relatives petition the chiefs for permission to sponsor various rites. Some rites are performed in groups, some in pairs, others individually; some rites are taken on tour to neighboring villages, others are performed solely at home. Although it is only men and initiated boys who perform in the dances, they require the support of the women of the clan, who prepare the food and gifts that the men distribute as part of the ceremony. These redistributions of food and other valuables among human beings are an image of the cycle of gift relations between spirits and humans.

The Kachina spirits are impersonated by masked, costumed dancers, who, like the Dogon dancers we discussed in chapter 6, may invent new personalities (there is a Mickey Mouse Kachina!) to supplement the existing repertoire of at least four hundred spirits. The masks are the most striking feature of the Kachinas. Again like the masks of the Dogon, they are of two kinds: winter masks (associated with men, winter, cold, and the killing of animals) and summer masks (associated with flowers, flutes, rain, and the growth of crops). Some Kachinas take on the role of chiefs or warriors or ogres to frighten and discipline children, but by far the largest and most sacred category have to do with the rain, earth, maize, beans, and squash: the life substances of the Hopi.

All this sounds very serious indeed – and solemnity is what we in the West expect from religious proceedings. It comes as something of a surprise to us to discover that in the middle of these ceremonies – usually during the spring or summer events – the privileged participants are in fact a troupe of clowns. These clown Kachinas – or anti-Kachinas, because, like sacred fools who embody wisdom, they represent everything the Kachinas are not – swarm into the plaza from the rooftops, climbing down the ladders head-first, falling, stumbling, rushing out to grasp the sacred paraphernalia for themselves, following behind spectators in merciless imitation of human pretension. Or they come creeping down, miming their great fear of stepping into the next world (the plaza with its spirit dancers). They act out life as it should *not* be – they are irreverent, ignorant, they squabble with their wives, they seek fame, they hoard food. They turn everything upside down, even such grave matters as the treatment of the dead. In fact the Hopi scholar and clown Emory Sekaquaptewa tells a story about a clown who requested a very unusual funeral as a final and supreme act of clowning. The town crier called for everyone to assemble for a funeral, but when the people arrived they saw the pallbearers up on a rooftop, bending over a person lying down. The clowns picked up the body by its arms and legs and swung it, as if to throw it down into the plaza. On the fourth swing they let go, laughing uproariously as the body landed with a thump near the astonished crowd that had come expecting a conventional funeral.

The point of all this is to stress that we are, in a sense, all clowns. "We are going to clown our way through life making believe that we know everything and when the time comes, possibly no one will be prepared after all to enter the next world," Sekaquaptewa explains. The clowns show us the futility of believing that we can be perfect, correct, or confident of ourselves. They behave scandalously and so they make us think about morality. They inspire the Hopi to protect their social and sacred values – the Kachinas shower the clowns with pebbles to teach them proper respect – and at the same time to laugh at their inevitable human weakness.

Hopi religion does not revolve around a quest for mystical experience; it focuses instead on occasions that combine social, ceremonial, and practical activities. The Kachina ceremonies require broad cooperation and participation. They are the forum for teaching the Hopi way of life to children. They also provide an opportunity for individual expression in singing, dancing, playacting, costume- and mask-making. The Hopi are famous for their hand-carved Kachina dolls, which they call *tihu* and are one of the many manifestations of the Kachinas in this world. The human world is thus tightly bound to that of the Kachinas and through the Kachinas to the universe.

It is this binding quality that lies at the heart of religion. The word "religion" itself comes from the Latin *religio*, meaning a bond or an obligation. The bond may be between a people and their god or gods, between them and their ancestors, between the people themselves, or all of these at once, but it is a contract in all the usual senses, entailing obligations and exchanges. The Romans thought of religion very much in social terms. It was essentially a family matter, since each Roman household had its own gods, but it was also a political and cultural matter. As Rome enlarged its empire, Romans encountered and conquered other peoples whom they perceived as being "bound together" by their own religious beliefs and customs. Rome was remarkably tolerant in matters of religion and that tolerance sprang from the peculiarly Roman emphasis on religion as being largely a social – not revealed or personal – institution.

The problem is that religion is not merely a social phenomena. It does indeed have its public and collective aspect; so much so that the French sociologist Emile Durkheim went so far as to describe it as society worshiping itself or, more precisely, worshiping the image of its own solidarity, projected onto a supernatural plane. There is another side to religious life, however. This is the aspect of it that is directed toward the total scheme of things, that seeks to imbue the universe with meaning. This universe can only be expressed in terms and symbols which come to us through our own language and culture and reflect the structure of our society; but it demands special means of communication. These have been developed, particularly, in the mystical, secret, or "esoteric" traditions. Where a religion has a supreme god, the esoteric tradition involves intimacy with that god. Sufism, the mystical form of Islam, has a long history of "brotherhoods" devoted to ecstatic and personal knowledge and love of god. In Islam as well as in

NIMAN KACHINAS

THE HOPI *NIMAN*, OR "GOING HOME" CEREMONY, IS A SIXTEEN-DAY EVENT THAT BEGINS AROUND THE TIME OF THE SUMMER SOLSTICE. THE NIMAN IS ONE OF THE MOST DRAMATIC AND SOLEMN OF ALL KACHINA CEREMONIES. IT IS AN OCCASION TO BID FAREWELL TO THE KACHINAS WHO RETURN HOME TO THE SAN FRANCISCO MOUNTAINS FOR ANOTHER WINTER. THE NIMAN HAS BEEN LIKENED TO CHRISTMAS BECAUSE SPECIAL CARE IS TAKEN THAT ALL CHILDREN RECEIVE GIFTS FROM THE KACHINAS BEFORE THEY LEAVE.

Painting on a Greek vase depicting ears of grain on a tomb. Grain was shown to initiates at the end of mystery rites to symbolize resurrection, happy afterlife, and man's compact with the gods.

Hinduism, Buddhism, Jainism, and Christianity, individual ascetics (literally, those who perform "exercises" in the pursuit of religious knowledge and experience) attempt to overcome the barriers between humanity and god through chanting, contemplation, and physical suffering.

In Greek antiquity this quest for resolution or knowledge took the form of what were called "mystery cults," rituals with a special objective – the care and tending of the soul – that set them apart from other ceremonial attentions to the gods. What also distinguished mystery cults from other kinds of ceremonies was that no matter how many initiates there were (and at the most famous cult, at Eleusis near Athens, there were thousands of initiates at one time) a special or personal relationship to the gods and the other world was established. The relationship was personal because it was not taught, in the usual sense, but *experienced*. Aristotle, himself an initiate, claimed that "those who are being initiated are not to learn anything but to experience something and be put into a certain condition."

We have little direct testimony of what actually went on at Eleusis, but we can guess at the general outline of the proceedings. The festival began with a grand procession from Athens to Eleusis, involving ritual washing in the sacred rivers and enlivened by much joking and laughter. This was followed by several days of sacrifices at minor sanctuaries. Finally the initiates gathered in a great hall, consumed a sacred drink, and witnessed the reenactment of a sacred drama concerning the goddess Demeter, her daughter Persephone, and Hades, the god of the underworld. The festival drew on ideas of fertility in agriculture – what is "underground" is the source of "wealth"; the grain is cut and dies but yields seed and grows again – to symbolize the journey of the soul. In this way, the promise was fulfilled that the initiate would find that death "is not only not an evil, but a good thing."

With the rise of Christianity, the mystery religions faded as institutions, but they influenced the practices of "gnostic" Jewish-Christian and Neoplatonic sects. *Gnosis* (meaning knowledge) was the particular knowledge of how the soul could journey through various spheres of matter and intermediary levels of spirit to be at one with God. As at Eleusis, this gnosis was not purely intellectual. Neither learning nor blind "faith," it was superior to both. Gnosis was an awareness or insight difficult to convey in words and more amenable to symbols and images. It was at once a revelation and a redemption of the human condition.

The gnostics had a radical solution to a problem that has troubled the religious mind for thousands of years. If god or the gods are powerful and good, then where does evil come from and why is it here? The gnostic answer was that humanity had fallen from the world of light to be trapped in creation, itself the product not of god but of a lesser power or demon. Expelled from paradise, we are strangers in this world, exiled from our true home. It followed, of course, that the life and martyrdom of Jesus did not, in the gnostic view, sanctify our world, nor did it bear witness to the power of God and of goodness in the universe. No wonder the Christian church persecuted the gnostics as dangerous heretics.

This desire to *know* the human condition through mystical experience is, if not universal, at least very widespread. Certainly it has been a very prominent part of all "world religions" as well as of indigenous cultures. What has happened, then, to the mystical impulse in our own pragmatic societies? Why is it that we do not give to our seers and mystics the respect and power we give to our political leaders?

The dynamics of organized religion have more than a little to do with it. What are called "revealed" religions – religions that begin as divine revelations to some chosen person, like Moses or Christ or Muhammad – assume, as they must, that people may know God directly. The chosen person or prophet is a charismatic leader who disseminates a message from God and gathers followers until there is a religious community that will carry on after his death. After the death of the prophet and his immediate followers, however, this charisma or grace begins to fade. As Max Weber, who made an exhaustive study of this process in world religions, discovered, religious inspiration becomes *routinized:* it eventually turns into a set of rules and practices that no longer require inner motivation. A kind of bureaucracy – the priests, the monks and nuns, the secular functionaries – has its own interests to advance and protect.

The Christian Church has never been very comfortable with mystical experience that is independent of corporate worship or conventional prayer. There is a long history of Church distrust of individual religious inspiration. While mysticism is at the heart of many religions, it is a zone of danger from the institutional point of view. It threatens the Church's established role as mediator between society and God. If mystical practice goes so far as to dissolve the individual ego of the devotee, it may even lead him to confuse himself with God. A mystic may seek union with God, but one famous Sufi was beheaded for saying that in the moment of ecstasy he "was God."

Organized religion, then, wants the faithful to be pious, but it wants them to channel their piety through its own institutions. Mystics threaten this arrangement by seeking direct access to the divine. From a church's point of view, therefore, they are acceptable in principle but subversive in practice. So ascetics have sometimes been persecuted in one century and canonized in the next.

Yet some societies, usually those that do not subscribe to a major religion with its attendant bureaucracy, continue to respect their mystics and seers, who are considered to be blessed with special powers. This is especially the case in societies that rely on shamans to communicate with the spirit world. A shaman, like an oracle, derives his powers from what is perceived to be direct contact with the extrahuman world. He or she is more or less drafted into the job by signs of a spiritual gift or sensibility. Sometimes the person so designated is reluctant to take on the role, because a shaman's training often consists of physically demand-

An enduring gnostic image is the tree as *axis mundi,* the center of the world. This fifteenth-century *Dream of the Virgin* shows Christ crucified on a dreamlike tree of life growing from his mother's side. The significance of tree worship persists in the Christian practice of erecting Christmas trees.

Ignacio, a Makuna
shaman, becomes a
jaguar in spirit form
as he experiences
the visions induced
by the hallucinogenic
yage.

An image painted by Makuna men on the village longhouse while under the influence of *yage*.

ing and frightening trials. Ultimately, however, the shaman has little choice because the spirit world does not let the candidate rest until this role has been accepted.

Among some peoples the taking of consciousness-altering drugs is a necessary adjunct to proper and effective shamanic practice. In South America, one of the most common of these drugs is *yage*, known to the Inca peoples of the Andean highlands as *ayahuasca*, "the vine of the soul." The Inca associated it with the special powers they believed the jungle-dwelling Indians possessed. Individuals react differently to yage, of course, but most people feel nauseated. They may vomit or experience acute diarrhea, or both at once. They feel numb about the jaw, and the pulse slows down. The body trembles and seems out of control, but the mind is released, soaring away in hallucinations that may be either exhilaratingly beautiful or quite terrifying. The terror, as much as the beauty, is very much part of the yage experience. People regularly see jaguars or anacondas, the huge and fearsome snakes that live along the rivers and crush unwary humans in their coils. They may feel clusters of snakes dropping onto them, twining around their extremities or otherwise threatening them while they are powerless to run away or resist.

If drinking yage is so unpleasant and terrifying, why then do people persist in using it? Because they believe the terror is something a person must overcome in order to attain knowledge. Needless to say, the insights acquired through taking yage depend very much on the training of the taker. An experienced shaman can

MYSTIC POETS

The quest for direct transcendental experience is not restricted solely to traditional or small-scale societies. In the West there is a vast body of mystical poetry associated with various devotional practices, some religiously orthodox and some unorthodox. The writings of the sixteenth-century Spanish mystic St. John of the Cross describe the journey of the soul through the *noche oscura,* the dark night, toward an inner god:

> On that glad night
> In secret, for no one saw me,
> Nor did I look at anything,
> With no other light or guide
> Than the one that burned in my heart;
>
> This guided me
> More surely than the light of noon
> To where he waited for me
> — him I knew so well —
> In a place where no one appeared.

see many things while under its influence. A novice may only be suffused with panic or lost in an ecstatic vision he cannot interpret.

A shaman may take yage in order to witness an unsolved case of murder or theft and to identify the culprit. He may also use it to see if another shaman is sending sickness to infect a patient whose illness does not respond to treatment. Among the Makuna, a shaman is called a jaguar because these creatures are thought to be the most humanlike of the animals, both intelligent and dangerous. The shaman becomes a jaguar-man in the defense of his community, traveling in the dark forest, dangerous to meet by accident. Shamans often feel in their visions as if their souls have left their bodies and are traveling as free spirits, soaring across the heavens, looking down on mountains, visiting cities. On these journeys, they may communicate with demons or deities or experience ecstatic union with god.

The Indians interpret these visions as clairvoyant experiences, enabling them to see beyond the limits of the ordinary reality that surrounds them. Their perceptions have occasionally been supported by outsiders. Ken Kensinger, an anthropologist working in eastern Peru, reported that the Cashinahua Indians gave him detailed descriptions of the town of Pucallpa (which they had never visited but had only seen in their hallucinations) that he was able to confirm himself when he went there. After another session of drinking yage, six of nine men told him that they had seen the death of his mother's father. Two days later he received confirmation of that news over the radio.

Shamans are normally less interested in clairvoyance, however, than they are in carrying out their responsibility to maintain the balance between the natural and the supernatural worlds. These realms are believed to be intimately related, and the shaman's mediation between them actually serves as a powerful check on disruptive behavior within the community. What yage-drinkers see, then, in their vine-induced visions, is not simply what is beyond but – if they have the experience and wisdom to perceive it – the relationship between the spirit world and this one. That is what they mean when they say that they take yage in order to know or when they say, more poetically, that taking yage is like spiritual coitus. It allows them to experience the union that they believe to be the true reality, instead of the discrete entities of the apparent reality in which they live their everyday lives.

The shaman's journey, when he leaves his body and travels in search of understanding, of a fuller experience of reality, is a kind of pilgrimage, and pilgrimage is common to religious traditions all over the world. Believers or seekers after belief in widely differing faiths have for centuries journeyed to sacred places, where the natural and the supernatural are thought to meet. They go in search of many things – of faith, hope, cures and favors in this life or good fortune in the next; but above all they seek to *know*, to put themselves and their lives in a cosmic context and to seek an understanding of their place in the scheme of things. This understanding is forged, not by each person alone, but by the experience of a collective journey and a collective endurance.

The Huichol Indians, who live in the Sierra Madre Occidental of central Mexico, are famous for their spectacular yarn paintings that form part of a tradition of sacred art that is intimately linked to their pilgrimages. Every year groups of Huichol, each led by a shaman-priest known as a *mara'akame*, set out on a sacred journey to Wirikuta, hundreds of miles away to the east. They do this to retrace the steps of their ancestors, the Ancient Ones who, in their pilgrimages, had knit together the sacred elements of the Huichol world: the ocean, the mountains, and the high plateau of Wirikuta. Modern Huichols make this journey so that they can "find their lives" after the manner of the Ancient Ones. The pilgrimage to Wirikuta is for them a journey to the core of their religious experience.

All Huichols have been prepared since childhood for this pilgrimage, and none more so than the mara'akame. The spiritual and therefore the physical safety of the pilgrims is in his hands. He must watch over them carefully so that they come through the ecstatic ordeal unscathed, so that they may "find their hearts." On the eve of departure he kindles a sacred fire and prays to it, asking its blessing, for it was Grandfather Fire in human form who led the first pilgrimage of the Ancestors to Wirikuta. The mara'akame becomes Grandfather Fire, ready to lead his people as they retrace the route of the Ancestors from the ocean to the sacred desert.

At dawn on the day of departure, the mara'akame leads the pilgrims out in single file. Traditionally, they set out on a rugged journey that took weeks to complete on foot. Nowadays they often go most of the way in the back of a truck, specially rented for the trip, with only the final and most sacred stages carried out on foot. Although the journey is physically less arduous for modern Huichols, it is becoming more and more difficult in other ways. Mexican landowners are fencing off portions of the Huichol route and occasionally refusing the pilgrims passage. The springs sacred to the Huichol are often polluted or surrounded by barbed wire to keep out animals.

Still, the Huichols persevere. As they near their destination, they must prepare themselves by cleansing themselves of all human failings. They gather one evening round the fire and each one makes a public confession of all illicit sexual escapades in which he or she has indulged since they last went on the pilgrimage. Each sexual transgression is recorded by tying a knot in a piece of string. New pilgrims (unless they are very young) may need long pieces of string to record a lifetime of transgressions. This ceremony is interspersed with hilarity as both men and women are prompted and cajoled into admitting all their liaisons.

Other ceremonies are more solemn. The pilgrims must cast off their mortal selves and be transformed into Ancestors – into gods – in order to enter Wirikuta. To do so they must give up, as far as possible, all human activities. They must forgo bathing and sexual relations and cut back severely on eating, drinking, sleeping, and even relieving themselves so that as little as possible of their mortality clings to them. As they draw closer to Wirikuta, they take leave of their own world by reversing it, turning it back to front and upside down. Old men act like little children. Men and women become each other, casting off divisions of gender. Sadness becomes happiness, ugliness becomes beauty; the moon becomes brighter, the sun darker, so that they too blend into each other.

By now the pilgrims, spiritually prepared, are nearing Wirikuta. They pass through little Mexican towns, leaving offerings in the churches at the feet of the Virgin Mary, whom they address as Grandmother Growth and believe was one of the Ancestors. For them, the statues of the Virgin mark the places where she stopped when she made her own pilgrimage to Wirikuta. Finally, after days of travel, the mara'akame stops the truck in the middle of the desert. The pilgrims are now at the "gates of Wirikuta" and must complete their journey on foot.

They spend their first night in Wirikuta in prayer, dancing, chanting, and fasting. They are excited to have arrived. The next morning the mara'akame leads the pilgrims on the sacred hunt for peyote. He takes out a small, diamond-shaped yarn weaving and with it he blesses the four directions before pointing it to the fifth direction – the heart, the center of all. Then he hunts the supernatural deer, whose footprints appear in the desert as buttons of peyote, a spineless cactus with tiny pink flowers. He fires a sacred arrow near the first plant, blesses it, and eats its crown. The pilgrims may now follow suit, gathering and eating their own peyote buttons.

The pilgrims scatter over the desert, scooping up peyote with digging sticks and long knives. They blend in with the cacti till their shimmering silhouettes, topped off by their feathered hats, are indistinguishable in the haze from the eerie trees. They hunt for hours till they have filled their baskets with peyote, enough for all the ceremonies of the coming year.

Now the pilgrims (peyoteros in Spanish) sit quietly, eating peyote and talking in low tones among themselves. The button of the peyote contains mescaline. It tastes bitter and, after causing initial feelings of nausea, it produces visions in those who eat it. Many of the pilgrims experience strong hallucinations there in Wirikuta. Others may taste the peyote too cautiously or be unready for it. They will not have any visions at all. But they will have other chances. The taking of peyote is central to Huichol religion and they will be invited to eat it again and again in their own villages, or if they should ever come back to Wirikuta.

Most Huichol both fear and yearn for the experience of taking peyote in a state of preparedness in Wirikuta itself, for then they truly become one with the Ancestors. Barbara Myerhoff, who was until her death one of the foremost authorities on Huichol religion, wrote that Huichol long for the ecstasy of Wirikuta, for the feeling of being at one with the Ancestors, of losing themselves in a state of fusion

**R
E
S
U
R
R
E
C
T
I
N
G

T
H
E

W
O
R
L
D**

Seventy-year-old Pancho was the leader of this pilgrimage – a journey he had made as many as forty times. The old shaman announced to the pilgrims gathered with him at the temple (*calihuey*): "When we go to Wirikuta, all of us together, we go to find our lives. We are all children of the same sun. This is the path of the gods. If we don't make the journey and leave our offerings, the world won't exist anymore."

Pancho blessed each pilgrim with his feathered baton (*movieri*). Then the two dozen Huichol companions – men, women, and children – gathered their offerings and their meager food supplies and walked single file out of the temple. The inexorable peregrination to Wirikuta had begun. Like the characters in an alternative *Canterbury Tales*, each pilgrim had his or her own story, his or her own reason for participating in the journey.

One family, Chalio, his wife Beatrice, and their infant son, were on their first pilgrimage. Chalio had only recently given up his dream of becoming the first Catholic priest among his people. Something was wrong in his heart, he said; he wanted to feel the faith of his Huichol heritage. Chalio's personal journey was an arduous pilgrim's progress. His companions doubted his sincerity and tested him in many ways. In the desert of Wirikuta rumors circulated that Chalio was afraid to eat the peyote (hallucinogenic cactus) because the visions would be too strong for him. However, Chalio found something on his pilgrimage that others did not. He was reassured of his commitment to work as the secular Huichol spokesperson to the outside world.

Pancho watched over all the pilgrims, including the anxious Chalio. Around the fire each night Pancho chanted, danced, and told stories, always guiding the listeners toward a greater understanding of their sacred journey. This was the time to remember one's path, to resurrect the world, and to renew one's relationship with the ancestors and the gods. On their last night together in the desert, Pancho called upon Grandmother Growth to ensure the survival of the peyote for the next pilgrims. Thirty seconds later a sudden rain – the only one in weeks – poured down. And then the shower ended as quickly as it had begun. Had Pancho brought the rains? He walked away expressionless – he wasn't about to tell. The pilgrims prepared for their return to the mountains, having secured the blessing of the gods.

with the universe and with their fellow humans. They fear it too, though, for they are tempted to linger in ecstasy, to remain in paradise, and if they were not strong enough to return, their souls would be severed from their bodies and they would die. It is the mara'akame who has the experience and the strength, acquired through years of preparation, to lead them out of their ecstatic union and bring them back to their ordinary lives. He does not let them linger. Sometimes they flee from Wirikuta, running, weeping, lamenting the loss of the paradise they long for and can only experience so briefly. Only the mara'akame is strong enough to move in and out of paradise at will. Others must do so in his care, or they risk being lost forever. The mara'akame helps the Huichol to accept the transient nature of the experience. They know that their own world is incomplete, but they also know it is made whole through their experience in Wirikuta. It is this knowledge that gives meaning to their lives and accounts for their insistence that the Huichol way of life is the most beautiful on earth.

This mystical ecstasy, the feeling of being one with a universe in which the ordinary oppositions between sun and moon, male and female, old and young have evaporated into a cosmic unity, is the central experience of Huichol religion. Huichols do not discuss its details (or their visions) with those around them, even though pilgrims on the way to Wirikuta must each make a knot in one long cord to show that they have given their hearts to one another and to the mara'akame. Yet it is a personal experience that must be sought only in the company of a congregation under the care of a mara'akame.

The contrasts between peyote use among the Huichols and drug use in the modern industrial world are instructive. Although the Huichol do indeed take peyote individually and more or less secularly for a variety of reasons on all kinds of occasions, their use of the drug is generally regulated by the communal and ritual nature of its most important function and by its symbolic importance. Use of hallucinogens in the Americas is very ancient and probably originated with the symbolic systems and religions of hunting peoples in Eurasia. Indeed, for the Huichol, peyote is associated in a trinity with deer and maize, and allows the Huichol to recover their identity as hunting peoples, for they say they "hunt" the peyote as their ancestors hunted deer. In ritually connecting peyote, deer, and maize, they place their own lives in the context of a sacred history. Hallucinogens are of great importance in societies that place a high value on transformation (for example the man-animal transformations of the shaman or the transformation of souls through transmigration) rather than on the fixity of species and on the barrier between the animate and the inanimate.

By contrast, when we speak of "drugs" in modern societies, we normally refer to substances that are illegal to buy and consume, such as opium, heroin, cocaine, and marijuana. We do not refer in this way to caffeine, tobacco, or alcohol, all of which produce physical changes in the bodies of people who consume them, can

THE OTHER DRUG CRISIS

Our current drug crisis is a tragedy born of a phony system of classification. For reasons that are little more than accidents of history, we have divided a group of nonfood substances into two categories: items purchasable for supposed pleasure (such as alcohol) and illicit drugs. The categories were once reversed. Opiates were legal in America before the Harrison Narcotics Act of 1914; and members of the Women's Christian Temperance Union, who campaigned against alcohol during the day, drank their valued "women's tonics" at night, products laced with laudanum (tincture of opium).

I could abide — though I would still oppose — our current intransigence if we applied the principle of total interdiction to all harmful drugs. But how can we possibly defend our current policy based on a dichotomy that encourages us to view one class of substances as a preeminent scourge while the two most dangerous and life-destroying substances by far, alcohol and tobacco, form a second class advertised in neon on every street corner of urban America? And why, moreover, should heroin be viewed with horror while chemical cognates that are no different from heroin than lemonade is from iced tea perform work of enormous compassion by relieving the pain of terminal cancer patients in their last days?

From Stephen J. Gould, "Taxonomy as Politics." *Dissent,* Winter 1990, pp. 73-78.

THE NEW AGE?

In the 1980s, a vast array of nontraditional spiritual beliefs achieved remarkable popularity throughout North America and Western Europe: channeling, benign witchcraft, shamanism, crystals, and many others gained adherents. There was renewed interest in Eastern religion and a quasi-religious devotion to the environment and world peace. Despite their differences, the new believers all agreed that Western life had become empty in the absence of spirituality. The spirituality they sought, however, was not found within the established Western churches that offered a transcendent deity. Rather, New Agers sought direct contact with the divine, often trying to find the divine within themselves or at least to feel part of a global and universal harmony.

What accounts for this shift in religious inspiration? Writing in the 1930s, Carl Jung observed an interesting parallel between the secular training one receives in the West and the type of alternative spirituality Westerners seek. Westerners are raised on the values of individualism and science; thus when they seek out spirituality they insist on direct experience of the divine. It is as though they are looking for a god whose presence can be "empirically" verified. It remains to be seen whether the New Age will coalesce into an enduring movement or whether it is part of a longer cycle of countercultural protests against the prevailing values of secular science.

be highly addictive, and can involve great medical and social costs. In other words, "drugs" for us are countercultural, whereas the use of hallucinogens in tribal societies is not only sanctioned but is actually sacred. As a result of these cultural and legal inconsistencies, the Native American Church, which has adopted white Christian ethics and theology, has been persecuted in the United States and its faithful occasionally prosecuted as drug users because they take peyote during their ceremonies. This criminalization of the Native American Church is a striking example of official obtuseness, but it is hardly surprising. Given that American society is uneasy about mystical experience and fanatically opposed (officially) to the use of certain kinds of drugs, the combination of the two is unlikely to be treated with much tolerance.

The point is that modern society is intensely secular. Even those who regret this admit it. Social theorists tend to assume that modernization is itself a process of secularization, which has not only undermined people's religious beliefs, but has also tended to deprive them of their spirituality. In the industrial nations of the West many of the people who believe in God do not expect to come into close contact with the divine, except after death – and some of them are not too sure about it even then. I suspect that many of us are comfortable with the point of view expressed by the philosopher Leibniz, who felt that god is a powerful figure but rather remote from the affairs of this world. Leibniz was sarcastic about Newton's feeling that God remained involved in the affairs of humankind even after he had established the laws of nature. Why, he asked, should God need to wind up his watch and clean it from time to time as if he had not had the foresight to set it in perpetual motion? This distant, almost abstract, conception of the divine is likely to appeal to people who are preoccupied with this world and do not want to worry too much about what lies beyond – to us moderns, in fact. Yet if we hold this view and act on it, busying ourselves with technological understanding and the accumulation of wealth in pursuit of pleasure, we are likely to feel that we have created a spiritual vacuum and to encounter that "great loneliness of spirit" of which Chief Seattle spoke so eloquently. Indeed it seems that those who live in the secular and industrialized West are already searching for ways to fill the vacuum in their lives left by "organized" religion and the numbing delights of mass society. We live in a world that prides itself on its modernity, yet is hungry for wholeness, hungry for meaning. At the same time it is a world that marginalizes those very impulses that might fill the void. The pilgrimage toward the divine, the openness to knowledge that transcends ordinary experience, the very idea of feeling at one with the universe, these are impulses which we tolerate at the fringes, where they are held at bay by our indifference. The irony is that, after excluding the mystical tradition from our cultural mainstream and claiming to find it irrelevant to our concerns, so many of us feel empty without it.

It seems that we denigrate our capacity to dream and so condemn ourselves to

The Nyinba people of north-west Nepal have passed down a prophecy for generations that there is a hidden valley near the sacred mountain of Helambhu. According to the prophecy, when chaos comes to rule the world a lama will lead the people to the hidden valley. Twenty years ago many people set out on the search, but they never found the valley. A Nyinban lama explains that the valley is only there when one is truly prepared. If one is ready, it may not be very far away.

live in a disenchanted world. Shorn of the knowledge that we are part of something greater than ourselves, we lose also the sense of responsibility that comes with it. It is this connectedness that tribal societies cherish and that we cannot bring ourselves to seek. But if we do not listen to other traditions, do not even listen to our inner selves, then what will the future hold for our stunted and overconfident civilization?

THE TIGHTROPE OF POWER

Evening in central Brazil. The accumulated heat of the day pressed down from a butter-colored sky. I was standing on the bank of the Rio das Mortes, longing for nightfall, when I heard a cry from the forest on the far bank. "Somebody coming back from hunting," I thought – and then I remembered that the Xavante Indians from our village were not trekking on the other side of the big river. Who could be over there? I peered at the jungle but could see no one. The call came again. This time I answered, using a shrill falsetto and then letting my voice slither down into the depths, the way the Indians had taught me to when I wanted it to carry a long way.

A Xavante stepped out from among the trees and then hesitated, startled to see a white man shouting back at him. For a moment it looked as if he might duck back again into the jungle, but he thought better of it. Instead he called again and gestured frantically for me to come over and fetch him in the canoe that was moored on our side. I noted that his voice cracked on the high notes as he hallooed across the river, and he could hardly manage the deep stops at all. He was obviously breathless and very nervous. What was he doing here? And why was he traveling with no rifle, no bow and arrows, nothing to hunt with?

As I and my fishing companion brought him over I noticed that he was bleeding from the shoulder and the thigh. My Xavante "brothers" Waarodi and Sibupa arrived and took charge of the newcomer. They marched off along the trail back to the village, with Waarodi in the lead and the stranger sandwiched between him and his brother. I brought up the rear, thinking that this looked like a posse that had just made an arrest, although I knew it was the way the Xavante always walked. Besides, they had sat down with the stranger in the canoe, all haste forgotten, and wept together, as Xavante do when a kinsman returns to his people after a long absence. Who was this mysterious stranger and why was he so nervous?

I had to wait until the senior men of the community gathered in their council at the center of the village before I learned his story. It came out in bits and pieces in the dramatic, barking rhetoric that the Xavante use on formal occasions. The stranger came from Marawasede, a community many days' journey to the north. I pricked up my ears at this, for his was one of the "unknown" Xavante villages that had not yet established any friendly contact with the outside world. The newcomer told us that the people of Marawasede were angry with him. He had run away in order to avoid being killed, but they had chased him along the trails. For days they had tracked him and fired arrows at him whenever they caught sight of him. They had wounded him in the shoulder and in the leg, but he had eluded them and succeeded in reaching the Rio das Mortes, though he had not slept at all for days and had eaten only what he could gather in his flight.

It seemed that the chief of Marawasede had died. His kinsmen suspected sorcery and used this as an excuse to carry out a purge of the men of another lineage who might have challenged them for control of the village. Our stranger, being of the threatened lineage, had prudently fled just in the nick of time. We would of course give him sanctuary. There was no question of that. Xavante custom dictated that political refugees should always be taken in. After all, nobody knew when they themselves might be needing such a favor from some other community. Besides, everyone had relatives everywhere. Not close relatives perhaps, but close enough that the relationship could be recognized and relied upon in time of need. So a Xavante fleeing from his village would always find relatives to live with in another community.

There was a constant ebb and flow of people between Xavante villages. Sometimes it was just a trickle of restless young men looking for a change of scene or a change of spouse; at others it could involve minor migrations, whole lineages splitting off from their villages and moving with women and children and all their worldly goods to other communities. These human eddies were carefully watched by the chiefs as they strove to maintain a precarious balance among their own people.

A Xavante chief has authority only in his own community and even there he has no real power as we understand it. He does not even have a clearly defined official position. He is simply the acknowledged leader of a strong lineage. To become such a leader, he must distinguish himself by his powers of persuasion, the wisdom of his suggestions, and, above all, the force of his oratory. But it is not enough for him to gain influence in this way. He must also be supported by a strong lineage, with enough men in it to back him up if his decisions are challenged. Occasionally a man from a small lineage may succeed, by sheer force of personality, in persuading stronger lineages to ally with his so that he becomes the leader of a dominant faction, but this is rare. Nor do communities necessarily have a single leader. There may be a number of men, leaders of competing lineages or factions, who are considered chiefs by their followers, and who vie for influence within the village.

The village in which my wife and I lived in 1958 had only one chief. Apewen, who bestowed his own name on me, was a man who inspired respect. He had been a famous warrior in his youth and was supported in his old age by a strong lineage, teeming with young men, and by plenty of allies from other families. Apewen, too, had carried out his purges. When his brother died, Apewen had directed that the dead man's son-in-law be killed as a sorcerer along with seven others of the same lineage. Apewen's actions had put his own faction firmly in the saddle, and there had been no internal strife in the community since then. Apewen, however, was unusual and was known throughout Xavante country as a strong chief.

Knowing all this, I was surprised that it was not he who stood up in the men's council to exchange speeches with the refugee stranger. It was his son-in-law Suwapte who did that. I soon understood why. Suwapte himself was a refugee from Marawasede who had come to our village, married Apewen's daughter, and settled down in Apewen's household. He was, therefore, the local expert on the dark intrigues of the Marawasede community. Besides, the newcomer was a member of Apewen's own people, and it is traditional in Xavante councils for two men to speak simultaneously, each representing half of the village. The newcomer was Apewen's kinsman and therefore belonged to his half of the village, so he was cross-questioned by Suwapte, speaking for the other side.

In this respect Xavante councils are similar to parliaments. There is a "government" supported by a majority, which may be a coalition of different groups, and an "opposition" consisting of a minority. But there is no state. There is nobody to enforce the decisions of the parliament except the people in it, who enforce the decisions against one another. What this means is that the community as a whole can only act against someone if he has done something so dreadful that even his own kin will not defend him. Otherwise, it comes to a test of strength between the kin of the accusers and the defenders of the accused. If the matter is sufficiently serious – an accusation of sorcery or some other kind of killing – the weaker group will often find it wise to move to some other village, or the person accused will flee. Banishing a person from the community is thus the major penalty in such a system, and the custom of giving sanctuary to outlaws provides the flexibility that makes it work.

A Xavante chief therefore walks a tightrope. In order to be recognized as a chief, he must be passionate, competitive, even ruthless. However, once he has achieved that status he is referred to as a watchman, a man who looks over and looks after his community, and then he needs to be a mediator and builder of consensus. Otherwise his community will break up, people will move away, and the very basis of his authority will be undermined.

I used to enjoy listening to Apewen in the men's council. He would get to his feet in the dying light of the evening, brush off the dust from the deerskin on which he had been sitting, and casually launch into a speech that held his audience spellbound. Not that Xavante ever display what we would call rapt attention. They would sit or lie in a wide circle, belching or commenting out loud when they felt like it. Occasionally a man would get to his feet and talk, too. Then Apewen and his opposing speaker would intertwine their oratory in a way that was intended to knit the village together. Apewen took mediation seriously and devoted to it all his skill as a leader and an arbiter. His people respected him and admired his wisdom even when they disagreed with him.

The whole setting reminded me of something I could not quite recall. One night I remembered what it was. Apewen was like a character out of the Icelandic sagas, those vivid epics that describe the lives and feuds of the Norsemen who settled Iceland in the tenth century. They, too, were strong-minded individualists. In fact, they had come to Iceland to escape the growing power of the Norwegian kings. In Iceland they were their own masters. How, though, does a society of strong-minded individualists work when there is no one in authority over them? The sagas provide the answer. They tell us of assemblies that all men were entitled to attend and where all disputes and grievances were debated. At first, assemblies were confined to particular districts, but eventually a general assembly was formed to which men could come from any part of the island. An assembly was called a *Thing*, referring to the public affairs it dealt with, and in concept it was similar to a *republic*, which also deals with *res* (things or affairs) *publica* (public). The general assembly, known as the *Althing*, met for the first time in 930, when the people of Iceland came together to establish their republic. The Althing was the first parliamentary assembly in the Western world, the ancestor of the modern parliaments in the Scandinavian countries, each of which is to this day known as the *Folkething* (*folketing* in the modern spelling) or people's assembly.

Nevertheless, in Iceland – as among the Xavante – there was no state. People were expected to fend for themselves, and the sagas explain that people cultivated friendship as well as kinship in order to broaden their alliances. When a boat arrived from Scandinavia, its captain had to choose carefully where he would put in and whose hospitality he and his crew would accept, for it would lock him into a system of friendships (and enmities) that he might be only dimly aware of. The same was true for those who traveled overland within the island. Accepting hospitality along the way was a necessity, but it was also a political act. People would sometimes push on in spite of bad weather when they knew that the local farmer was feuding with one of their friends. To complicate things even further, people were touchy about their honor and felt bound to pursue feuds, particularly blood feuds, endlessly through the generations.

There is a chilling passage in one of the most famous sagas of all, the Laxdaela Saga, where Gudrun, the beautiful and tragic heroine, is alone with her husband, Bolli, in a hut up by their pastures. She and Bolli send off their workers early in the morning but do not go with them. Gudrun is pregnant, so they go back to bed, which costs Bolli his life. They hear a group of men approaching. Realizing what this means, Bolli sends Gudrun to the stream to do some washing. He remains in the hut and defends himself until he is killed by the men who are taking blood vengeance on him in a feud. The men then speak with Gudrun who calmly continues her washing, all the while memorizing their names and faces so that her unborn child may one day exact vengeance in return.

Iceland in the tenth and eleventh centuries was unique among the countries of Europe. It was a relatively prosperous society of farmers, traders, and seafarers who managed their own affairs without submitting to the authority of a king. The republican experiment did not last, however, for ambitious men struggled to establish their power at the expense of the commonwealth. In their feuds with one another they sought the backing of outsiders, particularly the Norwegian kings, and plunged the country into a period of violence and anarchy against which the mediators of the Althing were helpless. Eventually, in 1262, the desperate Icelanders brought their own republic to an end by swearing allegiance to the king of Norway. It was not till nearly seven hundred years later that they got their republic back.

The sad end of the early Icelandic experiment seemed to indicate that people must sooner or later trade freedom for order. Medieval Europeans, at least, certainly saw it that way. When they came in contact with tribal societies, they were appalled by their anarchy. As a Spanish observer wrote disparagingly of the American Indians, they had "*ni rey, ni ley, ni grey*" (no king, no law, no community). For Europeans at that time, there could be no law without the coercive power of the king, and without law no orderly society was possible.

The early explorers were, however, quite wrong about tribal societies. The contrast between tribal democracies and the centralized societies that prey on them is not one of order and disorder, violence and peace. It is instead a contrast between societies in which no one has a monopoly on the legitimate use of force and others in which those rights are vested in a king or a state. As we all know, violence is by no means absent from modern societies. Our age has witnessed a fearful amount of brutality imposed by states on their own populations. In fact, the twentieth century has been one of the bloodiest in history, not only because of the wars between countries employing weapons of mass destruction but also because modern technology has been used by ruthless rulers to cow their own subjects. Hitler and Stalin are only the most notorious examples of dictators who directed violence against their own people in the name of the state. There are literally scores of shooting wars going on at the moment, most of them between states and their own subjects.

The state guarantees order, or is supposed to. This is expressed very well by the old saying about the coming of fascism in Europe. "There are no bodies in the streets and the trains run on time." Force is the monopoly of the government. It is applied massively but, once the system is in place, relatively invisibly. Its victims are hidden in concentration camps or banished to Siberias. In tyrannies more recent still, the victims simply disappear.

It seems that people will often acquiesce in despotism for fear of anarchy. Recent history seems to indicate that the most advanced countries are more afraid of anarchy than they are of oppression. The Russians, whose whole history is a struggle to create order on the open steppes of Eurasia, have a fear of disorder (which they call *besporyadok*, the condition of not being "lined up") that has frequently led them to accept tyranny. At the other extreme, the United States, whose whole history is a determination to avoid despotism, allows more internal chaos than most other industrial nations. It values individual freedom to the point of allowing private citizens to own arsenals of weapons and puts up with rates of interpersonal violence that would be considered catastrophic in other countries.

It seems that human beings are everywhere searching for the right balance between the cowboy and the sheriff, between chaos and tyranny, between the individual and society. Industrial societies give a monopoly of power to the state in exchange for a guaranty of peace. We take this social order for granted to the extent that we tend to assume that there is anarchy and perpetual warfare in tribal or stateless societies. What we do not realize is that such societies are acutely conscious of the fragility of the social order and of the constant effort needed to maintain it. Paradoxically, the people who live in societies that do not have formal political institutions are more political than those who do not since it is up to each individual to make sure that the system works, indeed to ensure that the system continues to exist at all. They avoid anarchy only through constant and unremitting effort.

Many tribal societies go to great lengths to try to prevent the concentration of power that would erode their versions of democracy – to prevent, in effect, the formation of anything like a state. They accord their leaders prestige but not power and abandon them if they appear to be seeking power for themselves. The Iroquois, for example, developed a sophisticated confederacy in North America in which leaders served at the pleasure of their followers and had to maintain their prestige – popularity in order to hold on to their positions. These libertarians formed a league of nations sometime in the fifteenth century, before Columbus set foot in the New World. The confederacy of the Five Nations united the Mohawk, Oneida, Onondaga, Cayuga, and Seneca peoples, all of whom spoke Iroquoian languages. (They were later joined by the Tuscarora and became the Six Nations.) Cadwallader Colden, writing in the eighteenth century, remarked, "The Five nations have such absolute Notions of Liberty that they allow of no Kind of Superiority of one over another, and banish all Servitude from their Territories." The alliance was expressly intended to embody the principle of unity in diversity in order to protect its member nations and their ways of life from external attack. The Council fires of each of the five nations continued to burn as before. Just as their fires were not quenched, so were their nations not extinguished. They came together by mutual consent in the Great Council, where strict rules protected their rights. Each nation, as Colden observed:

> is an absolute Republick by itself, govern'd in all Publick affairs of War and Peace by the Sachems of Old Men, whose Authority and Power is gained by and consists wholly in the opinions of the rest of the Nation in their Wisdom and Integrity. They never execute their Resolutions by Compulsion or Force Upon any of their People. Honour and Esteem are their principal Rewards, as Shame and being Despised are their Punishments.

Such a system required that Iroquois leaders be fine orators. Like the Xavante and the Icelanders, the Iroquois expected their leaders to be eloquent mediators, skilled in argument in defense of law and persuasive in maintaining agreement among their people. Unlike the Icelanders, the Iroquois made their federal republic work for a long time. They achieved lasting success by establishing an elaborate system of checks and balances that protected the rights of the member nations while striving constantly to maintain harmony among the peoples who comprised them.

It was not the rules so much as the spirit in which the Iroquois operated their system that made it so successful. All matters of any consequence were referred to a council and major issues to the Great Council. The councillors saw their task as achieving consensus, and their procedures were designed to guarantee it. This entire approach was informed by the Great Law of Peace, the constitution of the confederacy.

The first section of the Great Law refers to the planting of the Tree of the Great Peace, a white pine that symbolizes the unity of the league. All the provisions of the constitution were committed to memory and recited by the chiefs of the confederacy with the aid of the wampum belts that served as mnemonic devices. The Great Law did not need to be written down until 1880, when the chiefs began to worry that the wampum belts indicating the Great Law's provisions might be lost or stolen.

The law sets out the rules that govern the collaboration between nations. Each nation is given a ceremonial role in the Great Council, and all of the procedures for reaching decisions encourage consensus. Much of the law concerns the nomination of the chiefs, their solemn duties while they hold office and the procedures for removing them if they abuse their position. The rights of men and women are spelled out quite explicitly. Since the Iroquois traced descent in the female line, women and men belonged to their mother's clan. Women were expected to have an

**I circle around –
I circle around
The boundaries of the earth,
The boundaries of the earth –
Wearing the long feathers I fly
Wearing the long feathers I fly.**

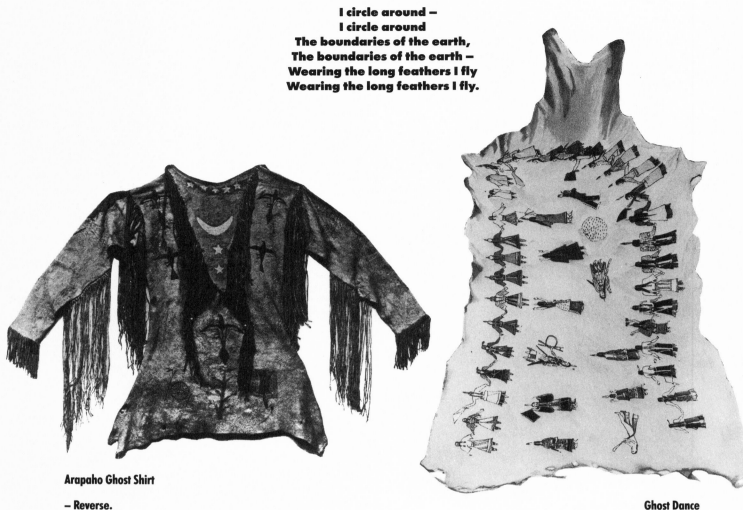

Arapaho Ghost Shirt

– Reverse.

Ghost Dance

painting on

buckskin.

THE GHOST DANCE

THE GHOST DANCE WAS A MOVEMENT THAT AROSE AMONG THE INDIANS IN THE WESTERN UNITED STATES IN THE LATE NINETEENTH CENTURY. IT WAS AN ATTEMPT TO RESURRECT A NATIVE WAY OF LIFE THAT HAD BEEN SHATTERED BY EUROPEAN EXPANSION. THE INDIAN PROPHETS OF THE GHOST DANCE LAID DOWN A MORAL CODE THAT WAS STRICTLY PACIFIST. THEY PROMISED THAT THE DANCERS WOULD COMMUNICATE WITH THE DEAD AND RECEIVE INFORMATION ABOUT THE IMPENDING RETURN OF THE ANCESTORS AND THE LIBERATION OF THE NATIVE PEOPLES FROM WHITE RULE. IN 1890, TWO HUNDRED SIOUX FOLLOWERS OF THE MOVEMENT – MEN, WOMEN, AND CHILDREN – WERE SLAUGHTERED BY PANICKING UNITED STATES TROOPS AT WOUNDED KNEE, SOUTH DAKOTA.

Burial of the Dead
at the Battlefield of
Wounded Knee S.D.
Photographed Jan 1st 1891
N.W. Photo Co. Chadron Nb.

Burial of the dead
after the battle of
Wounded Knee.

Arapaho Ghost
Dance.

important say in the affairs of this egalitarian society, and the position of clan mother was especially prestigious. Clan mothers formally inherited the titles of chieftainship and then nominated men in their clans to carry out the chiefly duties. Under a different section of the law they were entitled to admonish and remove the chiefs, if necessary. The law also made clear provisions for people or nations who wished to be adopted into the league.

The Iroquois were quite serious about the Great Law of Peace, and they had every intention of extending it to all the nations of the world, until all humankind was united in their confederacy. An astounded Jesuit father wrote in 1664 that the Iroquois were planning to send a peace embassy to the French, complete with women, children, and old men, in order to start on the process of uniting the two nations under the Great Law. The embassy was, however, ambushed by Algonquian allies of the French, and the Iroquois eventually became foes of the French and allies of the British. They were important allies to have, for their prosperous confederacy controlled most of what is now the state of New York. From New England to Illinois, the Iroquois maintained their peace, welcomed their friends, and fought off their enemies. Both the British and the French sought their help against each other in the eighteenth century.

During the protracted negotiations that the British colonists maintained with the representatives of the Six Nations, Benjamin Franklin came to know the Iroquois personally. He already knew *of* them, for he had printed the text of the treaty of 1744 on his own press and had been hugely impressed by the eloquence and wisdom of the Iroquois elders. Perhaps that was why he accepted an appointment to be one of the commissioners representing the Colony of Pennsylvania in further negotiations with the Six Nations in 1753. It was then that he met them in person and saw how their councils worked. He observed the dignity and courtesy of their procedures. They did not interrupt one another or the representatives of other peoples, even when they disagreed with them. Out of respect they always allowed a full day to elapse before giving a formal reply to any major question that was put to them.

Ben Franklin was particularly impressed by the Iroquois ability to create unity while respecting diversity, and he used them constantly as a model while urging and prodding his colleagues to opt for a union of the British colonies in North America. As he wrote in a letter to James Parker in 1751, "It would be a strange thing if Six Nations of Ignorant Savages should be capable of forming a Scheme for such an Union and be able to execute it in such a manner, as that it has subsisted Ages, and appears indissoluble, and yet a like Union should be impracticable for ten or a dozen English colonies."

Ben Franklin did not, in fact, think that the Iroquois were "ignorant savages." That was just sarcasm. On the contrary, he admired not only their political sagacity but also their way of life, and in this he was not alone. Thomas Jefferson was simi-

larly impressed, especially by the way in which the Indian leaders served their people rather than vice versa, as was the case in the "civilized" countries of the time. He came to the startling conclusion – reached by Jean de Léry before him with respect to the Indians of Brazil, as we saw in chapter 1 -- that the egalitarianism of the Indians and the absence of great differences of wealth among them ensured a higher level of happiness than was to be found in the European societies that presumed to despise them as "savages."

There is an argument raging currently about whether or not the founding fathers of the United States of America consciously modeled their new nation on the Iroquois confederacy. It seems to me, however, that the important thing is not whether they did or did not, but the fact that they *could* have. There were, after all, no models in Europe at that time for the kind of federal republic that the Americans established. Whether they did or not, the example of the League of the Iroquois was constantly in the minds of eighteenth-century American settlers. They could not forget the words of Canassatego, one of the most eloquent of the Iroquois chiefs, who told the colonial commissioners in 1744 about the peace and strength that had come to his people ever since their wise forefathers founded the league. Canassatego urged the colonists likewise to unite in a confederacy. In 1775 the colonists invited the chiefs of the Six Nations to come to Philadelphia because they were anxious to secure the support of the league in their war of independence. The colonial commissioners quoted verbatim the advice they had received thirty years earlier from Canassatego before telling the chiefs that they had now decided to take his advice. They had formed their own confederacy, which they hoped and believed would flourish and prosper as the League of the Iroquois had before them.

The League of the Iroquois, like most tribal democracies, strictly limited the powers of chiefs. Some tribal peoples go further. Feeling it is too difficult to combine the panache of a chief with the quieter skills of a mediator, they have hit upon the solution of mediators who are not chiefs. The Nuer, for example, are a fiercely democratic and individualistic people who live in the endless marshes and wide savannas of the southern Sudan. They were studied in the 1930s by Evans-Pritchard, a young Englishman who was to become one of the most influential anthropologists of his time. He admired their fierce independence and devoted his first book on them, entitled simply *The Nuer* (1940), to a description of their political institutions. These institutions were remarkable for being virtually nonexistent. The Nuer had no legal institutions and no organized political life. Evans-Pritchard's description of them is telling:

> That every Nuer considers himself as good as his neighbour is evident in their every movement. They strut about like lords of the earth, which, indeed they consider themselves to be. There is no master and no servant in their society, but only equals who regard themselves as God's noblest creation. Their respect for one another contrasts with their contempt for all other peoples. Among themselves even the suspicion of an order riles a man and he either does not carry it out or he carries it out in a casual and dilatory manner that is more insulting than a refusal.

How did these proud and egalitarian people organize their lives? Through the familiar means – a fierce loyalty to their kin, feuds when serious disagreements occurred, and accepted mechanisms for putting an end to these conflicts. This society that recognized no leaders nevertheless respected the judgment of people called leopard-skin chiefs, who mediated disputes and were able to put an end to the blood feuds that would otherwise have plunged Nuer society into violence and anarchy.

The leopard-skin chiefs derived their name from the hide they wore draped around their shoulders as the badge of their office. A leopard-skin chief had no power. His arbitration was not backed up by a powerful clan or community; it was effective only because a leopard-skin chief was revered and his person considered sacred. A Nuer who killed a man would often take refuge in the home of a leopard-skin chief, which served as a sanctuary. No one would touch the killer while he was thus protected, though they could lie in wait for him outside and take revenge if he ventured away from the confines of the chief's domain. Eventually, when tempers had cooled, the chief would visit the kin of the dead man and try to talk them into accepting cattle in payment for the life of their relative. This was not easy. It was a point of honor for Nuer to reject a settlement, saying they were determined to prosecute the feud and take vengeance on their kinsman's killer. The leopard-skin chief had to use all his powers of persuasion, which could be supplemented in extreme cases by his curse. Nuer feared the curse of a leopard-skin chief and would usually agree to a settlement rather than risk having it pronounced on them.

The remarkable thing is that this system kept a kind of order in a society of nearly a quarter of a million people. The Nuer thrived on their "anarchy" and only face a serious crisis now because of the onslaught of the state. They, like the other Nilotic peoples of the southern Sudan, have been fighting for years against the central government of the country, which is trying to incorporate them into an Arab-dominated, Islamic state. Meanwhile, the modern equivalent of their leopard-skin chief is the secretary general of the United Nations, but he does not receive the general respect that made the leopard-skin chief so effective. Nations, alas, do not fear his curse.

It may be time for modern industrial nations – even the most democratic of which insist on powerful central governments – to reconsider our centuries-old prejudice against such "primitive" forms of organization and take their central values of mediation and pluralism more seriously. Tribal societies themselves are discovering that if they are forced to play by the rules of the modern world, they are signing their own death warrants. They are therefore challenging the rules and urging the rest of us to do the same.

This realization on the part of tribal societies became clear when the Kayapo Indians of Brazil organized a meeting in the heart of the Amazon to protest the government's plans to build a dam that would flood Indian lands. It took place in 1989 in the little town of Altamira, which had not been in the public eye since the president of Brazil visited it twenty years earlier to launch the Transamazon Highway. The president's office boasted at the time that there were only two things on earth that were immediately visible from the moon – the Great Wall of China and the Transamazon Highway. Yet the First Congress of the Indian Nations of the Xingu River attracted even more international attention than the launching of the highway.

About two hundred journalists descended on the town, clogging the airlines and overflowing the area's modest hostelries. More than thirty Indian peoples sent representatives, some coming from as far away as Canada. Paiakan, the young Kayapo chief who called the meeting, had been in the hospital and arrived after most of the Indians had assembled in a large encampment outside Altamira. His own people met his plane and formed a double row of warriors between which he could walk to his car undisturbed. The next day Paiakan acted as master of ceremonies for the meeting, which was held in a huge hall in town. All of the Indian

BY THE TIME GUY JOHNSON DREW THIS MAP OF THE LANDS OF THE SIX NATIONS IN 1771, THE IROQUOIS CONFEDERACY WAS OVER THREE HUNDRED YEARS OLD. WARRIORS SUCH AS THE MOHAWK OTCHEEK, DEPICTED IN THE INSET DRAWING BY HENRY HAMILTON, FOUGHT A LOSING BATTLE TO RETAIN THEIR LAND. BUT THE IROQUOIS CONFEDERACY OF NATIONS COULD NOT BE STAMPED OUT AND LIVES TO THIS DAY.

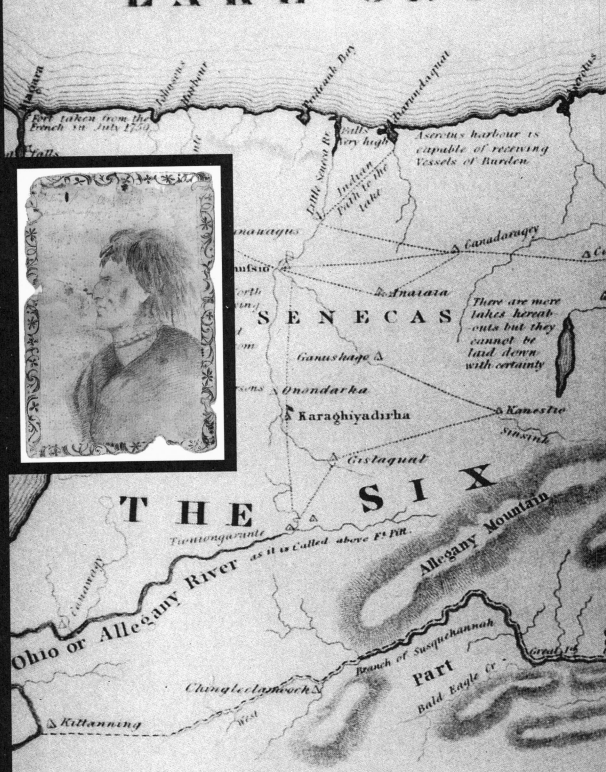

LAKE ONTAR

Fort taken from the French in July 1759

Aserotus harbour is capable of receiving Vessels of Burden

There are more lakes hereabouts but they cannot be laid down with certainty

SENECAS

Canadarager

Anarara

Ganushago

Kaneste

Onondarka

Karaghiyadirha

Eistaquat

THE SIX

Allegany Mountain

Tiononguarante

Ohio or Allegany River as it is called above Ft Pitt

Branch of Susquehannah

part

Chinagleclamioch

Bald Eagle Cr

Kittanning

West

By the Country of the six Nations proper is meant that part within which they principally reside
the rest which is of Vast extent being chiefly occupied by their dependants   The Mohocks are
as they reside within the limits of N York at Fort Hunter & Conajohare part of the Oneida
lies also within that Province the Tuscaroras who form the sixth Nation are omitted being
southern People that live on lands allotted them between Oneida & Onondaga

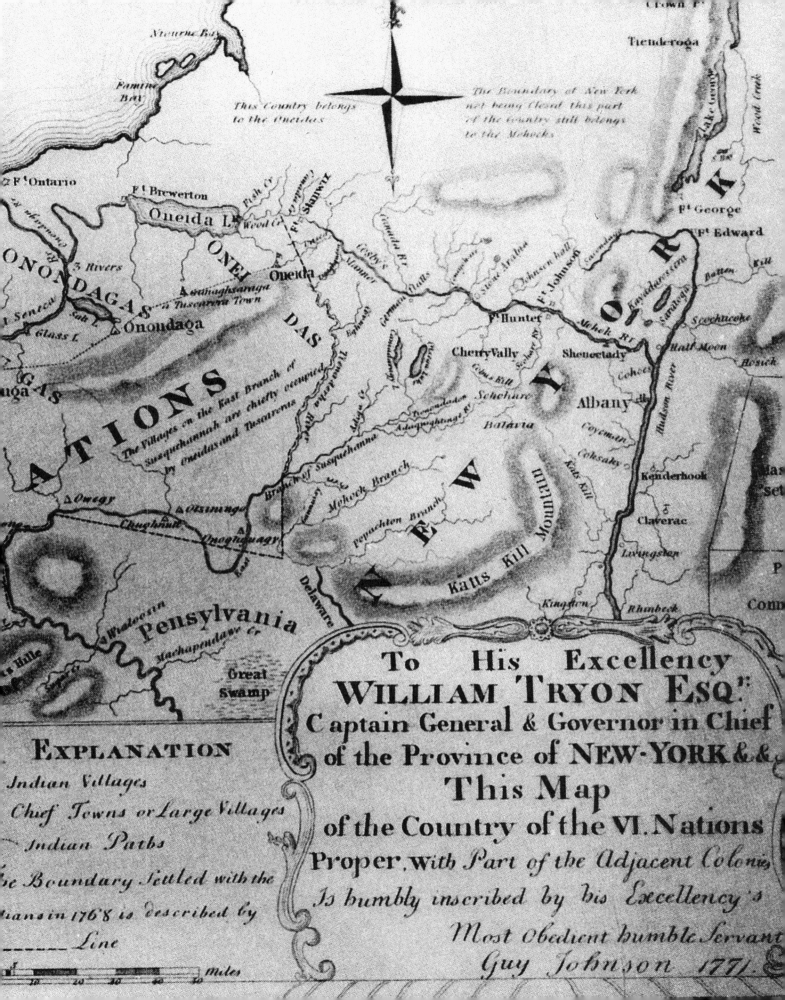

ETHNOCIDE OR ETHNOGENESIS?

Indigenous peoples around the world are beginning to see that they have something more in common than simply being victims of ethnocide — the destruction of their cultures. Despite differences in language and custom, they recognize that they are bound by commitment to a common way of life that is incompatible with the interests of the states against which they are struggling to survive. In South America, the Indians of the rainforest are organizing themselves in order to stop the expropriation of their lands. This was the message sent out to the world from Altamira. Through resistance, these people are actively engaged in the process of ethnogenesis — the forging of new cultural identities and social relationships.

delegations appeared in full ceremonial regalia and danced and sang before they were ushered to their seats on the palm fronds strewn across the floor. The leaders were escorted to the podium by Indian security men, armed for the occasion with bows and arrows. The security was not symbolic. Brazil's most conservative political party was organizing a counterdemonstration in favor of the dam, and bullets had been fired into the Indian camp on the eve of the meeting.

Paiakan introduced the Indian leaders one by one, and each spoke to the assembled gathering, which was swelling with townspeople coming in to watch the proceedings. After the Kayapo, it was the Xavante who sent the largest delegation. My brother Sibupa came with them but did not speak. That was left to the younger chiefs who spoke good Portuguese. Sibupa came looking for me and was sad to learn that I had been unable to come. He cheered up, though, when he found my son, his namesake, whom I had sent in my place. Or rather, when my son found him, for Sibupa could hardly have known that the bearded man who came up to the Xavante and asked after him was the toddler who had received his name so many years ago. Sibupa launched immediately into a formal speech of greeting in Xavante, which startled the chiefs among whom he was standing, for they did not know why a young stranger was receiving such honorific treatment. A younger Xavante translated into Portuguese, after which Sibupa embraced Biorn and presented him with a beautifully worked, ceremonial bow. In exchange, Biorn gave Sibupa his own watch which, fortunately, needed no batteries, since it was one of those that winds itself from the motion of the wearer. Sibupa showed me the watch with pride the next time I met him. Meanwhile Biorn's bow attracted a great deal of attention among the other Indians present. They knew it was no ordinary bow, and wondered how this young American had come by it.

Such meetings and greetings were soon pushed aside, however, by the serious business that had brought them all through days of journeying over rough roads

Kayapo representatives at the final meetings on the Indian rights section of the new Brazilian constitution, May 1988.

Western journalists attend a meeting in Altamira, Brazil, organized by the Kayapo Indians to protest government plans to build a dam that would flood Indian lands.

to this Amazon town. The Indians had sent personal invitations to various figures in the Brazilian government from the president on down, but the only one who accepted was the president of Eletronorte, the state-owned power company in charge of the dam. He explained that his company had surveyed all the river valleys in the heart of Brazil and had determined that the Xingu valley would be the best place for hydroelectric power plants. They had, over the course of the years, consulted with the appropriate people.... This was too much for the Indians. A Kayapo chief leaped to his feet in front of the speaker and made an impassioned speech in return, punctuated for emphasis by gestures with the war club he held in his hand. A Kayapo woman, painted and naked to the waist, rushed forward brandishing a long bush knife. She touched the flat of the blade to the cheeks of the power-company president, left, right, left, right, first one side and then the other. The photographers went wild, and the picture of the Indian woman giving the flat of her knife to the startled bureaucrat went out over the wires to symbolize the meeting in the world press. The Indians were outraged because Eletronorte had at no time spoken to them about the dams that were going to flood the lands on which they lived. Indeed, the company's plans were an eye-opener to many of the non-Indians in attendance, who had had no idea that they too were scheduled to be inundated.

The world focused on Altamira largely for ecological reasons. The Indians were victims all right, but what really attracted the press was the burning of the rainforest. To those outside Brazil, the struggle over the dams was only part of the larger story of the rape of the Amazon. Inside the country, the focus was different. Progovernment spokesmen had been trumpeting the virtues of development, but in Altamira some of the townspeople began to doubt whether their interests were really being represented as they listened to the Indians speak. They had not been consulted either, and they had not realized exactly what "development" would involve in their own region. The Indians had succeeded in highlighting the government's authoritarian disregard for its own citizens.

The First Congress of the Indian Nations of the Xingu River, while spectacular, marked only one stage of the paradoxical process undergone by the tribal peoples of the Americas: the process of becoming Indian. Members of tribal societies like the Xavante and the Kayapo were called Indians by outsiders as a result of Christopher Columbus's famous confusion, but they simply thought of themselves as people until they had to deal with the nations of which they had become unwilling citizens. Then they discovered that there were policies, attitudes, activities in the country at large that affected them as "Indians." Most of all, they realized that, whether or not they accepted this designation, they would have to band together if they were to have any say in their own future.

Therefore, the Amazonian Indians in the vast jungles that stretch from Bolivia and Peru to Ecuador, Colombia, Venezuela, and the heartland of Brazil are forming their own organizations. They are not, like the League of the Iroquois, confederacies set up to keep the peace. They are instead designed to enable Indian peoples to combine and defend their interests against the state. This goal poses a difficult challenge for tribal societies that have always wanted to be left alone and have as a result had as little contact as possible with the state. How can they suddenly become skillful players in the arena of national politics? The considerable political skills they often possess have usually been restricted to their local affairs. Even the eloquent speeches of their traditional leaders were delivered in languages unintelligible beyond their borders.

These groups have been able to respond to the challenge through a combination of their own political sophistication and outside help. In many countries the Catholic Church helped Indian organizations to get started, for instance the famous federation of the Shuar peoples in Ecuador. The Shuar had a reputation like that of the Xavante. They were regarded as fierce and warlike; they might well have been decimated in frontier skirmishes had they been forced to fight the state of Ecuador for their right to exist. Instead, the Catholic Church helped them to establish a federation that was able to negotiate with the state on behalf of the Indians of their region. This federation was soon receiving help from other organizations, including Cultural Survival, and has learned to become a political actor on the Ecuadorian scene. Meanwhile, Indian organizations were set up with outside help in the districts of Napo and Pastaza. Soon they were all collaborating in CONFENIAE (the Confederation of the Indian Nations of the Ecuadorian Amazon). Similar organizations, designated by tongue-twisting acronyms, sprang up in other countries. They were inspired by the example of the Shuar in Ecuador and the Kuna in Panama, societies known to have succeeded in working out a viable relationship between their peoples and the nations of which they formed a part, while also protecting their traditional ways of life.

While the world's attention was focused on the Amazon, on the jungles going up in flames and on the struggles of its native peoples, the issues raised by those struggles were being dramatically highlighted in the far north. It is ironic that the most glaring example of the struggle between indigenous peoples and the state should come from Canada, a nation that prides itself on its civility, and should involve the descendants of those same Iroquois whose egalitarian opposition to tyranny so impressed our eighteenth-century observers.

The story is complex and its implications even more so. The Iroquois originally controlled a huge territory covering parts of what are now the provinces of Ontario and Quebec in Canada, and stretching from New England to Illinois in the United States. Their lands have been whittled away over the last two hundred years. Canada and the United States now recognize only a minute fraction of those territories as belonging to the Six Nations, and major parts of that are in dispute. The particular dispute that jolted Canada and contributed to the disarray of its

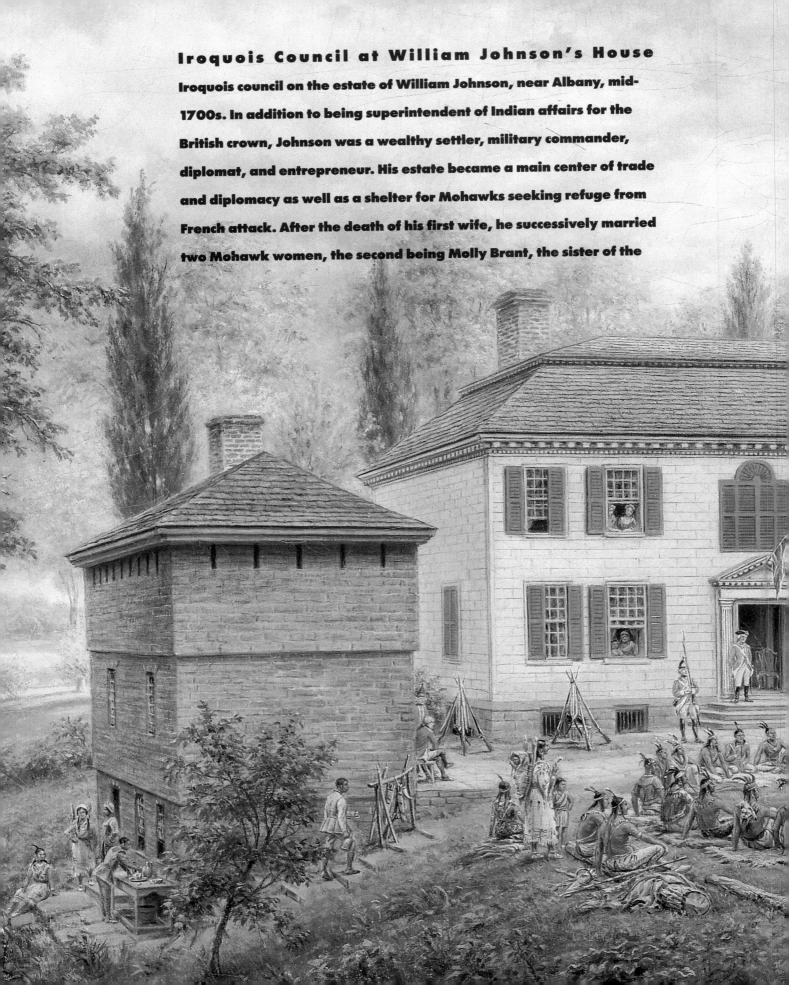

Iroquois Council at William Johnson's House

Iroquois council on the estate of William Johnson, near Albany, mid-1700s. In addition to being superintendent of Indian affairs for the British crown, Johnson was a wealthy settler, military commander, diplomat, and entrepreneur. His estate became a main center of trade and diplomacy as well as a shelter for Mohawks seeking refuge from French attack. After the death of his first wife, he successively married two Mohawk women, the second being Molly Brant, the sister of the well-known Mohawk leader Joseph Brant. Johnson promoted the acculturation of Indians through education and religious conversion. Through his friendship with the Iroquois he acquired tribal lands and furs for his own profit. He was chief negotiator in the 1768 Treaty of Fort Stanwix in which large tracts of protected hunting lands were promised to the Iroquois. Johnson did not foresee that the boundaries of the treaty would be ignored by waves of land-hungry settlers. Nor did he envision the bloodshed that followed.

federal system was provoked by an issue that seems absurd, especially when the momentous consequences of it are considered.

The town of Oka, near Montreal, decided to enlarge its golf course from nine holes to a full eighteen by extending it onto adjacent land. That land was, however, claimed by their neighbors, the Mohawk of the Kanesatake settlement, modern descendants of the original Six Nations. These Mohawk are also descendants of religious dissidents who were moved to Oka in the eighteenth century at the insistence of the Catholic Church. They came from Kahnawake, another Mohawk settlement across the river to the southeast. Many Mohawk gathered over the years at Kanesatake in a settlement run by the wealthy order of St. Sulpice. The order held the lands in trust for Indians under a grant from the king of France and was not originally entitled to dispose of them unless its Indian wards had died out or been persuaded to leave. As the lands on the riverfront at the outskirts of Montreal became increasingly valuable, the order tried in vain to persuade the Indians to leave. Finally the church began selling off parcels of the land, which changed hands repeatedly over the years even though the Mohawk still claimed that titles to them were invalid. The order of St. Sulpice was influential within the church and the church was influential within Quebec, so the Mohawk could get no redress for their grievances. The last straw, however, was the planned extension of the golf course.

The town of Oka intended to build the extension where the Mohawk had planted a sacred grove of pine trees (white pines, like the original Tree of the Great Peace), adjacent to their cemetery. The aboriginals refused to allow it and said they would fight to prevent the destruction of their sacred space. Oka went to court and established that the law regarded the land as town property. The town therefore announced that it would go ahead with the golf course and asked the Quebec police to prevent the Mohawk from interfering. The aboriginals, for their part, set up blockades to prevent the town from seizing the land. The police moved to expel the Mohawk from the disputed land, the Mohawk fought back, and in the firefight one policeman was killed. Now the Mohawk at Kahnawake decided they must act in solidarity with their brothers at Kanesatake. They seized the Mercier Bridge, connecting their reserve with the city of Montreal, and threatened to dynamite it if pressure were maintained to deprive their brothers of their sacred grove. Since the bridge is the main artery for commuter traffic out of Montreal, this action produced a stalemate. The province of Quebec supported Oka and told the aboriginals they must give up and accept punishment for their acts and the killing of the police officer. The Mohawk insisted they would not give up and argued that it was not clear who had killed the policeman. What was clear is that he died as a result of the battle that the province itself provoked.

The tense confrontation dragged on through the summer of 1990. Protracted negotiations failed to resolve the impasse, while the Quebec police and later the

Canadian army besieged the Mohawk. Men from the Mohawk warrior societies manned the barricades, and during the arguments and vituperation exchanged during that long, hot summer, the clash of values between the two sides became glaringly apparent. The besiegers insisted on the letter of their law. The Mohawk claimed that they were not bound by an alien law that had been systematically used against them and had never properly recognized or protected their rights. Besides, they added with good reason, it was just money that the whites were after. What kind of justice would elevate white profit over Mohawk religion? There was never any doubt about the outcome. The only question was whether the Mohawk would be martyred in a shoot-out or whether they could be quietly subdued. Still, during the seventy-eight days of the siege, before they were finally forced to give up, the Mohawk attracted worldwide sympathy and, to date, the golf course has not expanded beyond its original nine holes.

The showdown at Oka had been preceded by an extraordinary event in Canadian history, an event that united Canadian aboriginals as they had never been united before. A month earlier than the Oka uprising, thousands of miles away in the province of Manitoba, a Native Canadian leader managed to block passage of the federal agreement that was intended to hold the country together. The Native leader was Elijah Harper, an Ojibwa-Cree from Red Sucker Lake in northeastern

Contemporary work by Mohawk artist
Louis Hall celebrating the resurrection of
the Warrior Society. Traditionally,
members of the Warrior Society were
called into action when the hereditary or
elected chiefs were perceived to be
failing in their job to uphold the tenets of
the Great Law of Peace.

Manitoba and a member of the provincial legislature. The agreement was the Meech Lake Accord, championed by the prime minister of Canada himself, under the terms of which the province of Quebec would be recognized as a "distinct society" with its own language and culture (and newly defined provincial powers to protect them) within the Canadian federation. The agreement recognized "two founding nations" – French and English – in Canada, an idea that outraged Canadian aboriginals, whose historical priority and contributions were ignored. The Meech Lake Accord required amendments to the Canadian constitution, so it had to be approved by the legislatures of all of Canada's provinces before it could go into effect. The government set June 23, 1990, as the deadline for that approval. It was not easy to get the accord approved, however. Many English Canadians felt that it conceded too much to Quebec. Many French Canadians insisted that this was the final opportunity to restructure Canada to the satisfaction of Quebec. If the accord failed, Quebec would secede. The prime minister used that argument to coerce the provinces into approving it one by one. By the beginning of June 1990, only Manitoba and Newfoundland had failed to ratify.

Elijah Harper had opposed the agreement from the time it was hammered out behind closed doors in 1987. At that time, Native Canadians had tried and failed to have aboriginal peoples recognized and included as founders of Canada. Harper pointed out that under the terms of the Meech Lake Accord, Canada would acknowledge the linguistic and cultural distinctiveness of Quebec, while it systematically refused to do the same for all the aboriginal peoples who asked for similar consideration. In fact he had traveled to London ten years earlier as part of a Native Canadian delegation to ask the Queen not to sign the measure establishing the complete independence of Canada from Britain and the repatriation of the Canadian constitution. Harper did not want this done until that constitution guaranteed the rights of aboriginal peoples. The Native Canadians lost then and lost again when the Meech Lake Accord was drafted. In 1990, the Native Peoples of Canada knew this was their last chance to fight the accord. If Manitoba signed, the pressure on Newfoundland – the last holdout – would become almost unbearable. Meanwhile the pressure on Harper, the only Native in the Manitoba legislature, was equally intense.

It was then that Harper and the assembly of Manitoba chiefs discovered that they were entitled under provincial law to request a public hearing on the measure before it could be ratified. They instantly coordinated a grassroots movement to oppose the agreement and signed up thousands of people who asked to be heard. The hearings could not be completed before the deadline and the Meech Lake Accord was killed.

These stories pile irony upon irony – an Ojibwa-Cree using the full force of European parliamentary procedure to defeat legislation born of European notions of the state; Quebec asking for greater sensitivity on the part of English

CANANDAIGUA TREATY OF 1794

In 1794 at Canandaigua a treaty was signed between President Washington's Indian agent, Colonel Timothy Pickering, and the chiefs of the Six Nations Confederacy. It recognized the Iroquois as a sovereign nation and guaranteed that the United States would never encroach upon what was left of Iroquois territories in western and central New York. The treaty was never honored, despite persistent complaints to the United States government by Iroquois chiefs. Recently an original copy of the treaty was discovered by confederacy chiefs in a forgotten safe-deposit box. They argue that the document is conclusive proof of the legitimacy of their claim to the lands in question.

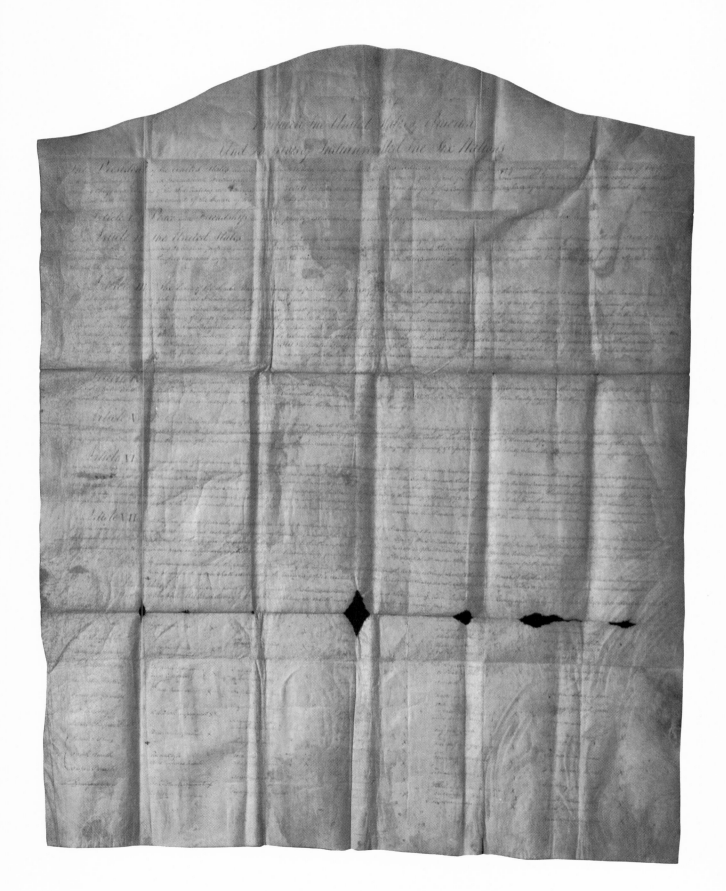

STATES AND PEOPLES

We tend to assume that the world is made up of states, countries with recognized governments and boundaries and seats in the United Nations. The word *state* is often used interchangeably with the word *nation* (as it is in the name of the United Nations) and when we speak of someone's *nationality* we refer to the state to which he or she belongs. This equation of state with nation is a modern phenomenon that is the cause of much confusion. Traditionally, *nation* referred to a distinct people, identifiable by certain characteristics — a common language or history, or a feeling of common descent, among others. Nations, spoken of in this sense, do not necessarily correspond to states, and conversely states usually contain a number of nations. That is why nationalism is often thought of as threatening the state, because it may advocate the cause of nations that are dissatisfied with their situation within states. *Self-determination* is also usually taken to mean the right of a people to govern itself *in its own, separate state.* So tribal or indigenous peoples that demand the right to control their own affairs are normally accused of wishing to secede from the state that surrounds them, or at the very least of acting to undermine that state. Our vocabulary reflects a way of thinking that contrasts the interests of the state with those of the nations or peoples contained in it. An alternative way of looking at things would be to envision more flexible states that permitted considerable local autonomy to nations and peoples within them.

The following statistics illustrate the complexity of these issues:

World population in 1830:	1 billion
World population in 1930:	2 billion
World population in 1975:	4 billion
World population in 1990:	Over 5 billion
Number of states in the world:	170
Number of nations in the world:	15,000
Number of wars currently being fought in the world as of 1987:	120
Number of wars being fought as of 1987 that involve conflicts between nations and states:	86
Number of officially recognized refugees in the world:	15 million
Number of people displaced from the lands they have traditionally occupied:	150 million
Number of nations in Nigeria:	450
Number of nations in Indonesia:	over 300
Number of nations in Cameroon:	320
Number of nations in Brazil:	180
Number of known living and extinct languages:	4,522
Number of languages spoken by more than 1 million people:	138
Number of languages spoken by between 1,000 and 10,000 people:	708
Number of languages spoken in the United States before 1492:	1,000
Number of languages spoken in the United States today:	200
Native North American language with the greatest number of speakers:	Navajo (100,000)

Elijah Harper, the Ojibwa-Cree leader and member of the Manitoba provincial legislature who helped scuttle the Meech Lake Accord. Harper's use of legislative procedure prevented the accord from being passed in Manitoba, and because constitutional amendments need the unanimous approval of Canada's ten provinces, the accord failed. Harper and other Native Canadians objected to the constitutional accord because it did not guarantee the rights of aboriginal peoples.

Canadians toward the French-speaking minority, yet supporting the town of Oka in its desire to extend a golf course onto a Mohawk sacred site; the Canadian government insisting that the future of the nation depended on its ability to provide a framework in which the Anglophone and Quebecois cultures could coexist, yet refusing to extend this framework to aboriginal cultures as well.

The Canadian crisis makes clear what is only dimly perceived in other countries, namely that the destiny of the majority in any nation is intimately linked to the fate of its minorities. The tragedy at Oka and the collapse of the Meech Lake Accord have forced Canadians to think about what kind of a nation they live in and what kind of a society they want theirs to be. These are the same questions that Brazilians are debating in the aftermath of Altamira, and that the Aborigines are trying to put on the Australian agenda.

Obviously it is not only in authoritarian states that these questions arise, although the dramatic events in Eastern Europe have led some people to think so.

Once the heavy hand of Communist dictatorship was lifted, the nations of Eastern Europe started to unravel. Old ethnic loyalties surfaced and ethnic rivalries threaten to dismember one nation after another. The problem in Eastern Europe is not that it is made up of more peoples than states, but rather that the states have not been successful in working out federal solutions that could enable those peoples to live together amicably, or at least without serious conflict. Authoritarian regimes avoid such solutions until they are in grave trouble, at which point it is usually too late to turn to them. But neither do democratic regimes find it easy to create more imaginative federal solutions.

The reason for this failure is that such solutions require us to have a different idea of the state, a kind of new federalism which, after the manner of the League of the Iroquois, permits each people in the nation to keep its council fire alight. This requires more than rules; it requires commitment. The Great Law of the Iroquois was remarkable because it was a constitution that had the force of a religion. People were willing, indeed eager, to subscribe to it, because they saw it and revered it as the source of peace. Is it too much to hope that in a world riven with ethnic conflict we might search for federal solutions more energetically than we have in the past? That we will not continue to expect strong states to iron out ethnicity, even if it means wiping out the "ethnics"? A new federalism is in our own interest, for it offers the hope of peace and the prospect of justice. Nations that trample on the rights of the weak are likely to end up trampling on the rights of everybody. As we wring our hands over the fate of tribal peoples in the modern world, we would do well to remember John Donne's words: "Never send to know for whom the bell tolls; it tolls for thee."

AT THE THRESHOLD
An Interview with David Maybury-Lewis

A serious consideration of tribal ways of life should lead us to think carefully and critically about our own. What would it take for us to try to live in harmony with nature or to rehumanize our economic systems? How can we mediate between the individual and the family, between genders and generations? Should we strive for a less fragmented view of physical reality or of our place in the scheme of things? These questions revolve around wholeness and harmony, around tolerance and pluralism. The answers are still emerging, but they too are variations on a grand theme that can be summed up in E. M. Forster's famous phrase: "Only connect."

Modernization is a process that started with the splitting of the social atom that unleashed the furious energy of individualism. We cannot go back on that, nor do most of us want to. Modern regimes that have tried systematically to suppress the individual have committed fearful crimes against humanity. But now that the artificial polarity between capitalism and communism has disappeared, we need no longer be paralyzed by the impossible choice between the social horrors of the former and the political nightmare of the latter.

Humankind possesses a vast store of knowledge and experience about how to live together in responsive communities. In our times, this knowledge has been dismissed as archaic or utopian, while capitalists and Communists alike focused on the relationships between the individual and the state. The project for the new millennium will be to reenergize civil society, the space between the state and the individual where those habits of the heart flourish that socialize the individual and humanize the state.

There are no instant solutions to our dilemmas, but the first step is to understand them. The *Millennium* television series, and this book that accompanies it, are intended to present these issues to a wide audience. In May 1991 I met with a team of colleagues from the *Millennium* series to discuss them further. What follows is the text of that interview.

MILLENNIUM TEAM[1] (MT). Aside from the literal fact that we are approaching the year 2000, what do you think is millennial about this moment in history? Are we in fact at a threshold?

DAVID MAYBURY-LEWIS (DM-L). My immediate temptation is to reply that the moment has no special significance. We cross into the year 2000 and in the great span of time it doesn't mean a thing. It's an artificial construct. No doubt future historians will look back and try to give the year 2000 some special meaning, simply because it's such an important-looking date, but in reality it doesn't have much meaning.

Yet, on second thought, I think it does have some meaning and the meaning is this. I believe that this is a moment when we in the modern world are beginning to discover that the ideas and attitudes and activities that have seemed to serve us so well for the past five hundred years are not working very well anymore. Since the expansion of Europe, the invasion of the Americas, and the growth of science – first in the West but later spreading all over the world – a whole set of attitudes and practices have grown up that we associate with modernity. It seems to me that these have now run their course. We are beginning to discover that we can easily destroy all of humankind in a fit of pique or incompetence. We are also starting to perceive that, through our own blindness about the way we live, we can destroy the very environment on which we depend to support life. We are beginning to understand as well that we are not doing a very good job of organizing the societies in which we live.

As Daniel Bell put it not too long ago, the nation-state has now become too big for the small problems of this world and too small for the big ones. For that reason we have to rethink the societies we live in, the way they relate to the environment, and, in general, the way all of us interact with the world around us. I feel that people are coming vaguely to realize this, and that this realization is going to take the world by storm in the next decade. In this sense, the millennium may very well be an important watershed.

MT. So would you describe the time we're living in as a time of cultural disintegration, as many say? A time of uncertainty and of insecurity? Or does it have within it the promise of renewal, the birth of something new? In other words, are we talking about an apocalypse or a millennium?

DM-L. Well, I certainly think that this is a time of promise, of great hope for renewal. I do think as well that there is a great deal of uncertainty in our times, but then we have to remember that uncertainty is part of the human condition. If there is (or if we feel there is) more uncertainty at the moment than there used to be, then it may be because of the trends I have just referred to. People are becoming aware of megatrends that seem to be drastically altering the circumstances in which they live, yet they feel powerless to do anything about them. They don't even know very well how to *think* about them. But I don't feel that we are hurtling

[1] Victor Barac, Laurie Hart, Richard Meech.

toward the apocalypse. On the contrary, this is a time of promise, because I sense that people are yearning for change. They are willing to consider new ways of relating to one another, of going about their business, of dealing with our planet. That is why I thought it worthwhile to found Cultural Survival and to work with it over all these years.

MT. So how is Cultural Survival designed to help us think about those problems and in what context?

DM-L. I'm glad you said "to help us think about them" because, to my mind, one of the most important things Cultural Survival does is to try to help people look at things from a new perspective. Until people do that, they are not going to be able to change anything. When my wife and I first founded Cultural Survival, we did it with strong, "activist" intentions. We were outraged by what we saw happening to tribal peoples and other powerless groups around the world. We wanted to do something about it. Scholars are often accused of studying problems to death or, worse still, just using them as an excuse to get research funds. We were determined not to be like that. We wanted to show that people who were serious scholars could also be concerned enough to try to make a difference in the "real world."

So it came as something of a surprise to us to discover, once we were up to our armpits in the work of Cultural Survival, that the "real world" needed the theory of the scholars as much as it did their commitment. It did not so much need another organization to innoculate babies or get food to people suffering from famine; these are terribly important things to do, but there are organizations already trying to do them. It needed people willing and able to find better ways of thinking about the causes of such problems and about the solutions to them. Cultural Survival is not an organization that is trying to rethink *all* the problems of the world – our commitment is to tackle the problems that face tribal societies in particular and to make the point that what affects them affects us all.

MT. Does Cultural Survival deal only with tribal societies, then?

DM-L. No, we have always placed the problems of tribal societies in the wider context that is necessary if we are to understand them and come anywhere near solving them. Nowadays our projects are not confined either to those very small-scale societies that prompted us to found the organization. As an individual, I feel a general responsibility to do what I can about human rights abuses, so I support organizations like Amnesty International. As an anthropologist, however, I felt a particular responsibility to the kinds of societies that anthropologists like me were working with, societies that seem particularly vulnerable in the modern world and for whom there did not seem to be many advocates. They had no lobby of any kind in any state in those days, not even in the United Nations. Few of them had their own organizations or could make their voices heard when their rights and sometimes their very lives were threatened. Nor did there seem to be many other people speaking up for them, and certainly nobody seemed to have much idea of what might be done for them. In fact, even well-intentioned people around the world – and thank goodness there are plenty of them – tended to wring their hands and say, "Well, it's sad, what's happening to societies like those, but it's inevitable, isn't it? They're bound to get wiped out by the march of progress, aren't they? By development?" I heard these lines so often – in boardrooms, at the World Bank, in foundations and other organizations – that I wanted to jump to my feet and shout at the top of my voice, "No, it's not so! This is not a necessary part of some abstract process over which none of us has any control. It's an *unn*ecessary part of the politics with which we are all familiar." So it was working through these intellectual problems and getting people to understand them that was our primary task.

MT. A lot of people, though, still believe in the idea of societal evolution, that all cultures have to move from something primitive to something more modern. Doesn't this affect your arguments?

DM-L. It's a popular misconception that societies pass through an inevitable series of stages, that they move from one phase to another unavoidably and that everybody has to pass through them. It is also a popular misconception that we are the most advanced people on earth and that tribal societies are either cases of arrested development – people who haven't got there yet – or people who have quite simply failed, flunked the test, been left behind. We now know that this is not true. Other societies make different choices. Compared with them, we excel in some things, but fall behind in others. I simply don't believe in any linear progression, and nor do social or cultural anthropologists in general.

Having said that, I think certain trends may well be more or less irreversible. Societies are becoming more and more industrialized, more and more urbanized and so on. I can't imagine a society deindustrializing, for example, as part of the future. It's conceivable, I suppose, that societies could actually deurbanize to a certain extent. People are, after all, seriously thinking of breaking up huge metropolises that seem to have outgrown their usefulness. When I was a boy, large cities were considered the sign of a very advanced society. When I was growing up I was told that London was the largest city in the world. It hasn't been for many years now. Maybe it wasn't even then, but people *thought* it was and the British took pride in it. That was supposed to tell us that we were living in a very advanced society. Nowadays very large cities tend to be signs of societies that are having serious problems. There are cities like Mexico City, New York City, Calcutta, São Paulo – places that we do not associate with enormous social success. If people figure out ways to shrink these cities, it would show that even the trend toward bigger and bigger metropolises is not irreversible.

MT. You are talking about the city as the old paradigm, and yet Cultural Survival was founded on a vision of pluralistic societies, a vision that comes perhaps from your interest and experience in smaller-scale tribal societies. Is there a way to incorporate these societies, these cultures, within larger states to create pluralistic societies?

DM-L. I think that question has to be answered in two parts. One concerns the fate of the small societies and the other concerns the future of the larger ones. Their destinies are linked and that is an important part of the message of Cultural Survival. I'll talk about the larger societies in a moment, but first I want to say something about the small, relatively isolated ones that, according to traditional evolutionary thinking, should just "naturally" vanish. They should either evaporate, be absorbed into the mainstream of the wider culture, or be wiped out (just how is left conveniently vague here) by the "forces of progress." What we have been arguing and demonstrating in the last few years is that this is not necessary. It's *not* part of some abstract historical process. It's actually the result of simple political expediency. Since these people are too small and too weak to fight back, it's convenient and very easy to stomp on them – to take their lands and just shove them out of the way.

MT. You don't think it's patronizing to assume that we in the developed countries have to help them?

DM-L. No more patronizing than to help anyone else as a matter of conscience. Furthermore, in helping them we help ourselves. That's what I am coming to in a moment. You see, the same kinds of arguments about the "inevitable" fate of tribal peoples were used a hundred years ago to defend slavery. People used to say: "Well, it's the way of the world. The strong have always enslaved the weak and there's no way to get around that because there are always going to be stronger and weaker people. Therefore, there are always going to be masters and slaves and there's nothing much you can do about that. It's the law of God, or nature, or what have you." From Aristotle to the southern planters in the United States in the nineteenth century people have been using that argument. Yet we now regard slavery as an anachronism. There may be a few corners of the world where it still exists but, by and large, it had been eradicated, rather like smallpox. We no longer regard it as tolerable, reasonable, or even thinkable and certainly not as one of the unalterable laws of nature.

I like to think that in the next century we'll come to the same way of thinking about our treatment of smaller societies. That the present injustices they suffer are simply intolerable, that there *are* alternatives and that the alternatives can be explored and should be explored and are being explored. Tribal societies, if they're not physically exterminated, and if they're not deprived of their lands and their way of making a living, are quite capable of coexisting within the larger political units and making their own way in the modern world. Just look at the societies of the American Southwest. The Hopi and the Navajo, for example, have a very strong sense of themselves, of their culture. They've fought hard. They're still there. They've maintained a cultural identity under quite adverse circumstances, which shows that it is possible. But the prospects for most tribal societies depend on their living in a world that is sufficiently enlightened to think about living with them, rather than just rolling over them, steamrollering them, if you will. That presupposes a world that is willing to allow that and that's what the future comes to for us all.

I think the future belongs to a world where people are going to be much more willing to live and let live, to coexist in states where interethnic relations are a matter of multiculturalism and tolerance for other peoples' ways of life. This is by no means easy and I'm not pretending it is, but it's possible. After all, it has not been easy for people to thrive under the old system – which insisted you had to have a nation-state, which had to have a dominant culture, which had to eradicate all other cultures that were not considered to be in the mainstream. That has not been easy either. It has led to extraordinary levels of repression, violence, revolt, and upheaval that are still going on to this day. In our preoccupation with nuclear Armageddon, we tend to forget that we live in an extraordinarily violent century, in which nation-states vent unprecedented destruction on one another and particularly on the minorities in their midst. Yet people tend to argue as if this were the natural way to do things and any other way is too difficult to think about. I disagree.

MT. Well then why is there so much negative reaction from both the far right and the far left when people talk about pluralistic societies? What do they fear? Why has ethnicity been given such a bad name?

DM-L. I'll talk about far-left position first because I see it as having been more influential in past years, whereas the far-right position, at least in the United States, is more influential right now. In the past, there was a sort of orthodox Marxist position that maintained that ethnicity was atavistic, a false consciousness. Indeed, if you believed the orthodox Marxist theory that the real relations in human society were actually class relations and that they were determined by your position in the productive system, then it followed that ethnicity was not so important. It would follow, as Marx argued, that if the inequities between the owners of the means of production and the rest of the people, who were just proletariat and laborers within the system, were ironed out in the society of the future, then all the other evanescent relationships that had grown up around this inequality, this dichotomy, would themselves evaporate. Marx gave a great deal of thought to this society of the future and tried to sketch it out in his works. He considered the state to be another of those institutions that owed its existence to the inequalities of the present; it would evaporate once those inequalities had been eliminated.

Marx has been much criticized for this theory of the "withering away" of the state, but you can see how it made sense – in theory. If you see the state as encapsulating the rule of the bourgeoisie, then when the inequalities between the bourgeoisie and the proletariat are ironed out you are not going to have that kind of state anymore. I think he was wrong, because I don't think these things are solely economic. I think that politics is an independent principle, related to but not simply determined by economics. I think the state is unlikely to wither away even if we ever have a fairly egalitarian distribution of wealth, and nobody's yet figured out how to achieve that in industrial societies. Nor is ethnicity likely to wither away. I'm not quite sure what you could do to make that happen. The fact of the matter is that orthodox, leftist parties that have come into power in recent years and have thought this would be an opportunity for everybody to lay aside their ethnicity, to cast aside their ethnic differences and come into the popular fold, have been terribly disappointed. They have found out that ethnicity is a deeply ingrained way of defining oneself and one's relationships to others, and that human beings cling to it.

One of the most interesting, and in a way most tragic, examples of this is what happened in Nicaragua when the Sandinistas took over. The Sandinistas really thought that once the revolution had triumphed, once the rotten dictators of the Somoza variety were got rid of, then the Miskito and other Indians of the Caribbean coast would just join in the business of building the new Nicaragua and shuck off this whole nonsense of being Indian. There was no further necessity to be Indian – except that the Miskito and other Indians of the Caribbean coast did not see it that way; they felt that this was their primary identification. As soon as they realized what the Sandinista agenda was and how it differed from their own, they got into battles with them. The Sandinistas realized their mistake later on, as a matter of fact, and came to terms with the Indians.

MT. What about the far right? What do they fear?

DM-L. The far right, I think, fears ethnic pluralism because it threatens their hegemony. It's fairly clear in the United States that what they resent most is people paying attention to – empowering, if you will – the ideas and attitudes of minorities within the country. It seems to me that the not-very-hidden agenda of the far right is to keep these people as second-class citizens. For the far right, it is the thin end of the wedge to say that Hispanic writers should be seriously studied along with Anglo writers in the core curriculum, that students should learn about African-American culture along with mainstream white culture and so on. Their objections are often cloaked in the rhetoric of the American way, interestingly enough.

There was an article published recently in the *Boston Globe* by two men from the Free Congress Foundation, who argued that a new tribalism was growing up in the United States and that this represented everything that was antithetical to the American Dream. After all, they insisted, America, the very name of which we in the United States have appropriated to refer to ourselves, was built as a nation of individuals, a place where an individual was judged on his or her own merits. So people should not be assigned to "tribal" categories and judged on the basis of their race or ethnicity, as they are in affirmative-action programs. They said this was a terrible thing to do and would only lead to the kind of ethnic strife that we see elsewhere in the world. They then went on to stress that America was a meritocracy, where people were promoted on merit – all of which made me gasp in amazement. Here are people who apparently think they're writing seriously about the United States and they've missed the whole point of the civil rights movement. I mean, why was it necessary to have a civil rights movement? Precisely because people were being judged by the color of their skin rather than on merit. Precisely because Blacks could not vote in many places and so on. To say that meritocracy is the American way simply ignores history. It is the American *ideal*, but one that has not been lived up to in practice.

As for the new "tribalism," that again is the kind of nonsense that I was talking about earlier. The idea that taking other peoples' cultures seriously and making an effort to coexist with them will lead to endless ethnic strife is simply not true. By and large we have been too fearful even to try doing this seriously. If we had devoted anything like the amount of energy to making federalistic systems work as we have to trying to stamp out "the ethnics" and to homogenize large-scale societies, I think we would all be in much better shape today than we are.

MT. With the sweep of neoconservatism throughout the Western world in recent years, pluralism seems to be under attack as part of liberalism. Is pluralism part of the classic liberal philosophy? What are the prospects for ethnic pluralism in the current climate of opinion?

DM-L. That's a complicated question – actually three or four questions collapsed into one. Classic liberal philosophy placed a great deal of emphasis on freedom – on freedom for the individual, free trade, free enterprise, freedom of religion, an open political system, and so on. It therefore tended to defend the rights of minorities to "do their own thing," but I don't believe that classical liberalism had much to say about ethnic or cultural pluralism. In fact, I don't think political philosophers, or politicians for that matter, have paid a great deal of attention to ethnic pluralism until quite recently. Now that they are beginning to, they almost invariably regard it as a terrible threat and danger – something to be avoided at all costs. The idea of relative autonomy for ethnic groups within the state has had a very bad press.

I argued, in a paper I wrote some years ago, that we have two traditions in Western thinking. One, stemming from French theorists around the time of the French revolution, holds that a strong, centralized state is the best and most rational way to run a country, and that the fewer intermediate organizations you have between the individual and the state, the better. Another line of argument was largely pioneered by German thinkers. Writers like Fichte and Herder were much less convinced of the inherent virtues of the state. Germans in the eighteenth and early nineteenth centuries lived in a plethora of little states. Their problem was how to get Germans together in spite of the boundaries between all the states in which they lived. So German thinkers tended to be more interested in the ethos of peoples than in the supposed advantages of a strong state, for states, in their experience, were usually imposed on peoples with little regard for the wishes of the governed. What were seen in the nineteenth century as two legitimate ways of looking at things very rapidly became the good way and the bad way. People came to think of the idea of giving any autonomy – however regional, however local, however limited – to ethnic groups as backward and conservative. They condemned it because they thought it stood in the way of political and economic development. Finally they came to think of it simply as a prelude to violence, war, and all the bad things of this world. Their pessimism seemed to be confirmed by World War I, which was triggered off by ethnic antagonisms in the Austro-Hungarian empire. Between the two world wars President Wilson and others argued for self-determination (in Europe at least!) and the League of Nations oversaw the creation of smaller and more ethnically homogeneous states. But the world did not seem ready to protect these smaller states. The international community set up an independent Czechoslovakia, for example, but then could not protect its integrity. Then the Nazis cynically manipulated the entire idea of ethnic self-determination, so once again it became associated with all the nastiest and most atavistic trends in recent history. As a result, when the United Nations was founded in 1945 and came out with its ringing universal declaration of human rights, it talked a lot about the rights of individuals. It was meticulous about the rights of states and the rights of individuals within states, but said nothing at all about the rights of peoples who did not happen to be in the mainstream of or control a state. That is the difficulty – it's the lack of correspondence between states and peoples – or between states and nations, if you will – that we are dealing with in the modern world. What we think we're dealing with is "tribals" – people clinging to their own groups and fighting their neighbors – but in fact, people have been clinging to their own groups for their identity ever since the beginning of human history and they're going to go on doing that as far as I can see. The problem in the modern world is not "tribalism." The problem is that we have so systematically and unsuccessfully attempted to suppress these units of identity that human beings appear to need.

There, I hope I've answered your question!

MT. Just for clarification, is tribalism the same thing as ethnicity and, if not, what is the difference between them?

DM-L. Tribalism is a dirty word now used, all too often, as a pejorative way of referring to ethnicity. Ethnicity is no more than the sense, however strongly or weakly felt, of belonging to a certain people. Tribalism is used to emphasize the divisive effects of ethnic affirmation. In Africa they talk about tribalism as being the terrible legacy of European rule. Europeans, they say, adopted the divide-and-rule principle and therefore African states are riven with tribalism because that's the way the colonial authorities wanted it. Now the new African governments are not going to have any truck with tribalism and therefore they're going to deny the existence of the tribe. But this is a rewriting of history. Europeans certainly did divide and rule, but they also did find groups of people in Africa who considered themselves different from one another. Whether you want to call them tribes or not doesn't matter, but those groups are still there and they still consider that there are important differences between them. The African leaders who refuse to acknowledge these differences in order to deny tribalism usually have a hidden agenda, and the hidden agenda is very often a desire to conceal the fact that they and members of their own tribe are running their particular country. So, in the name of not having anything to do with tribalism they are in fact operating a hegemonic system that keeps down members of other tribes.

MT. But is Cultural Survival, then, protribalism?

DM-L. No. Again, one has to be very clear about this because tribalism is always used in the pejorative sense and Cultural Survival is not in favor of any of the reductio ad absurdum positions that are normally meant when people talk about tribalism. The consequences of standing up for tolerance and multiculturalism are not what you're going to get in the nightmares of the American right and they're not the kind of thing you're going to get in the rhetoric of African elites. This is not what Cultural Survival stands for. Cultural Survival defends the right of a people to maintain its own culture and have a say in its own future. It advocates the kind of tolerance and pluralism that can make this work. The second point is as important as the first. Our whole philosophy is the complete opposite of what is normally meant by "tribalism."

MT. What happens to people who don't have those units of identity, those ethnicities – those people who have left their ethnic group or identity behind? Like a lot of people in the modern world. Because of individualism we've all become individuals. How do we fit in?

DM-L. You may think you're an individual, but everyone has a potential ethnic affiliation of some kind. You may not be aware of it, because the situation doesn't call for it, but if the situation did, you would very soon discover your ethnicity. In Canada, for example, you can go through life thinking you're just an individual until a problem arises between Anglophone and Francophone Canadians. Then you discover you're one or the other, unless you happen to be a Sikh or an aboriginal Canadian and you say, "Hey, what about me?" There's always the potential for ethnic identification, and that's the point I'm trying to make. What governments have banked on in the past was the idea that if you stamped on all the specific manifestations of ethnicity, somehow you could prevent that potential from flowering into a full-blown sense of ethnicity. I think this is a hopeless task.

In fact, people need these identifications and they have them even when (indeed most especially when) they think they don't have them at all. The people in the United States who go around saying terrible things about "tribalism" usually belong to the white Anglo-Saxon tribe that happens to have run the United States up until now. The reason they don't like what they call "tribalism" is because it might let the other tribes in.

MT. People often say that tribal people themselves are at least as xenophobic as anyone else, perhaps even more so. Does their sort of xenophobia differ from ours? Tribal peoples often identify themselves by a word that in their own language means "human," while the word for others outside their culture often means "nonhuman" or "subhuman." Is xenophobia a constant in human nature?

DM-L. No, I don't think it's a constant. When I talk about tribal societies I'm talking about relatively isolated societies. I use the world "relatively" advisedly because very few societies in this day and age are totally isolated. There may be some, and for obvious reasons we don't know much about them.... Anyway, the ones we're talking about are only relatively isolated. Now if you live in relative isolation it's very difficult to have tolerant multiculturalist views about your relationships with all sorts of other people in the world whom you don't know. So it's fairly understandable, I think, that they do have a sort of firm insistence on their own identity and their own lives because that is what they know. In fact, it's not true that tribal peoples routinely consider outsiders less than human in the moral sense. They may think outsiders are not *properly* human, because they don't take part in the exchanges and rituals that, for them, define humanity. But that's not to say all of them are xenophobic. Some of them are definitely not. There are areas of the world, for example, where tribal peoples interact with one another in such a complex way that it puzzled anthropologists who couldn't figure out where one society began and the other left off. Edmund Leach's book entitled *Political Systems of Highland Burma* became a classic because he analyzed a complex instance of this. He described how a number of peoples living along the Sino-Burmese frontier interacted with one another so intensely that it made sense to consider them part of a single, flexible social system. Yet these peoples would conventionally have been regarded as different tribes, speaking different languages and even living in different countries. The tribes of central Brazil along the Xingu River are a similar case. There are about eight or nine different tribes who come together there. They speak different languages – not only different languages, but languages drawn from different language families – as if you have one society speaking a Germanic language, one a Slavic language, another a Latin language – and they all come together for mutual ceremonies. Interestingly enough, they've developed common rituals and myths, and exactly how they've done that is something I don't quite understand yet. But here are these societies coming from quite different perspectives, speaking different and mutually unintelligible languages, which have worked out a way of living together in some sort of a multicultural system. Quite an interesting experiment.

MT. Yes, I think that's probably been going on a long time, a lot longer than we know.

DM-L. In this case, not an awful long time – a mere hundred years or more. But I agree. This kind of thing has probably been going on all over the place for a long, long time.

MT. That's an interesting case of pluralism – different languages, common myths. Is there some kind of a lesson in this for us? Do you think there are things we can learn from tribal peoples? We associate the values of community, spirituality, even spontaneity with tribal societies. Have these been irrevocably lost in the course of modernization, or is there some way of reincorporating them into our own industrial societies?

DM-L. These are not things that the modern world has lost entirely. If we'd lost them entirely we would find them almost inconceivable. That, to my mind, would be a sort of sci-fi nightmare world, or dystopia. I don't want to pretend for one minute that the modern world is like that. We ourselves do feel, I think, that we've lost a great deal of our sense of community and that individuals are very lonely in modern society, and that they certainly are not in tribal societies. Tribal people may be suffocated by the companionship that is forced on them, but they are certainly not lonely. So there are things that tribal societies emphasize that we have deemphasized (I prefer to put it that way). Very often this is partly a result of scale. If you live in a village with three hundred people and that is the boundary of your universe, clearly you know everybody and everybody knows you. So the alienation of coming as a young adult to New York, maybe for your first job, and not knowing anybody and not knowing your neighbors, and walking down the street and being surrounded by thousands of people who don't know who you are and don't care, is simply not in their world and is not likely to be. So then the question is: what do you do in societies that have New Yorks? You're not going to turn them around and make them into Xavante villages and certainly the Xavante are not particularly interested in making their villages into New Yorks, although they might like some of the modern conveniences.

So, the question we are asking is whether or not it is possible to incorporate some of the more enviable features of tribal societies into a modern way of living, and I believe it is possible. I don't have recipes to offer you but I really think it is. But in order to do so – I keep repeating this because I think it's terribly important and it's actually the spine of all the remarks I've made – we have got to be determined to do it! We have to know that this is what needs doing and we have to get on with it. If you refuse to acknowledge that there is a problem, then you're certainly not going to solve it. If, for example, you refuse to admit that there is any problem in a society which declares people redundant (the phrase used in Britain when people are laid off), if you think that's perfectly natural and that's the way things are going to be, then you're going to go on having societies which declare people redundant and you are going to have all the alienation that follows from it. You are going to have societies where people step over or walk around the homeless in the street and so on. Now I don't think that this is necessary in a modern industrial society. It may be a necessary result of the way we organize modern industrial societies right now. But I think it's not beyond the wit of mankind to figure out better ways of organizing our societies. In fact, some smaller societies in Europe are beginning to move in that direction. People talk about the Scandinavian societies – they're industrial, they're capitalist, presumably the same kinds of constraints apply to them as apply to us – yet you don't find the homeless lying around in the streets there. Why not? Worth thinking about.

MT. There seems to be built into modern society the notion that somebody has to win and somebody has to lose.

DM-L. When you talk about winners and losers it's difficult to see how a big gap could be opened up between absolute winners in a society like that of the Xavante and absolute losers, even supposing they thought in those terms. There's no way one Xavante can make 18 million dollars in one year while another Xavante is sleeping in the street. It's not possible in their system, but it is possible in ours. That possibility is a fact of life. What we do about it is not a fact of life – it's a choice. Other industrial societies (other than the United States, I mean), don't have these phenomenal differentials and they are often as successful as industrial societies. It was pointed out just recently that the differentials between the salaries of CEOs and workers in Japan are nowhere near as great as they are in the United States. I'm not quite sure what conclusion you draw from that. The conclusion I draw from it is that these astronomical salaries are not an indispensable feature of the industrial world, and they are not even indicative of very successful capitalist systems.

MT. Tribal peoples seem to have a broader perspective on the human condition than is generally accepted here in the West. They have well-developed notions of spirituality and a profound sense of connection to the natural world. Does this way of looking at things have any relevance for us in industrial society?

DM-L. Yes, absolutely. For nine-tenths of the history of humankind, people lived in small societies that felt themselves and knew themselves to be part of the natural order of things. They were not the lords of the earth. They might have felt they had a certain advantage over the predators in their region, but not much. To take one example, the Indians in the Amazonian jungles have a very healthy respect for jaguars. They consider jaguars to be the equivalent of shamans – extremely powerful people who mediate between this world and the next. Human beings have traditionally thought they were very much on a par with the other creatures of this earth; they were very much a part of the natural order of things. They depended on the natural order and so were extremely concerned with maintaining the balance of it. Now one of the joys and excitements of the whole scientific, industrial revolution was it seemed to release humankind from its bondage, from its natural bondage. What we have seen in the last five hundred years or so is an unbelievable explosion of creative energy in modern society.

This led, unfortunately, to the hubris of believing that at last humankind was free, that we were masters of the earth or masters of the universe. And we are now discovering that this is simply not true. We cannot do anything we want. Our will, or rather willfulness, and our scientific know-how are actually digging a trap for us all into which we may very well fall through our sheer inability to change our way of thinking. So I think it would indeed be good for us to recover some of that sense of connectedness, some of that spirituality that tribal peoples have cultivated and that is absolutely essential for our own survival.

MT. What specifically do you hope that the *Millennium* series can achieve for tribal peoples?

DM-L. I think the *Millennium* series will bring the ideas of tribal peoples before a much wider audience than organizations like Cultural Survival could otherwise hope to reach. That to me is an extremely valuable and worthwhile thing to do. Remember, in answer to an earlier question, I said one of the reasons why it is so difficult to deal with these "others" (the tribal peoples) is because one doesn't meet them. The average person in his average life is never going to meet tribal peoples. "Tribal people" is an abstraction and if tribal people are being eradicated at the frontier, well it's just another statistic, as impersonal as the weather. What *Millennium* will do is to bring these people into the living rooms of the public and give the public a sense of them as human beings, a sense of them as people who are interesting, who represent another possibility of life, people who might be interesting to talk to, interesting to think about. Tribal peoples are, after all, massacred or dispossessed at the frontiers of our civilization because their very humanity is denied. So I think it's very important to humanize them and bring them into our moral sphere of reference, which is what I hope the *Millennium* series will do.

MT. You suggest that the more exposed you are to differences – at least in a context where those differences are not threatening – the more tolerant you become. But many people are afraid that a greater exposure to differences will cause them to be less secure in their own identities, perhaps cultural hybrids. Do you see this as a problem?

DM-L. There is always that fear. There is always the fear that if I get too involved in other societies, I lose my own center of gravity, my own frame of reference, I lose myself. I've said this often myself about anthropologists. If you go and immerse yourself in another society and you become deeply interested in and involved in what they do, you come back having lost your firm moorings in your own society without having gained a place in another one – so you are sort of floating halfway in between. For anthropologists, this is a creative uncertainty, leading to a deeper reflection not only about them but about us, and about one's own self. I think it would be the same kind of mind-broadening experience for other people, too. That's not always the case, of course. Plenty of people travel and come back just as narrow-minded as they were before they went. But those people who travel intelligently and come back with their minds broadened, yes it does affect their view of their previous comfortable certainties. They're no longer so comfortable. I feel that that's a good thing. We should not cling to our beliefs and close our minds to outside influences, merely because they make us feel uncomfortable. Isn't it this dogmatism and refusal to be open-minded that we disdain in the mentality of the Middle Ages? When we talk about the Middle Ages as the Dark Ages what we mean is that they were closed and they were reluctant to accept other ideas. They put people to death if they were too imaginative about other alternatives. We, I think, are in the position to be able to accept those alternatives, to allow them to influence our own way of looking at the world without losing our center of gravity. If we're so insecure that by simply considering other ways of looking at the world we're going to lose our own sense of ourselves, then I would submit that our own sense of ourselves is probably not worth having.

Curiously enough, tribal peoples who are given a chance – who are not physically massacred or economically or socially overpowered so they are reduced to destitution – seem to have much less problem maintaining their own identity than we do. We are the people who are constantly worried about our own identity and feel it is threatened by diversity, multiculturalism, and so on. I find it an interesting irony that tribal peoples seem to be more confident of their identity than we are of ours. Of course tribal ideas about identity change and, since this actually bears on the work of Cultural Survival, I'll say something about it. Cultural Survival is an organization that does not believe in cultural *preservation*, and it's very important to make that clear. What we mean by cultural survival is a process through which a people, any given people, has an important say in its own future. Ideally I would have said "a process through which a people *controls* its own future." But no people that I know of in this world has total control over its own future, not even the United States, which thinks it's the most powerful nation in the world. There are all sorts of external forces that impinge on the United States. Tribal societies certainly don't have that kind of control; but what we argue for, fight for, and try to help them fight for is to gain the maximum possible say in their own future, to participate in it. Now that implies a process of defining their own future and their own future is not going to be the same as their past. So Indians don't cease to be Indians when they abandon the bow and arrow any more than Americans ceased to be Americans when they abandoned the horse and buggy – they move on to something else. Indians don't cease to be Indians when they have Ph.D.s, as I'm happy to say an increasing number of them do. Or when they become members of parliament, or whatever. But then the question is: does there come a time when their culture, their way of life, ceases to make sense to a people? It's conceivable, just as it's conceivable there'll come a time when our own way of life doesn't make sense to us. After all, isn't that one of the things we're worried about right now? I mean, when we talk about our own way of life leading us into ecological disaster, leading us into wars and things, aren't we saying that there is something wrong with our own way of life that we would like to correct? And if we correct it, won't we make substantial changes in the way we ourselves live? We look forward to that as something positive, as something that we have within our power if we have the good sense to do it. We believe we can make changes in our own way of life, and I think we ought to give other people credit for being able to do this as well without assuming that if they do so, they are losing their own souls, losing contact with themselves.

I think, if I can go on editorializing on this point, that what we so often see is that people do lose their own souls, do lose contact with themselves, when they are forced to make changes that they don't want to make and aren't ready for. That is when you find tribal peoples driven to drink or to suicide – there has recently been a rash of suicides among the Kaiuwa Indians of Brazil, for example. These are people who are reduced to despair by being forced to make changes they can't deal with.

MT. One of the most general and devastating consequences of modernization seems to be that individuals feel they have no home, not only literally (as in the case of refugees) but emotionally. They feel rootless and "alienated." In contrast, tribal societies – if they are able to maintain their land and their sense of identity – have a very strong sense of place, of home, which seems to satisfy an important human need. How do you feel that people will find a sense of place, a sense of belonging, in the modern, pluralistic world that you hope for and envision?

DM-L. It's interesting that we talk about it as a sense of place because of course tribal people do have a very strong feeling about the land and their relationship to it. But that is also folded into their relationship to one another. It's a sense of place and a sense of people simultaneously. We talk about it as a sense of place, implying somehow that if we could just get back to the ancestral acre, to that place where we were born and relate to it in some mystical way, this would solve all our problems. But we leave out the people part of it. And I think they're both necessary.

I think in the modern world there is a sense of rootlessness, not in everybody, of course, but in a number of people. Many people feel rootless because in fact they *have* been uprooted – they have moved from one place to another. They may have emigrated; they may have been forced out as refugees and so on. These are aspects of modernity that are just facts of life and they have to be dealt with.

Other people feel lonely, isolated, and alienated because in their own society processes are taking place that produce these results. Our very emphasis on individualism has led to a certain isolation of individuals within mass society and a feeling in those individuals that they are not very strongly connected to other peoples and other groups within the society.

So I think that one aspect of a sense of place – or the recovery of a sense of place, if you will, for those who have lost it – is a recovery of that sense of connection. And that means, of course, that we've got to start thinking about the ways in which we relate to people, not just the ways in which we are plugged into the productive system of the whole society. It's clear that unless we're unemployed or marginalized (and unfortunately there are too many such people in modern societies) we have a role within the society, however modest it may be. But it's an economic role, as producers and as consumers. It seems to me that we haven't paid as much attention lately as we might to the other aspects, the human needs for social connectedness in families, in communities, in neighborhoods, and so on. Speaking of the United States, where I live, it's sort of assumed, very interestingly, that this is a natural thing that human beings will be able to do regardless of what goes on around them. In other words, you can make it as difficult as possible for people to stay close to their families, yet it is assumed they will nevertheless. That's what all the conservative rhetoric is about – family values. Families are supposed to stick together even though it's economically impossible for them to make do unless everybody is out at work, and then they agonize about who is going to look after the children.

We hear an enormous amount of rhapsodizing around election time about how communities will hang together. We'll have a thousand points of light and all this altruism will somehow arise instinctively and spontaneously from the people. But the systems this society sets up actually thwart people's attempts to fulfill their very human desires for connection. It seems to me we've got to start thinking seriously about making it easier for people to achieve these human aims, which they want and need so badly. It is in that way that they will recover their sense of people and, with it, their sense of place.

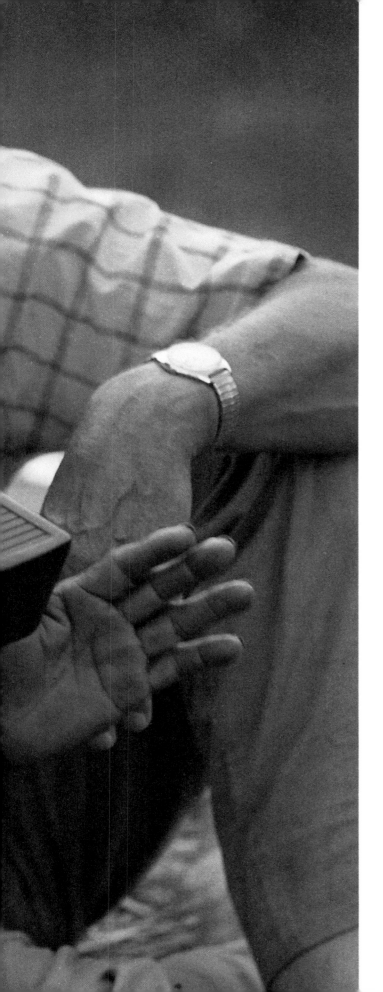

I was given the chief's name, Apewen, meaning "beautiful return." But it was the old man's son, Sibupa, whom I considered my special friend. When he spoke in the men's council his speeches touched on the essence of what it means to be Xavante in a time when that was becoming increasingly difficult. I was delighted when the Xavante decided that his name ought to be continued in our son, to be known thereafter as Sibupa.

PHOTOGRAPHIC

ESSAYS

DOGON

The way in which tribal art is woven into the fabric of society is rooted in something that the modern world has lost, a cosmic confidence in ourselves and in the whole scheme of things. Tribal art is a means of reconciling what is otherwise irreconcilable, of making the painful crises of life manageable – even of overcoming the ultimate disjunction between life and death. The Dogon masked funeral dances are great communal rituals that are as much about life as they are about death. The dances are performed to please the dead and speed them on their way, but they also serve to instruct the living and to incorporate them into the cosmic flow of Dogon being. The masks come from the bush, the source of power and wisdom, the wild place that contrasts with the civility of Dogon communities. For the Dogon, art must be lived.

MALI, WEST AFRICA

POPULATION: 300,000

XAVANTE

How do you know who you are? Western societies offer maturity piecemeal to their growing children — and prolong a period of adolescence that seems to be as confusing and painful for the parents as it is for their offspring. Such considerations do not complicate growing up in tribal societies like the Xavante, where the transition to maturity is made more clearly and is marked with greater ceremony. Initiation rituals are intended to provoke anxiety. They act out the death and rebirth of the initiate, which is a stressful process. His old self dies and he is separated from his society. He is in limbo. While he is in this marginal state he learns the mysteries of his society, instruction that is enhanced by fear and deprivation, and by the atmosphere of awe that his teachers seek to create. Then, some time later — for the ceremonies may last many months — he is reborn as an adult.

MATO GROSSO, BRAZIL

POPULATION: 10,000

The initiate, stripped of his previous identity,

is held in the shadow world

of betwixt-and-between,

A creeping sickness had struck the village. Sizapi, the shaman, was dreaming intensively, traveling through space and time to track down the cause of the disease.

Each day he marshaled the villagers, men, women, and children, and they danced to combat the plague. Each night I danced with them, till I lost all notion of time and space and felt myself wheeling and reeling with the starlit sky.

This went on for days – how many I do not remember – until the dancing stopped. The dancers squatted around their fires. Nobody spoke. We sat there for hours. The fires stopped crackling and glowed like wounds in the night.

At last a sighing movement ruffled through the lines of men. My companion nudged me.

"Listen!" he said. "Can you hear it?"

"Hear what?"

"The souls of the dead. They are whistling all around us."

ABORIGINES

The Aboriginal view of reality appears strange to us because we are accustomed to thinking in Newtonian terms. The Aboriginal system rejects our separation of the visible world into discrete objects, just as it denies that matter is the primary level of reality. Ironically, it is in the pursuit of the ultimate building blocks of matter that our scientists have encountered a world that exhibits traits found in Aboriginal epistemology. The world of quantum physics suggests that objects are somehow interrelated without any force acting on them or any communication between them. Moreover, it appears that "matter" relies on an observing consciousness to dictate where it should materialize. Thus, the phenomenal world, which we take to be so firm and real, is actually unstable and is always changing, spending most of its time as potential. In many respects, this theory sounds like a paraphrase of what the Aborigines call the Dreamtime.

AUSTRALIA

POPULATION: 300,000

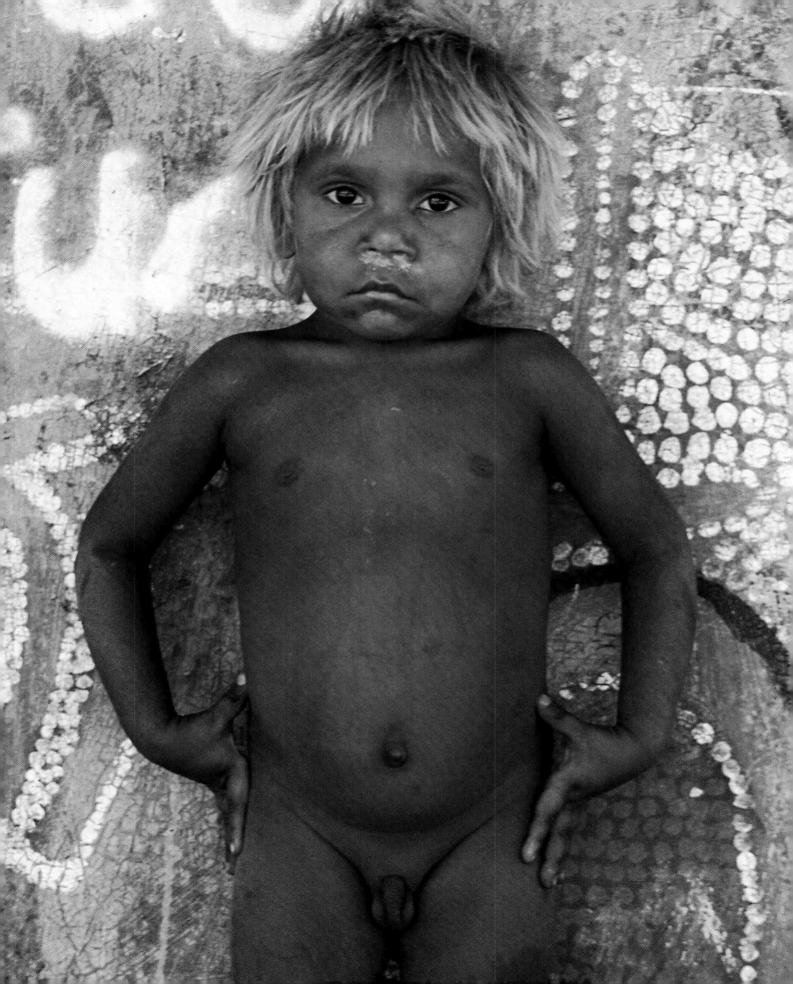

The Dreamtime bears little resemblance to our ordinary notions of time. Past, present, and future fold into one another, and time and space are in flux. We have experienced this in our dreams. Aborigines live it in their reality as they continue to shape their world.

MAKUNA

The idea of the interconnectedness of all things is central to the tribal way of looking at the world. Practical knowledge of the environment, of crops and medicines, of hunting and fishing, is a byproduct of it. For us, it tends to be the other way around. We have prospered both intellectually and materially by separating ourselves from our environment and by seeking to dominate it. The Makuna believe that human beings, animals, and all of nature are parts of the same One. Animals and fish live in their own communities, which are just like human communities, with their chiefs, their shamans, their dance houses, their songs, and their material possessions. When human peoples dance in this world, the shaman invites the animal people to dance in theirs. If humans do not dance and shamans do not offer spirit food to the animal people, the animals will die out and there will be no more game left in the world. For the Makuna the radical disjunction so characteristic of Western thought between nature and culture, men and animals, dissolves.

COLOMBIA

POPULATION: 600

GABRA

The prejudice against nomads is very old. While sedentary peoples have often envied nomads their freedom and political independence, nomads are often stigmatized as being "obstacles to development." In Africa, nomadic pastoralists are accused by their governments of contributing to ecological degradation by overgrazing their animals. In fact, nomads like the Gabra take elaborate care of their grazing lands. Their very survival depends on it. People become restless once the decision to move has been made, and women often get up in the middle of the night to begin dismantling their households. All of the packing and loading is done entirely by women. Men take no part in it other than to restrain the camels if they become unruly or to help lift some item that is too heavy for the women. Gabra live their entire lives in unending cycles of migration. They know how to use their land and to conserve its resources. They move even before they have to in order to ensure that the land is replenished for the future.

The Gabra philosophy of life is summed up in their idea of *finn*, meaning fertility and plenty. Human beings contribute to finn as they care for the earth and their animals, as they exchange livestock, nourish friendships, tell tales, or sing songs. Finn is the earth and the cycle of life that takes place upon it.

WODAABE

Most tribal societies are keenly aware that love and sexual attraction are an explosive mixture when combined. Such societies are amazed by the Western ideal of romantic love as the proper foundation for marriage. They consider it very strange that something as important as marriage be based exclusively on such an irrational and volatile passion. The problem is that love is ecstatic and personal, while marriage is sober and social. The Wodaabe strive for the best of both worlds. They allow two kinds of marriage – *kobgal* marriages, arranged at birth and *teegal* marriages, made "from the heart." A man can have many wives but Wodaabe women can leave their husbands without stigma to seek a happier marriage. Children, however, always remain in the man's lineage. Members of both sexes are often on the lookout for possible liaisons leading to teegal marriages. Their greatest opportunity is at the annual Geerewol celebrations where hundreds gather to watch young men compete to be chosen as the most charming and beautiful dancers.

NIGER, WEST AFRICA

POPULATION: 45,000

WEYEWA

In tribal societies people are enmeshed throughout their lives in systems of gift exchange. A person who gives a gift compels the recipient to make a return gift or to reciprocate in some other way. In such societies a rich person is not someone who accumulates wealth in money or goods but rather someone who has a large network of people beholden to him. In modern societies these networks have shrunk. There are fewer people to whom we feel obligated and, more ominously, fewer who feel obligated to us. The notion of wealth that comes from giving things away is strange to us. Not so for the Weyewa who say, "It is the custom of life that we exchange our belongings and we do not hang on to what we have." At a feast, a guest might bring a water buffalo and receive a small pig in return. Yet everyone is happy. A guest would be mortified if he received an equivalent countergift for it would mean that his exchange relationship was over, that the accounts were balanced. The endless cycle of reciprocity, of mutuality, would be broken forever.

SUMBA, INDONESIA

POPULATION: 85,000

NYINBA

The stability of the family — this is the constant preoccupation of societies the world over. Among the Nyinba of Nepal, a woman is expected to have a number of husbands at the same time. It is normally an arrangement where a woman marries a group of brothers and moves into their household. Passionate attachment to any one of them is frowned upon, for it risks alienating the others and threatens to break up the family. While the practice of polyandry has been explained as a special adaptation to a land where resources are limited — family property does not have to be divided up when all brothers are married to the same woman — the Nyinba, in fact, tolerate a variety of marriage arrangements. They prefer polyandry but permit polygyny, monogamy, and even "conjoint marriages," where a man in a polyandrous marriage marries another woman on the side. Their tolerance contrasts sharply with the Western insistence on monogamy as the only "natural" family arrangement.

NEPAL

POPULATION: 1,300

HUICHOL

We live in a world that prides itself on its modernity, yet is hungry for wholeness, hungry for meaning. The openness to knowledge that transcends ordinary experience, the very idea of feeling at one with the universe, these are impulses we tolerate only at the fringes, claiming to find them irrelevant to our concerns. Ironically, after excluding the mystical tradition from our cultural mainstream, many of us feel empty without it. Every year the Huichol Indians go on a pilgrimage to Wirikuta, retracing the steps of their Ancestors, so that they can "find their lives." They spend many nights in prayer, dancing, chanting, and fasting. Then the shaman leads the pilgrims on the sacred hunt for peyote, the hallucinogenic food of the gods. The pilgrims yearn for the feeling of being at one with the Ancestors, of losing themselves in a state of fusion with the universe and their fellow humans. Yet they fear it, too, for they are tempted to linger in ecstasy, to remain in paradise, and if they were not strong enough to return, their souls would be severed from their bodies and they would die.

MEXICO

POPULATION: 15,000

When we go to Wirikula, the land of the Ancient Ones, it is like the first morning.
Everything is fresh again. When we make offerings to the gods, when we sacrifice our
animals, we pray for the world. We pray for everyone — the Japanese, the Chinese,
the Mexicans, the Americans, even the Europeans. We must keep praying or the world

NAVAJO

Curiously enough, tribal peoples seem to have much less problem maintaining their own identity then we do. It is we who are constantly worried by our identity and feel it is threatened by diversity, multiculturalism, and so on. Tribal societies, if they are not deprived of their lands and their way of making a living, are quite capable of coexisting within larger political units and making their own way in the modern world. The Navajo, for example, have a very strong sense of themselves and their culture. They have fought hard to maintain their cultural identity under quite adverse circumstances. They still exist. But the cultural survival of most tribal societies in the world requires the rest of us to think in more enlightened ways about living with our fellow human beings. A world that is willing to embrace tolerance and pluralism can ensure not only the survival of traditional peoples but also our own.

UNITED STATES

POPULATION: 150,000

BIBLIOGRAPHY

CHAPTER ONE:
THE SHOCK OF THE OTHER
Readings referred to in the text:
Galeano, Eduardo. *Memory of Fire: Genesis.* New York: Pantheon Books, 1985.

Herodotus. *The Histories.* Harmondsworth: Penguin Books, 1972.

de Léry, Jean. *History of a Voyage to the Land of Brazil.* Berkeley: University of California Press, 1990.

Montaigne, Michel de. *The Complete Essays of Montaigne.* Stanford: Stanford University Press, 1958.

Sahagun, Frey Bernardino de. *A General History of the Things of New Spain.* Trans. by Arthur Anderson and Charles E. Dibble. Salt Lake City: University of Utah Press, 1963–79.

Additional readings:
Bodley, John. *Victims of Progress.* Menlo Park, Calif.: Cummings Pub. Co., 1975.

"Brazil: Who Pays for Development?" *Cultural Survival Quarterly* 13 (1989).

Brotherton, Gordon. *Images of the New World: The American Continent Portrayed in Native Texts.* London: Thames & Hudson, 1979.

Denevan, William, ed. *The Native Population of the Americas in 1492.* Madison: University of Wisconsin Press, 1976.

Geertz, Clifford. *Works and Lives: The Anthropologist as Author.* Stanford: Stanford University Press, 1988.

Hanke, Lewis. *Aristotle and the American Indian.* (An account of the Las Casas – Sepúlveda debate, but now out of print.) Chicago: H. Regnery Co., 1959.

Hodgen, Margaret. *Early Anthropology in the Sixteenth and Seventeenth Centuries.* Philadelphia: University of Pennsylvania Press, 1964.

Kamin, Leon. *The Science and Politics of I.Q.* Potomac, Md.: L Erlbaum Associates; distributed by Halsted Press, New York, 1974.

Lévi-Strauss, Claude. *Tristes Tropiques.* New York: Criterion Books, 1961.

Stocking, George. *Race, Culture and Evolution.* New York: Free Press, 1968.

Thornton, Russell. *American Indian Holocaust and Survival: A Population History Since 1942.* Norman: University of Oklahoma Press, 1987.

Wolf, Eric. *Europe and the People Without History.* Berkeley: University of California Press, 1982.

CHAPTER TWO: AN ECOLOGY OF MIND
Part of this chapter is based on unpublished materials kindly furnished by:
Aneesa Kassam on the Gabra
Kaj Århem on the Makuna

Readings referred to in the text:
Breslin, Patrick, and Mac Chapin. "Conversation Kunastyle." *Grassroots Development* 8 (1984): 26–35.

Forsyth, Adrian. *Portraits of the Rainforest.* Camden, Ontario: Camden House, 1990.

Gould, Stephen J. "Is a New and General Theory of Evolution Emerging." In *Self-Organizing Systems: The Emergence of Order,* eds. Francis E. Yates *et al.* New York: Plenum Press, 1987.

Horowitz, Michael. *The Sociology of Pastoralism and African Livestock Projects.* United States Agency for International Development, Washington; GPO, 1979.

Lévi-Strauss, Claude. *The Savage Mind.* Chicago: University of Chicago Press, 1966.

United Nations. Food and Agriculture Organization. *Preliminary Suggestions for an Integrated Approach to Long-Term Development in the Sahelian Zone of West Africa.* 1973.

Additional readings:
Århem, Kaj. *Makuna: Portrait of a Culture.* In press.

———. "Ecosofia Makuna." In *La Selva Humanizada,* ed. F. Correa. Bogotá: ICAN, 1989.

Bateson, Gregory. *Steps to an Ecology of Mind.* San Francisco: Chandler Pub. Co., 1972.

Gordon, Anita, and David Suzuki. *It's a Matter of Survival.* Cambridge: Harvard University Press, 1991.

Ibn Khaldūn. *The Muqaddimah.* New York: Pantheon Books, 1958.

Khazanov, A. M. *Nomads and the Outside World.* Translated by Julia Crookenden. Cambridge: Cambridge University Press, 1983.

"Land and Resources." *Cultural Survival Quarterly* 14 (4) (1990).

"Nomads Stopped in their Tracks." *Cultural Survival Quarterly* 8 (1) (1984).

Wallace, Alfred Russel. *A Narrative of Travels on the Amazon and Rio Negro.* London and New York: Ward, Lock, 1953.

CHAPTER THREE:
A POOR MAN SHAMES US ALL
Part of this chapter is based on unpublished materials kindly furnished by: Joel Kuipers on the Weyewa

Readings referred to in the text:
Durkheim, Emile. *The Division of Labor in Society.* New York: Free Press, 1933.

Malinowski, Bronislaw. *Argonauts of the Western Pacific: An Account of Native Enterprise and Adventure in the Archipelagoes of Melanesian New Guinea.* New York: E. P. Dutton, 1961.

Marx, Karl. *Capital.* Trans. by Dona Torr. New York: International Publishers, 1947.

Mauss, Marcel. *The Gift: The Form and Reason for Exchange in Archaic Societies.* London: Routledge, 1990.

Weiner, Annette. *Women of Value, Men of Renown: New Perspectives in Trobriand Exchange.* Austin: University of Texas Press, 1976.

Additional readings:
Lukes, Stephen. *Individualism.* New York: Harper & Row, 1973.

Schama, Simon. *The Embarrassment of Riches: An Interpretation of Dutch Culture in the Golden Age.* New York: Knopf; distributed by Random House, 1987.

Weber, Max. *The Protestant Ethic and the Spirit of Capitalism.* New York: Charles Scribner's & Sons, 1976.

CHAPTER FOUR: STRANGE RELATIONS

Part of this chapter is based on unpublished materials kindly furnished by: Carol Beckwith on the Wodaabe

Readings referred to in the text:

Confucius. *The Analects*. Trans. by D.C. Lau. Harmondsworth and New York: Penguin Books, 1979.

Lévi-Strauss, Claude. *The Elementary Structures of Kinship*. Boston: Beacon Press, 1969.

Levine, Nancy. *The Dynamics of Polyandry: Kinship, Domesticity, and Population on the Tibetan Border*. Chicago: University of Chicago Press, 1988.

Sappho. *The Poems and Fragments*. New York: E. P. Dutton, 1926.

Additional readings:

Beckwith, Carol, and Marion von Offelen. *Nomads of Niger*. New York: H. N. Abrams, 1983.

Bellah, Robert N. *Habits of the Heart: Individualism and Commitment in American Life*. Berkeley: University of California Press, 1985.

Goody, Jack. *The Development of the Family and Marriage in Europe*. Cambridge: Cambridge University Press, 1983.

Halperin, David, John Winkler, and From Zeitlin, eds. *Before Sexuality*. Princeton, N.J.: Princeton University Press, 1964.

James, Wendy. "Matrifocus on African Women." In *Defining Females: The Nature of Women in Society*, ed. Shirley Ardener, London: Croom Helm in association with the Oxford University Women's Studies Committee, 1978.

McCall, Daniel. "The Dominant Dyad: Mother-right and the Iroquois Case." In *Theory and Practice*, ed. Stanley Diamond, The Hague: Moutan, 1980.

Morgan, Lewis H. *Ancient Society*. Cambridge: Belknap Press of Harvard University Press, 1964.

Lasch, Christopher. *Haven in a Heartless World: The Family Besieged*. New York: Basic Readings, 1977.

CHAPTER FIVE: MISTAKEN IDENTITY
Readings referred to in the text:

Bamberger, Joan. "The Myth of Matriarchy: Why Men Rule in Primitive Society." In *Woman, Culture and Society*, eds. Michelle Rosaldo and Louise Lamphere. Stanford: Stanford University Press, 1974.

Gilligan, Carol. *In a Different Voice*. Cambridge: Harvard University Press, 1982.

Huntington, Richard, and Peter Metcalfe. *Celebrations of Death*. Cambridge: Cambridge University Press, 1979.

Ortner, Sherry. "Is Female to Male as Nature Is to Culture?" In *Woman, Culture and Society*, eds. Michelle Rosaldo and Louise Lamphere. Stanford: Stanford University Press, 1974.

Richards, Audry. *Chisungu: A Girls' Initiation Ceremony Among the Bemba of Zambia*. London and New York: Taristock, 1982.

Additional readings:

Bachofen, Johann J. *Mother Right*. Frankfurt am Main: Suhrkamp, 1975.

Ehrenreich, Barbara. *The Hearts of Men: American Dreams and the Flight from Commitment*. New York: Anchor Press, 1983.

Foucault, Michel. *A History of Sexuality*. Translated by Robert Hurley. New York: Pantheon Books, 1978.

Henry, Jules. *Culture Against Man*. New York: Random House, 1963.

Maybury-Lewis, David. *The Savage and the Innocent*. Boston: Beacon Press, 1988.

Mead, Margaret. *Sex and Temperament in Three Primitive Societies*. New York: W. Morrow and Co., 1935.

Rosaldo, Michelle and Louise Lamphere. *Woman, Culture and Society*. Stanford: Stanford University Press, 1974.

Segal, Lynne. *Slow Motion: Changing Masculinities, Changing Men*. London: Virago, 1990.

Van Gennep, Arnold. *The Rites of Passage*. Translated by Monika Vizedom and Gabrielle Caffee. Chicago: University of Chicago Press, 1960.

"Women in a Changing World." *Cultural Survival Quarterly* 8 (1984).

CHAPTER SIX: THE ART OF LIVING

Part of this chapter is based on unpublished materials kindly furnished by: Walter van Beek on the Dogon

Readings referred to in the text:

Griaule, Marcel. *Conversations with Ogotemmeli: An Introduction to Dogon Religious Ideas*. London: Published for the International African Institute by Oxford University Press, 1970.

Witherspoon, Gary. *Language and Art in the Navajo Universe*. Ann Arbor: University of Michigan Press, 1977.

Additional readings:

Beckwith, Carol. "Geerewol: The Art of Seduction." In *Fragments for a History of the Human Body*, ed. Michael Feher. New York: Urzone; distributed by MIT Press, 1989.

Berger, John. *Ways of Seeing*. Harmondsworth: Penguin, 1972.

Ezra, Kate. *Art of the Dogon*. New York: Metropolitan Museum of Art; distributed by H. N. Abrams, 1988.

Graburn, Nelson. *Anthropology of Tourism*. New York: Pergamon Press, 1983.

Guss, David. *To Weave and Sing: Art, Symbol, and Narrative in the South American Rain Forest*. Berkeley: University of California Press, 1989.

Maybury-Lewis, David, and Uri Almagor. *The Attraction of Opposites*. Ann Arbor: University of Michigan Press, 1989.

Ong, Walter. *Orality and Literacy: The Technologizing of the World*. London and New York: Methuen, 1982.

van Beek, Walter. *Dogon Restudied: A Field Evaluation of the Work of Marcel Griaule*. In press.

CHAPTER SEVEN: INVENTING REALITY
Readings referred to in the text:

Evans-Pritchard, E. E. *Witchcraft, Oracles and Magic Among the Azande*. Oxford: Clarendon Press, 1937.

Frazer, James. *The Golden Bough: A Study of Magic and Religion*. London and New York: Macmillan, 1980.

Lévi-Strauss, Claude. *The Savage Mind*. Chicago: University of Chicago Press, 1966.

Shirokogoroff, Sergei. *Psychomental Complex of the Tungus*. London: Trench, Trubner, 1935.

Additional readings:

Chatwin, Bruce. *The Songlines*. New York: Penguin, 1987.

Davies, P. C., and J. R. Brown. *The Ghost in the Atom: A Discussion of the Mysteries of Quantum Physics*. Cambridge and New York: Cambridge University Press, 1986.

Stanner, W. H. "The Australian Aboriginal Dreaming as an Ideological System." *Pacific Science*. Honolulu: University of Hawaii Press, 1963.

————. *White Man Got No Dreaming*. Canberra and Norwalk, Conn.: Australian National University Press; distributed by Books Australia, 1979.

Stanton, John E. *Painting the Country: Contemporary Aboriginal Art from the Kimberly Region, Western Australia*. Nedlands: University of Western Australia Press, 1989.

Yates, Frances. *The Art of Memory*. Chicago: University of Chicago Press, 1966.

CHAPTER EIGHT:
TOUCHING THE TIMELESS

Part of this chapter is based on unpublished materials kindly furnished by: Juan Negrin on the Huichol

Readings referred to in the text:

Berrin, Kathleen, ed. *Art of the Huichol Indians*. New York: Harry Abrams, 1978.

Frazer, James. *The Golden Bough: A Study of Magic and Religion*. London and New York: Macmillan, 1980.

Kensinger, Kenneth. "Banisteriopsis Usage Among the Peruvian Cashinahua." In *Hallucinogens and Shamanism*, ed. Michael Harner. New York: Oxford University Press, 1973.

Myerhoff, Barbara. *Peyote Hunt: The Religious Pilgrimage of the Huichol Indians*. Ithaca: Cornell University Press, 1974.

Reichel-Dolmatoff, Gerardo. *Beyond the Milky Way: Hallucinatory Imagery of the Tukano Indians*. Los Angeles: UCLA Latin American Center Publications, 1978.

Additional readings:

Berman, Morris. *The Reenchantment of the World*. Ithaca: Cornell University Press, 1981.

Douglas, Mary. *Purity and Danger: An Analysis of Concepts of Pollution and Taboo*. New York: Praeger, 1966.

Durkheim, Emile. *The Elementary Forms of the Religious Life*. New York: Free Press, 1947.

Evans-Pritchard, E. E. *Theories of Primitive Religion*. Oxford: Clarendon Press, 1965.

Gerth, H. H., and C. W. Mills, eds. *From Max Weber: Essays in Sociology*. New York: Oxford University Press, 1958.

Knight, Gareth. *A History of White Magic*. London and Oxford: Mowbrays, 1978.

Ladurie, E. Le Roy. *Montaillou: Cathars and Catholics in a French Village*. London: Scolar, 1978.

Mooney, James. *The Ghost Dance Religion and the Sioux Outbreak of 1890*. Chicago: University of Chicago Press, 1965.

Reichel-Dolmatoff, Gerardo. *The Shaman and the Jaguar*. Philadelphia: Temple University Press, 1975.

Wasson, R. Gordon. *The Road to Eleusis: Unveiling the Secrets of the Mysteries*. New York: Harcourt Brace Jovanovich, 1978.

Turner, Victor. *The Forest of Symbols: Aspects of Ndembu Ritual*. Ithaca, N.Y.: Cornell University Press, 1967.

Worsley, Peter. *The Trumpet Shall Sound: A Study of "Cargo" Cults in Melanesia*. New York: Schocken Books, 1968.

CHAPTER NINE:
THE TIGHTROPE OF POWER

Readings referred to in the text:

"Brazil: Who Pays for Development?" *Cultural Survival Quarterly* 13 (1) (1989).

Colden, Cadwallader. *History of the Five Indian Nations of Canada*. New York: Allerton Book Co., 1904.

————. *History of the Five Nations Depending on the Province of New York in America*. Ithaca, N.Y.: Cornell University Press, 1958.

Evans-Pritchard, E. E. *The Nuer*. Oxford: Clarendon Press, 1940.

Johansen, Bruce E. *Forgotten Founders: How the American Indian Helped Shape Democracy*. Boston: Harvard Common Room Press, 1982.

MacLaine, Craig, and Michael Baxendale. *This Land Is Our Land: The Mohawk Revolt at Oka*. Montreal and Toronto: Optimum Publishers, 1990.

"Nation, Tribe and Ethnic Group in Africa" *Cultural Survival Quarterly* 9 (3) (1985).

Additional readings:

Clastres, Pierre. *Society Against the State*. New York: Zone Books, 1987.

Fried, Morton. *The Notion of Tribe*. Menlo Park: Calif.: Cummings Pub., 1975.

Hallberg, Peter. *The Icelandic Saga*. Lincoln: University of Nebraska Press, 1962.

Kuper, Adam. *Anthropologists and Anthropology: The British School, 1922–1972*. New York: Pica Press, 1973.

Sahlins, Marshall. *Tribesmen*. Englewood Cliffs, N.J.: Prentice-Hall, 1968.

Urban, Grey and Joel Scherzer, eds. *Nation-States and Indians in Latin America*. Austin: The University of Texas Press, 1991.

CHAPTER TEN: AT THE THRESHOLD

Readings referred to in the text:

Bell, Daniel. *The Winding Passage*. Cambridge, Mass.: Abt Books, 1980.

Leach, Edmund. *Political Systems of Highland Burma*. London: Athlone Press, 1977.

Maybury-Lewis, David. "Living in Leviathan." In *The Prospects for Plural Societies*, ed. David Maybury-Lewis. Washington: American Ethnological Society, 1984.

Additional readings:

Lévi-Strauss, Claude. "Race and History." In *Structural Anthropology*, Vol. II. New York: Basic Books, 1976.

INDEX

PHOTO AND ILLUSTRATION CREDITS

Chapter 1. p. 5: Courtesy of the Library of Congress; 5: Courtesy of Fisher Rare Books Library, Toronto; 10: Rosenthal, Franz, *The Muquaddimah*, Ibn Khaldun, © 1958-1967 by Princeton University Press. Reproduced by permission of Princeton University Press; 11: Bibliothèque Nationale, Paris; 13, 21: Rare Books Collection, The New York Public Library; 16 Metropolitan Toronto Reference Library; 19, 27: Courtesy Department Library Services, American Museum of Natural History; 22, 23: Michael Grant; 24, 26: Peabody Museum, Harvard University; 28: Thomas Kelly; 30: Courtesy, Museum of Fine Arts, Boston.

Chapter 2. p. 39: Bancroft Library, University of California, Berkeley; 42, 43, 50, 56, 57: Thomas Kelly; 48, 49: Hans Silvester; 52: Sue Cunningham; 58: Glenbow Archives, Calgary (NA-2520-67); 60: Washington State Historical Society, Tacoma.

Chapter 3. p. 64: Peabody Museum, Harvard University; 67: Argonauts of the Western Pacific, Bronislaw Malinowski, Routledge; 69: By permission of The British Library; 70, 71: Edward Parker; 75: Jan Breughel, Frans Haismuseum, Haarlem; 76: Reproduced by courtesy of the Trustees, The National Gallery, London; 79: Roxby Press, London; 82, 84: Thomas Kelly.

Chapter 4. p. 97, Bibliothèque Nationale, Paris; 98: CNMHS 1991/VIS*ART Copyright Inc.; 103, 104, 105: Carol Beckwith; 111: Thomas Kelly; 112: Susanne Page; 115: Rick Gerherter, Impact Visuals; 117: Peabody Museum, Harvard University; 118: Courtesy of the Board of Trustees of the V & A.

Chapter 5. p. 125: The Hermitage, St. Petersburg; 126, 127: Edward Parker; 129: Phillip Galgiani; 131: Susanne Page; 135: Carol Beckwith; 138, 139, 144, 145: Thomas Kelly; 143: National Museum of the American Indian.

Chapter 6. p. 149: Thomas Kelly; 150, 151: Stark Museum of Art, Orange, Texas; 155: By permission of Institut d'Etudes Médiévales, Université de Montréal; 156, 158, 159, 161 (lower): Susanne Page; 161 (upper): © Hans Namuth; 164, 165: Carol Beckwith; 168, 169: Edward Parker.

Chapter 7. p. 178, 179: Antonio Vizcaino; 182: Edward Parker; 184, 185: Reproduced by permission of Johannes Fabricius from Alchemy; 188, 189: Peabody Museum, Harvard University and Musée de l'Homme; 192, 193: The Huntington Library; 199: Michael Grant.

Chapter 8. p. 209: Trans. 1524(2) Courtesy Department Library Services, American Museum of Natural History; 211: "Clowns Getting Ready", California Academy of Sciences, Elkus Collection (catalog #370-1215); 214, 215: From the Collection of Bill and Frances Belknap; 216: Kerenyi, C., *Eleusis: Archetypal Image of Mother and Daughter*, trans. by Ralph Manheim, © 1967 by Princeton University Press. Reproduced by permission of Princeton University Press; 219: Reproduced by permission of Dr. C.A. Meier, Zurich; 220, 221: Michael Grant; 226, 227: Antonio Vizcaino; 232, 233: Thomas Kelly.

Chapter 9. p. 242: Smithsonian Institution Photo No. 55,660; Photo No. 75-4305; 243 (upper): Montana Historical Society, (lower) Smithsonian Institution Photo No. 36; 245: Pitt Rivers Museum, Oxford; 248, 249: Courtesy New York State Library; 251: (upper) Ricardo/CEDI and (lower) Jason Clay 254, 255: Albany Institute of History and Art; 257: Canapress; 258: Courtesy Watertown Daily Times with permission from the artist; 261: © National Geographic Society; 263: Winnipeg Free Press. Photographer Wayne Glowacki.

Picture Essays
Dogon: Edward Parker; Xavante: Thomas Kelly; Aborigines: Claude Coireault; Makuna: Thomas Kelly; Gabra: Thomas Kelly; Wodaabe: Carol Beckwith; Weyewa: Edward Parker; Nyinba: Thomas Kelly; Huichol: Antonio Vizcaino; Navajo: Susanne Page.

THE BODY OF THIS BOOK WAS SET IN THE DIGITIZED VERSION OF THE FACE CALLED BODONI, DESIGNED BY THE PRINTER AND PROLIFIC TYPE DESIGNER GIAMBATTISTA BODONI (1740-1813) OF PARMA, ITALY. OTHER TYPE FACES APPEARING IN THE CHAPTER HEADS, PHOTO CAPTIONS AND PRINT BOXES ARE COPPERPLATE GOTHIC (FREDERIC WILLIAM GOUDY, 1905), FRANKLIN GOTHIC (VICTOR CARUSO, 1980), FUTURA BOLD CONDENSED (PAUL RENNER, 1930), FUTURA EXTRA BOLD (EDWIN SHAAR, 1952) AND UNIVERS 55 AND 63 (ADRIAN FRUTIGER, 1957). TYPE WAS PRODUCED ON THE SCANGRAPHIC SYSTEM.

COMPOSED BY
CHARACTER COUNT INCORPORATED, TORONTO, CANADA

THE PRODUCERS OF THE TELEVISION SERIES
MILLENNIUM: TRIBAL WISDOM AND THE MODERN WORLD
GRATEFULLY ACKNOWLEDGE THE CONTRIBUTIONS OF THE FOLLOWING:

THE BODY SHOP
PBS
THE CORPORATION FOR PUBLIC BROADCASTING
THE JOHN D. AND CATHERINE T. MACARTHUR FOUNDATION
THE FORD FOUNDATION
ESPRIT INTERNATIONAL

JOSHUA MAILMAN

ELA ALFORD
THE BELDON FOUNDATION
PATRICK BERMINGHAM
ELREEN BOWER
JEFFREY BRONFMAN
GEORGE BUTTERFIELD
PENNY CALDWELL
THE DAMIEN FOUNDATION
MARK ELLIS
MARNEY GRANT
CAROL MACLEAN GRAY
DAVID HARRIS
J.D.H. HUME
MRS. J.D.H. HUME
THE HUNT FOUNDATION
RICHARD M. IVEY
RICHARD W. IVEY

CHARLES KENNEDY
NANCY KENNEDY
SONJA KOERNER
MELA LEAVELL
BOKHARA LEGENDRE
CAROL MEECH
RICHARD C. MEECH
DEREK PHILLIPS
HENRY ROLFS
AZAD SHIVDASANI
ARMAN SIMONE
NORTON SMITH
THRESHOLD FOUNDATION
MARION WEBER
THE WENNER-GREN FOUNDATION
SANDRA WILSON
ROBERT WISENER

LIVINGSTON CUSTOMS BROKERS
PATAGONIA, INC.

MILLENNIUM: TRIBAL WISDOM AND THE MODERN WORLD
IS A CO-PRODUCTION OF
BINIMAN PRODUCTIONS LIMITED, ADRIAN MALONE PRODUCTIONS, INC.
KCET, LOS ANGELES AND BBC-TV
IN ASSOCIATION WITH
THE GLOBAL TELEVISION NETWORK
WITH THE PARTICIPATION OF
ROGERS TELEFUND AND TELEFILM CANADA